DATE DUE

NOV 1 4 1988 LCS		
APR 1 9 1989		
NOV 1 5 1999		
MAR 1 0 2008		
MAY 2 6 2009		
WITHDRAWN		

HIGHSMITH 45-220

ENTERED DEC 2 2 1987

William Carlos Williams
and the Maternal Muse

Studies in Modern Literature, No. 72

A. Walton Litz, General Series Editor

Professor of English
Princeton University

Consulting Editor:
Paul Mariani

Professor of English
University of Massachusetts/Amherst

Other Titles in This Series

William Carlos Williams and the Maternal Muse

by
Kerry Driscoll

U·M·I Research
Press

Ann Arbor / London

Grateful acknowledgment is given to New Directions Publishing Corporation for permission to quote from the following published works of William Carlos Williams: *The Autobiography of William Carlos Williams* (Copyright 1948, 1949, 1951 by William Carlos Williams); *The Build-up* (Copyright 1946, 1952 by William Carlos Williams); *The Collected Earlier Poems* (Copyright 1938 by New Directions); *The Collected Later Poems* (Copyright 1944, 1948, 1950 by William Carlos Williams); *Imaginations* (Copyright © 1970 by Florence H. Williams); *In the American Grain* (Copyright 1925 by James Laughlin); *I Wanted to Write a Poem* (Copyright © 1958 by William Carlos Williams); *Paterson* (Copyright 1946, 1948, 1949, 1951, 1958 by William Carlos Williams; copyright © 1963 by Florence H. Williams); *Pictures from Brueghel* (Copyright © 1949, 1951, 1952, 1953, 1954, 1955, 1956, 1957, 1959, 1960, 1961, 1962 by William Carlos Williams); *A Recognizable Image: William Carlos Williams on Art and Artists* (Copyright © 1978 by the Estate of Florence H. Williams); *Selected Letters of William Carlos Williams* (Copyright © 1957 by William Carlos Williams); *Yes, Mrs. Williams* (Copyright © 1959 by William Carlos Williams).

Previously unpublished material by William Carlos Williams, Copyright © 1987 by William Eric Williams and Paul H. Williams. Used by permission of New Directions Publishing Corp., agents. Grateful acknowledgment is also given to the various libraries housing the unpublished Williams manuscripts which are quoted in this text: The Poetry/Rare Books Collections, University Libraries, State University of New York at Buffalo; Collection of American Literature, The Beinecke Rare Book and Manuscript Library, Yale University; Harry Ransom Humanities Research Center, University of Texas at Austin; Brown University Library; The Lilly Library, Indiana University.

Portions of this work appeared, in somewhat different form, in the *William Carlos Williams Review*, vol. 11, no. 2 (Fall 1985), and *William Carlos Williams: Man and Poet* (Orono, Maine: National Poetry Foundation, 1983).

Produced and distributed by
UMI Research Press
an imprint of
University Microfilms, Inc.
Ann Arbor, Michigan 48106

ibrary of Congress Cataloging in Publication Data

Driscoll, Kerry.
  William Carlos Williams and the maternal muse.

  (Studies in modern literature; no. 72)
  Bibliography: p.
  Includes index.
  1. Williams, William Carlos, 1883-1963—Criticism and interpretation. 2. Williams, Raquel Hélène Rose Hoheb, 1847-1950, in fiction, drama, poetry, etc. 3. Mothers in literature. 4. Mothers and sons in literature. 5. Poets, American—20th century—Mothers. I. Title. II. Series.
  PS3545.I544Z5863 1987   811'.52   87-13855
  ISBN 0-8357-1801-8 (alk. paper)

British Library CIP data is available

For Dan

There was one place in the world that stood solid and did not melt into unreality: the place where his mother was. Everybody else could grow shadowy, almost non-existent to him, but she could not. It was as if the pivot and pole of his life, from which he could not escape, was his mother.

D. H. Lawrence, *Sons and Lovers*

Figure 1.   Raquel Helene Rose Hoheb Williams, ca. 1895

Contents

Figures

All photographs are courtesy of Dr. William Eric Williams.

Acknowledgments

In bringing this project to fruition I have received the encouragement and support of many people. I would especially like to thank Neil Schmitz, Marcus Klein, and William Warner, all of the State University of New York at Buffalo, for their insightful criticism which helped, early on, to shape my thinking about Williams. Each has been, in his own respect, a tremendously influential teacher. I am also greatly indebted to Paul Mariani, of the University of Massachusetts, Amherst, who generously shared with me both his time and vast scholarly knowledge not only of Williams but modern poetry in general. He has offered invaluable guidance and assistance throughout all phases of my research.

Special thanks are due to my colleagues at the University of Heidelberg, especially Dieter Schulz, Karl Schubert, and Dietmar Schloss, whose friendship and cordiality made my Fulbright year in Germany a richly rewarding one. I am also grateful to Doctor William Eric Williams for allowing me to reproduce here photographs of his father and grandmother, and to my dear friends, Ashley Miller and Gene Endres, who made the pilgrimage to Rutherford to secure them in my stead.

Lastly, deepest gratitude goes to my husband, Dan Bailey, for his patience and unwavering support. In more ways than I could name, this work would have been impossible without him.

Abbreviations

The following abbreviations have been used throughout the text in citing works by William Carlos Williams:

A   *The Autobiography of William Carlos Williams* (1951)

BU   *The Build-up* (1946)

CEP   *The Collected Earlier Poems* (1951)

CLP   *The Collected Later Poems* (1963)

IAG   *In the American Grain* (1925)

I   *Imaginations,* ed. Webster Schott (1970; contains *Kora in Hell,* 1920; *Spring and All,* 1923; *The Great American Novel,* 1923; *The Descent of Winter,* 1928; *January: A Novelette* and *Other Prose,* 1932)

Int   *Speaking Straight Ahead: Interviews with William Carlos Williams,* ed. Linda Welsheimer Wagner (1976)

IW   *I Wanted to Write a Poem: The Autobiography of the Works of a Poet,* reported and edited by Edith Heal (1958)

ML   *Many Loves and Other Plays* (1961)

P   *Paterson* (1963)

PB   *Pictures from Brueghel and Other Poems* (1962; contains *The Desert Music,* 1954; *Journey to Love,* 1955)

SE   *Selected Essays of William Carlos Williams* (1954)

SL   *Selected Letters of William Carlos Williams,* ed. John C. Thirlwall (1957)

YMW   *Yes, Mrs. Williams* (1959)

Introduction

Williams and the "Female Principle"

The subject of women perennially intrigued and mystified William Carlos Williams. "Women!," exclaims "Doc," the poet's persona in the play *Many Loves*, "With their small heads and big lustrous eyes. All my life I have never been able to escape them" (*ML*, 84). As this statement suggests, Williams' irresistible attraction to the feminine involved a strongly sexual component; however, it was not restricted to an appreciation of physical appearance or superficial charms. Rather, the poet's fascination with women stemmed from a recognition of their essential otherness—the fact that the female, while closely akin to the male, was nonetheless a distinct entity, a creature at once familiar and inexplicably foreign. This paradox of simultaneous resemblance and divergence, which he termed "the riddle of a man and a woman" (*P*, 107), was deepened by his belief in the androgyny of all artists. Williams associated the feminine with creativity and the unconscious, asserting, for example, in the 1914 poem "Transitional":

> It is the woman in us
> That makes us write—
> Let us acknowledge it—
> Men would be silent

(*CEP*, 34)

The poet's curiosity about women and desire to understand the ways in which gender affected perception were thus partially motivated by a quest for self-knowledge. To this end, he explored a diverse range of female characters in both his poetry and prose, attempting to transcend the limits of his own male consciousness and imaginatively become the "other." Yet, as he explained to Edith Heal in *I Wanted to Write a Poem*, the task proved virtually impossible:

Women remained an enigma; no two had the same interest for me; they were all different. I was consequently interested in too many of them, and trying to find out about them all. What made them tick? It was a fascinating experimentation. I would draw back from them

and try to write it down. . . . I'll die before I've said my fill about women. I feel I am saying
flattering things about them but they won't take it. After all there are only two kinds of us,
men and women, the he and the she of it, yet some antagonism, some self-defense seems
to rise out of a woman when a man tries to understand her. I am so terribly conscious of
woman as woman that it is hard for me to write about a woman—I become self-conscious—
too aware that she is there ready to tell me I've got her all wrong. *(IW,* 64–65)

The self-consciousness Williams refers to here, combined with the alleged
readiness of female associates to blanketly condemn the inaccuracy of his portrayal of women, effectively prevented the poet from achieving the holistic understanding of the opposite sex that he desired. One confronts both the ubiquity
of this ambition and signs of its inevitable frustration throughout his writing,
from the inclusion of Marcia Nardi's scathing letter at the end of *Paterson,*
book 2, to his own poignant expression of defeat in "To Daphne and Virginia":

> All women are fated similarly
>   facing men
>   and there is always
>   another, such as I,
>   who loves them,
>   loves all women, but
> finds himself, touching them,
>   like other men,
>   often confused.
>
> *(PB,* 76)

Despite his deep affinity for women and sensitivity to their plight, Williams was unable, except in a few rare instances, to surmount an inherently patriarchal bias involving notions of male primacy and dominance, and hence
could not make the psychic transition from sympathy to truly empathic identification. Trapped by what he labeled "a counter stress, / born of the sexual
shock" *(PB,* 78), the poet viewed women from a compassionate, but external—
and therefore "confused"—stance. The exteriority of his position is reflected
in a tendency to depict them in two antithetical, but equally idealized ways.
The first, illustrated by the above remark to Edith Heal, proclaims the bewil-
dering multiplicity and variation of feminine traits—"they were all different."
The second, as the following passage from *January: A Novelette* reveals, reduces all women to a single, symbolic archetype, a Botticellian vision of
beauty:

> And what is a beautiful woman?
> She is one.
> Over and over again, she is one . . .
> So she—building of all excellence is, in her single body, beautiful; enforcing
> the mind by imperfections to a height. Born again, Venus from the confused sea.
> Summing all the virtues. Single. Excellence. Female.
>
> *(I,* 282)

These conflicting modes of representation are reconciled in Williams' later work, where female characters, though individuated, are treated primarily as avatars of this archetype. The convergence of the two styles can be clearly seen in the poet's nostalgic recollection in *Paterson* 4 of girls to whom he'd been attracted in his youth. His litany of praise to "Margaret," "Lucille," "Alma," and "Nancy," each of whom is delineated by a few specific details (which, quite tellingly, consist mostly of body parts—"big breasts and daring eyes," "gold hair," "steady hand," and a "mouth [that] never wished for relief"), concludes in this manner:

> All these
> and more—shining, struggling flies
> caught in the meshes of Her hair
>
> (*P*, 192)

These lines typify the technique of "drawing back" that Williams mentioned in the excerpt from *I Wanted to Write a Poem* quoted earlier. Through a sudden, distancing shift in authorial perspective, the four women lose not only their individual identities, but their humanity itself. They become helpless "flies," entrapped in and serving as adornments for the "invisible net" covering the hair of a primordial earth goddess who is associated throughout the poem with Garrett Mountain. The distinguishing personal features of Margaret, Lucille, Alma, and Nancy are thus subsumed into a single attribute of a mythic entity who incarnates the universal "female principle."

This same mythicizing tendency can also be observed in two of Williams' most celebrated later poems, "Of Asphodel, That Greeny Flower" and "For Eleanor and Bill Monahan." In "Asphodel," which is addressed to his wife Flossie, he states:

> All women are not Helen,
> I know that,
> but have Helen in their hearts.
> My sweet,
> you have it also, therefore
> I love you
> and could not love you otherwise.
>
> (*PB*, 159)

Though Williams stops short of literally equating all women with Helen of Troy in this passage, he nevertheless predicates his love for Flossie upon a subjective mythic association, namely, that "all women . . . have Helen in their hearts." Moreover, he insists on the necessity of this imaginative projection in order for love to exist and survive: "I could not love you otherwise." For the poet, the figure of Helen represents a male fantasy of female beauty, desirability, and possession; she epitomizes the concept of woman as object and prize.

In asserting that all women somehow partake of Helen, he obliquely alludes to the possibility of their seduction, thereby unconsciously revealing more about himself (e.g., as a modern-day Paris) and his perceptions of women than about Flossie, his intended subject.

Fantasy also plays a significant role in "For Eleanor and Bill Monahan," although in this case, the poet's subject is not a female intimate but rather a religious deity, the Virgin Mary. Throughout the lyric, Williams humanizes the Mother of God by imaginatively describing her as a palpable, sexually attractive woman, "young / and fit to be loved" (*PB*, 85). This strategy, which anticipates his characterization of the virgin and the wore in book 5 of *Paterson* as dual facets of a single female identity, initially seems presumptuous, even irreverent; however, as the poem's concluding lines indicate, the piece is in fact a prayer, a plea for mercy and forgiveness, addressed to a being whom Williams clearly worships. Rather, the radicality of his interpretation lies in locating the source of Mary's divinity not in her remote, inviolable aura of virginity, as the Christian church has traditionally done, but in an attitude of tenderness, vulnerability, humility, and love which he considers quintessentially feminine:

> Mother of God
>   I have seen you stoop
>   to a merest flower
> and raise it
>   and press it to your cheek.
>   I could have called out
> joyfully
>   but you were too far off.
>   You are a woman and
> it was
>   a woman's gesture.
>
>   (*PB, 84*)

The implications of this description are far-reaching: by emphasizing the womanly qualities of the Virgin Mary's character, Williams suggests that the archetypal feminine is in itself divine. All women, in addition to having "Helen in their hearts," resemble the Mother of God in the gentleness of their gestures and largesse of their spirits. The poet, in this instance, moves beyond the bounds of mythicizing into pure deification, declaring: "The female principle of the world / is my appeal / in the extremity to which I have come" (*PB*, 86). Interestingly, this exaltation of the feminine creates a corresponding diminution of his own status within the lyric. Williams portrays himself as a devotee and supplicant who willingly "submits" to the "holy rule" (*PB*, 83) of the redemptive female force embodied in Mary. The generosity of women and their capacity for forgiveness become for him synonymous with emotional salvation; hence, they are to be treated as objects of veneration. The archly romanticized nature of his depiction, though intended to be flattering, proves ultimately counterproductive in that it deepens the "riddle of a man and a woman" rather than taking steps to resolve it. In this respect, the glaring inequity of the relationship he proposes between himself and the "female principle" reaffirms the exteriority of his perceptual stance—that women are indeed the "other."

The attitudes Williams expressed about women in his writing range over a wide emotional spectrum, from candid acknowledgment of their potent erotic appeal to the mythic idealization so evident in the later poems. After lecturing to a predominantly female audience at Vassar, for example, he told a friend: "I [always] find it rather difficult to take the girls seriously enough except on the one topic";[1] similarly, in *I Wanted to Write a Poem*, he recalled a reading at Wellesley, commenting to Edith Heal, "The girls . . . were so adorable. I could have raped them all!" (*IW*, 95). Although many of his statements, like the following passage from *Paterson*,

> Say I am the locus
> > where two women meet
>
> One from the backwoods
> > a touch of the savage
> > and of T.B.
> > (a scar on the thigh)
> The other—wanting,
> > from an old culture
> —and offer the same dish
> > different ways

                                                                (*P*, 110)

are both distasteful and flagrantly sexist from a contemporary feminist standpoint, the openness with which Williams attempted to record his varied responses to women, even when they were objectionable or taboo in nature, must also be taken into consideration. He describes, for example, his lust for little girls in a number of poems such as "The Ogre," where, upon viewing a "sweet child . . . with well-shaped legs," he contemplates thoughts which would "burn [her] to an ash" (*CEP*, 154). Whereas another writer might have suppressed such feelings, or at least chosen not to publicly commemorate them in print, Williams understood that passion was an integral component of his identity, and defied the prevailing puritanical morality of his time to repeatedly assert it. In the foreword to his *Autobiography*, he states unequivocally: "I am extremely sexual in my desires: I carry them everywhere and at all times. I think that from that [*sic*] arises the drive which empowers us all" (*A*, i). The intensity of this innate drive was, in his estimation, augmented by the isolated circumstances of his childhood: "I never had a sister, no aunts and no female cousins, at least within striking distance. So that aside from Mother and Grandma I never knew a female intimately for my entire young life. That was very important. It generated in me enough curiosity to burn up fifty growing boys" (*A*, 4–5).

Despite the poet's endeavor in this statement to minimize the importance of his mother, Elena Hoheb, and paternal grandmother, Emily Dickenson Wellcome, in formulating his early impressions of women, these two individuals undoubtedly comprised his primary female role models. Significantly, their relationship to one another was far from harmonious; another childhood memory recounted in *Autobiography* concerns the fierce rivalry that developed between the two women over the possession of little Willie himself. Immediately following the birth of his younger brother, Edgar, Williams had been begrudgingly surrendered to the care of his grandmother, who lived at home with the family; as a result, Emily came to think of him as "her boy": "Grandma took me over or tried to. But once Mother lost her temper and laid the old gal out good with a smack across the puss that my mother joyfully remembered until her death" (*A*, 5).[2]

The legendary slap with which Elena ended her mother-in-law's attempt to usurp her eldest son had extensive repercussions for the poet's personal development. Through this act of symbolic reclamation, she asserted the primacy of the maternal relationship above all others, and established a hierarchy of familial bonds and devotion which was never again overtly challenged. Moreover, the incident's sexual configuration (a triangle, involving two females and a male) influenced and, to some extent, determined the pattern of Williams' mature interactions with women by revealing to him, at an early and impressionable age, that females "desired" him and would quarrel among themselves over the right to his possession. One of the most famous passages in *Paterson* illustrates how fundamental this notion of male singularity as the magnetic center of a multiplicity of females was to the poet's self-image:

> A man like a city and a woman like a flower
> —who are in love. Two women. Three women.
> Innumerable women, each like a flower.
>   But
> only one man—like a city.
>
> (P, 7)

Even in old age, Williams remained confident of his ability to charm women, telling Robert Lowell with characteristic aplomb: "I am sixty-seven, and / more attractive to girls than when I was seventeen."[3]

Within the large cast of female figures who populate Williams' writing, there stands a triumvirate of characters notable for both the careful detail with which they are delineated and the frequency of their appearance. Beyond the generic appeal that all women had possessed for the poet, these three—his mother, grandmother, and wife—are distinguished by the intimacy and long duration of their relationships with him, as well as by the powerful influences they exerted on his imagination. The poet's fictive representations of these three individuals offers a logical starting place for critically examining the evolution of his attitudes towards women and theories about "what made them tick" (*IW*, 64) for the simple reason that they were the ones whom he himself knew best and had the most extensive opportunities to observe.

To a certain extent, Williams consciously mythologized these three women in his work; each is elevated and ennobled in the process of transmutation from life into art. His grandmother, for example, who appears as the haggard old muse in his important early poem "The Wanderer," is by Williams' own admission, "raised to heroic proportions . . . [and] endowed with magic qualities" (*IW*, 26). She flies through the air with the poet, initiating him, through a series of visionary experiences, into the sordid realities of the modern world, and finally baptizes him in the filthy waters of her "old friend" (*CEP*, 11), the Passaic River. In a less fantastic, but still idealized manner, he describes her in the eulogy, "Dedication for a Plot of Ground," as a tough, adventurous individual who voyaged from the old world to the new and fought tirelessly to defend herself "against thieves / storms, sun, fire," as well as "against the weakness of her own hands" (*CEP*, 171). The great admiration Williams felt for his grandmother's passion, independence, and determination did not, however, allow him to transcend the exteriority of his male perceptions and penetrate to the hidden, inner core of her being. Emily Dickenson Wellcome remained, to the end, a mystery to him.

Similarly, Williams' treatment of Flossie in both his poetry and prose is also externalized. His trilogy of novels about her childhood and family background, *White Mule, In the Money,* and *The Build-up,* is narrated, significantly, from a limited third-person point of view. Little attempt is made to enter into and explore the development of the young girl's consciousness; instead, the narrative chronicles a progression of purely external events. Even in the heart-wrenching love poems of the 1950s, Flossie is a veiled, passive presence. Williams variously describes and interprets her, evokes tender moments in their long life together, and pleads for her forgiveness, but her responses to these overtures are unfortunately not recorded; as a result, she is elusive and inaccessible to the reader, a subjective "dream of love" (*ML*, 105) created within the poet's imagination.

The one instance in which Williams successfully overcame his perception of female "otherness" was the portrayal of his mother, Raquel Helen Rose Hoheb Williams. Aside from the poet's ubiquitous representations of himself, she is arguably the most fully realized of all his "characters," appearing regularly throughout his work from the very earliest pieces to the last. He upheld her, for example, as a symbol of the imagination in the prologue to *Kora in Hell,* related bits of her biography in *The Descent of Winter* and *January,* made her the subject of numerous poems ("Eve," "All the Fancy Things," "Two Pendants: for the Ears," "The Horse Show," "An Eternity," "The Painting," to mention only the most prominent), and devoted a book-length memoir, *Yes, Mrs. Williams,* to her stories and aphorisms.

The source of Williams' abiding fascination with Elena, which served as a crucial factor in his surmounting of the perceptual barriers typically imposed by gender difference, was his intuitive recognition of the extensive physical, spiritual, and psychic similarities that existed between them. Because the poet believed that he and his mother were, in many respects, fundamentally alike, he came to regard her as a living text in which he could read and discover the secrets of his own identity. The concept of female "otherness" thus yielded in the case of Elena to a perception not only of resemblance, but symbolic convergence. Within the fictive universe of Williams' writing, the figures of mother and son complement one another, conjoining male and female elements to form a single, unified whole; as Doc Thurber explains to his wife Myra in the play *Many Loves,* the process is one of reciprocal imaginative completion: "Just as a woman must produce out of her female belly to complete herself—a son—so a man must produce a woman, in full beauty out of the shell of his imagination and possess her, to complete himself also . . ." (*ML,* 200).

This analogy between the literal act of giving birth and artistic creation has particular relevance for the poet's depiction of Elena, in which the roles of "parent" and "offspring" are thoroughly conflated. The mother is engendered, "in full beauty," out of the womb of her son's imagination, in much the same way that she earlier gave life to him. As "Eve," the title of his 1936 poem about her, suggests, Elena represented the first, archetypal female for Williams, the Ur-mother from whom all other women are descended. In this respect, his characterization of her parallels Freud's theory of the three symbolic forms assumed by the figure of the mother as a man's life proceeds: "the mother herself, the beloved who is chosen after her pattern, and finally the Mother Earth who receives him again."[4] For Williams, Elena not only supplied the "pattern" for the beloved, but fulfilled that role herself in his imagination; as a young man studying medicine in Leipzig, he had written a letter to her, enclosing a poem that he described as "a pure love song and all the truer because of the impossibility of passion."[5] Through the intensity of this "impossible," multifaceted passion, Elena became the foundation upon which her son's later concept of a generic "female principle" was erected; following her example and instruction, he learned how to live, how to love, and ultimately, how to die. "What do I look for in a woman?" he asked in *Autobiography.* "Death, I suppose, since it's all I see anyhow in those various perfections. I want them all in lesser or greater degree" (*A,* 222).

But who exactly was this obscure woman to whom Williams ascribed such monumental significance? The answers are diverse: an immigrant to the U.S., born and raised on the island of Puerto Rico; a frustrated artist and musician; a misfit; a spiritual medium who fell into periodic trances; an isolated suburban housewife who bore two sons. Petite in stature and ethereal in temperament, Elena was also very much a lady, fond of fine dresses and polite society, extremely vain about her slender waist and size 4½ feet. The fragility of her appearance, however, concealed a tough, resilient inner fiber and potential for emotional volatility that manifested itself from time to time in violent, impetuous actions, like slapping Grandma Wellcome in the face or "whaling [the] hell" out of Williams and his brother with a piece of cord wood (*A*, 11–12). Yet, in terms of her son's poetry, Elena was most compellingly a voice—indeed, the primal voice of human contact, that of the mother. As nurturer and guardian, singer of lullabies and teller of bedtime tales, it was she who largely introduced Williams into the mysteries of language, and the powerful impression created in his mind by the exotic rhythms of her ungrammatical immigrant speech later became the wellspring of his interest in the American idiom.

Elena's centrality in the poet's life and imagination is illustrated by the following passage from *I Wanted to Write a Poem:*

> I was conscious of my mother's influence all through this time of writing, her ordeal as a woman and as a foreigner in this country. I've always held her as a mythical figure, remote from me, detached, looking down on an area in which I happened to live, a fantastic world where she was moving as a more or less pathetic figure. Remote, not only because of her Puerto Rican background, but also because of her bewilderment at life in a small town in New Jersey after her years in Paris where she had been an art student. Her interest in art became my interest in art. I was personifying her, her detachment from the world of Rutherford. She seemed an heroic figure, a poetic ideal. I didn't especially admire her; I was attached to her. I had not yet established any sort of independent spirit. (*IW*, 16)

Although these remarks pertain specifically to Williams' first two books, *Poems* (1909) and *The Tempers* (1913), they also attest to the enduring nature of his preoccupation with Elena. "I've *always* held her as a mythical figure," he states, suggesting that her appeal did not suddenly diminish at the end of his apprentice period, but continued throughout his career. Moreover, in attempting to describe the extent of his mother's early influence, Williams makes several revealing comments, the most significant of which is, "I was personifying her, her detachment from the world of Rutherford." Initially, he seems to be sketching a rather conventional portrait of spiritual legacy ("Her interest in art became my interest in art"), yet the weight of the mother's inheritance is so strong that it unsettles the poet's sense of personal identity and autonomy. From a semantic standpoint, his use of the verb "personify" is incorrect, since only inanimate objects can be personified, not people. But in this context, the verb accentuates the extent of Elena's imaginative hold on Williams: in his poetry, he is incarnating and acting out her interests, her ideals, her plight. This strange configuration is reinforced by two statements which occur at the end of the passage: "I was *attached* to her. *I had not yet established any sort of independent spirit*" (emphasis mine).

The exaggerated nature of these assertions implies that Williams' statement is more than an idle reminiscence; even at this late stage in his life, almost a decade after Elena's death in 1949, his identification with her remained active and unresolved. Furthermore, the subtle blurring of identities in the passage is not an aberration produced by the casual, oral quality of *I Wanted to Write a Poem,* but a motif that characterizes all the poet's descriptions of his mother. For this reason, I believe that Williams' textualization represents more than an extended illustration of the way life is mysteriously metamorphosed into art; rather, it exposes the essence, the "radiant gist" (*P,* 186) of his identity. Williams' mother was his muse, the spiritual source from which his creative genius sprang. As such, his numerous portrayals of her, especially the memoir, *Yes, Mrs. Williams,* have a dual resonance, simultaneously revealing essential facets of his own personality. In analyzing the memoir's genesis and slow evolution over the course of the poet's career, this study explores not only the complex configuration of the mother-son relationship, but Williams' progressive understanding of himself, particularly in terms of the androgynous, "female" aspects of his character.

The intimate and assiduous detail in which Williams delineated Elena was the result not only of psychic affinity but physical proximity. Because he spent his entire life within a few miles of the house where he was born, the poet was able to maintain extraordinarily close contact with Elena right up until the time of her death. When, for example, he left home in 1912 to marry Flossie, the newlyweds rented rooms which adjoined his parents' residence, and took meals with them. And in 1924, Elena, who was growing increasingly infirm, moved in with her eldest son at 9 Ridge Road, and lived there most of her last twenty-five years. Through the daily regularity of their contact, Williams became steeped in his mother's personal mythos—the figure of the defeated romantic "clinging desperately to the small threads of a reality which she thought to have left in Paris" (*YMW,* 33). He could not, however, easily reconcile Elena's sentimental self-image with his firsthand knowledge of her toughness and ability to survive adversity, and so resolved to break through this mythic facade and excavate her "true life, undefeated if embittered, hard as nails, little loving, easily mistaken for animal selfishness" (*YMW,* 33). Much of Williams' writing about his mother can thus be viewed as a hermeneutic exercise—an attempt to come to terms with conflicting interpretations of her identity and character which, by extension, offered insight into his own. The 1927 poem, "Brilliant Sad Sun," offers a concise example of the way in which he approached and articulated this dilemma:

> Lee's
> Lunch
>
> Spaghetti   Oysters
> a Specialty   Clams
>
> and raw Winter's done
> to a turn—Restaurant: Spring!
> Ah, Madam, what good are your thoughts

romantic but true
beside this gaiety of the sun
and that huge appetite?

Look!
from a glass pitcher she serves
clear water to the white chickens.

What are your memories
beside that purity?
The empty pitcher dangling

from her grip
her coarse voice croaks
Bon jor'

And Patti, on her first concert tour
sang at your house in Mayagüez
and your brother was there

What beauty
beside your sadness—and
what sorrow

(*CEP*, 324)

This impressionistic poem concerns the disparity between past and present, memory and direct experience. The unusual arrangement of the first four lines mimics an advertisement, perhaps the signboard of an unpretentious local eatery. Although the dramatic situation of the poem is unclear, the sense of vividness and immediacy created by the opening stanzas suggests that mother and son may in fact be dining at Lee's Lunch or simply out for a drive in the spring weather. In any event, the text's focus and progression depend largely on Williams' pun on the word "restaurant," which derives from the French verb, "restaurer," meaning to restore, refresh, or reestablish. He moves deftly from the subject of food to the changing of the seasons by using the term simultaneously as a noun and verb, "raw Winter's done / to a turn—Restaurant: Spring!" This double entendre metaphorizes the concept of "restaurant" by linking it with a natural process of renewal; moreover, the highly kinetic quality of the phrase, "turn—Restaurant: Spring!" parallels the quick leap in the poet's train of thought.

The questions Williams poses to Elena are also intended to produce a "restaurant," drawing her out of a futile absorption with the past into an appreciation of the sensuousness and diversity of her present environs. He openly challenges the validity and worth of his mother's attitudes ("What good are your thoughts / romantic but true / beside this gaiety of the sun / and that huge appetite? . . . What are your memories / beside that purity?"), but does so in a polite, respectful manner. Indeed, he even calls her "Madam," as a waiter would a female customer. In lieu of Elena's direct response to these questions,

Williams presents a pair of enigmatic images which form a veiled parable about the dangers of her condition. The first scene he enjoins her to observe, "Look! / from a glass pitcher she serves / clear water to the white chickens," is a pastoral paradigm of grace, plenitude, and order. And yet its pristine clarity, accentuated by the modifiers "glass," "clear," and "white," is ultimately deceptive, since the image is idealized and atemporal, as its degraded counterpart reveals: "The empty pitcher dangling / from her grip / her coarse voice croaks / Bon jor'." This anonymous female figure represents two antipodal aspects of memory—its benign ability, on the one hand, to crytallize, refine, and preserve individual experience, and its treacherous vacuity and insubstantiality on the other. As Williams states in the poem's conclusion, it is precisely this combination of beauty and sadness that makes the snare of memory so difficult to escape. He understands Elena's attraction to the distant, irretrievable past of her youth in Puerto Rico, but also recognizes its concomitant hazards. The sorrow he alludes to in the last line is thus not his mother's, but rather his own, arising from the failure of his "restaurant" to effect any change in her outlook on the present.

Like "restaurant," the poem's title, "Brilliant Sad Sun," is a double entendre that plays on the concept of turning. This celestial image refers most obviously to Elena, who occupies the center of the text and, in her old age, resembles the diminished splendor of the setting sun. Yet there is another possibility as well, that of "brilliant sad *son*." The sun's "gaiety," which Williams evokes in line 9 as a symbol of the beauty and vitality of the physical environment, epitomizes all that he seeks to restore to his mother. In this respect, the poet himself becomes the sun, the primary source of light in Elena's memory-bedimmed world. The title's ambiguity thus reflects the richness, complexity, and dynamic reciprocity of influence which characterizes the poet's depictions of himself and Elena throughout his work. Together, mother and son comprise an imaginative universe, "the he and the she of it" (*IW*, 65), spinning in perpetual orbit about one another, seeking coalescence. This book is, in its broadest sense, an exploration of that strange, uncharted realm.

1

Son and Mother:
"Something Else the Same"

Listen while I talk on
against time.
It will not be
for long.

"Asphodel"

For William Carlos Williams time was always a precious commodity. Because the rigors of his medical schedule rarely allowed him to spend extended periods working in his attic study, he seized what little spare time he had—waiting at traffic signals while driving, in between examining patients at his office—to jot down ideas for stories and poems. Although he claimed the hectic pace of this dual existence stimulated him, Williams often longed for the opportunity to devote all his energy to writing. In fact, he seriously considered early retirement from medicine at various points in his career, but a combination of economic factors and tireless dedication kept him doctoring until well past the age of sixty-five.

At the beginning of the 1950s, however, the poet's elusive dream of having the leisure to write as he wished finally appeared within reach. His eldest son, also a physician, had just assumed full control of the busy practice at 9 Ridge Road, thereby freeing his father to plunge headlong into the completion of book 4 of *Paterson*. Yet even with the exigencies of medicine behind him, Williams found that his time was still not entirely his own. He was now beset by equally insistent demands of a different nature—innumerable requests for lectures, readings, and interviews. After years of critical neglect, the American literary establishment had decided that Williams was, if not a great poet, at least a venerable one worthy of their recognition, and began honoring him with awards and academic degrees. Williams greeted this flurry of unexpected attention with wry bemusement, commenting to his friend Charles Abbott: "All my life I've sought a little leisure. Now that I may get a taste of it, they're after me—on all sides."[1]

Despite his understandable exasperation, Williams seems to have been pleased by the prospect of an active retirement in which long, unhurried stretches of writing were punctuated by occasional travel and public appearances. Unfortunately, however, the poet's idyllic plans never fully materialized. By his seventieth birthday in 1953, Williams' physical condition was precarious: he had suffered two serious strokes which impaired his vision and partially paralyzed his right side; in addition, he was recovering from a severe depression brought on largely by the controversy surrounding his appointment as the Consultant in Poetry at the Library of Congress.[2] During the lengthy periods of convalescence following these strokes, Williams was often unable to either read or write, and so had ample opportunity for introspection. Faced with the imminence of his own demise, he carefully reexamined the past, and was deeply troubled by many of his previous actions. These disquieting memories filled Williams with an urgent need for summation, to explain himself and his poetic theories to the world before death permanently silenced him. As he wrote in a letter to Louis Martz shortly after his first stroke, "I must now, in other words, make myself clear. I must gather together the stray ends of what I have been thinking and make my full statement as to their meaning or quit."[3]

In this manner, the physical and emotional havoc wrought by Williams' illness became a powerful stimulus for creative expression. Rather than lulling him into the mute despondency of invalidism, the poet's thoughts spurred him on to a possible spiritual recovery through the act of writing. "The mind is the cause of our distresses," he wrote in a poem dating from this period, "but of it we can build anew" (*PB*, 75), and this is precisely what he did. As soon as he regained sufficient strength after each stroke, Williams went determinedly back to his typewriter and sat, his limp right arm folded on his lap, diligently pecking at the keys until the letters blurred beyond recognition and it was necessary to stop. Thus, in his last years Williams was not, as he claims in book 5 of *Paterson*, "learning with age to sleep my life away" (*P*, 239), but hard at work composing many of his finest lyrics. His poetic achievement during the fifties is prodigious by any standard: *The Desert Music* (1954), *Journey to Love*, which includes "Of Asphodel, That Greeny Flower" (1955), and book 5 of *Paterson* (1958). These works, which concern old age, memory, and the permanence of art versus the transcience of human life, reflect Williams' acute awareness of his own mortality. Yet as factual proof of his continued ability to write, they are also a defiant assertion of life. Though he was unable to change his situation, the act of recording it became a source of personal redemption for the poet; as he states in "To a Dog Injured in the Street":

> I can so nothing
>   but sing about it
> and so I am assuaged
>   from my pain.

(PB, 86)

As part of this endeavor to sum up his life and work before time ran out, Williams turned his attention to a manuscript which had occupied him intermittently for nearly thirty years. It was a memoir of his mother, Elena Hoheb, who died in 1949 at the astonishing age of 102. The poet had long been fascinated by the intricacies of her character, particularly by the fact that in her youth she had aspired to be an artist and studied painting in Paris for three years before her family's financial problems brought her education to an abrupt end. Beyond their obvious blood ties, mother and son shared an aesthetic kinship. Williams believed his creativity was an extension of Elena's artistic impulse, and looked to her as both a muse and poetic ideal. In the early 1920s, he began recording unusual bits of Elena's conversation which he intended to use as the basis of her biography. Over the years, he assembled a vast number of her proverbs and anecdotes, but was uncertain of the proper form in which to present them, and so the book remained unfinished.

Returning to the memoir within a few years of his mother's death was no doubt a strange emotional experience for Williams. While the passage of time allowed him to perceive her in a more objective light, it also introduced a new, unsettling element into his own relationship to the text. In rereading his detailed accounts of Elena in old age—her horror at the degenerative changes of her body and pervasive fear of death—Williams could not have failed to notice an uncanny parallel between his mother's previous state and his present one. Like her, he too was crippled, nearly blind, and dependent on others to perform even the simplest tasks. Moreover, Elena's stubborn resistance to her plight and reliance on the power of memory as a means of recovering the world she could no longer perceive through her senses closely resembled the poet's methods for coping with old age. The memoir thus assumed an almost prophetic quality for Williams; in striving to depict Elena's life and personality, he had unconsciously prefigured his own fate. Now as he faced death himself, the poet realized that he was in a sense becoming his mother, repeating the same painful process of her decline.

This discovery, which I believe Williams made while revising the memoir for publication in the mid-fifties, significantly changed its status in his mind. He began to view the text as more an autobiographical document than biography, and wrote to a friend in 1958 expressing the hope that it would help explain his nervous disposition, in other words, "how I got that way: honestly out of my mother."[4] Yet when the memoir was printed the following year under the title, *Yes, Mrs. Williams,* it did not appear overtly autobiographical in either content or scope. Elena is the central focus of the work, while Williams in his role as editor, arranger, and occasional commentator lurks in the background throughout. The autobiographical dimension of the text derives rather from the poet's belief that his representation of his mother was implicitly a self-portrait as well.

The fundamental premise underlying this belief is explored in a 1952 essay entitled "The Portrait," written after Williams was painted by the Italian artist

Emanuel Romano. Originally intended as the introduction to a catalog of Romano's work, the piece is more a meditation on the genre of portrait painting and the complex relation which exists between a painter and his subject than a critique of the Italian's art. There are two strategic reasons for this: first, by subsuming his remarks on Romano in a generalized discussion of the status of post-Cubist portraiture, Williams felt he could honestly evaluate the artist's achievement without exaggerating its importance. Also, his mother's primary ambition in life was to become a master portraitist, and her considerable skill in this field had been recently reaffirmed in the poet's mind by his discovery in an old trunk shortly after her death of three medals she received from L'Ecole des Arts Industrielle. Although Elena is never specifically mentioned in the essay, her memory inspires and suffuses it, much in the same way that Romano observed her features and "silky independence" in Williams' face as he painted it.[5]

It is therefore appropriate that the central thesis which the poet advances in "The Portrait" concerns the self-reflexivity of all art. He states: "What the artist will paint is his creation, the hidden work of his own imagination; what he is—painted in the subtly modified contours of the sitter's face. It is his own face in the terms of another face."[6] While the concept of art as an imaginative projection of its maker's emotions is fairly commonplace, Williams radicalizes it by insisting on a physical projection of identity as well: "It is his own face in the terms of another face." He stresses this mysterious conflation of self and other throughout the essay, declaring at one point that no matter what subject the artist chooses to depict, it ultimately becomes an image of "Himself—in all its multiple implications."[7] This idea can be easily extended to literature, and more specifically to Williams' own work. As a verbal artist, he too engages in a double-edged activity wherein "the imagination work[s] subtly with the flesh, representing extraordinary cominglings between two images,"[8] himself and his subject.

In *Yes, Mrs. Williams,* the poet achieves an "extraordinary co-mingling" of himself and Elena by deleting all proper names and personal pronouns from various sections of the text, thereby making it impossible to determine the source and subject of certain statements. This technique, as the following passage reveals, blurs the distinction between mother and son gives the memoir a rich, ambiguous resonance:

> Begins with an attack upon old age, what it does, what it does to others—sclerosis—faces expressionless—the mumbled word—
>
> —and the mind, as if enclosed, signaling alive from within—better than ever—ripened— every fault exaggerated, witnessed, and unable to check it. (*YMW,* 49)

The complete anonymity of this statement universalizes it; rather than describing a particular individual, it evokes a human condition equally applicable to Williams and Elena at the end of their lives. The passage is also openly polemical, proclaiming itself as "an attack upon old age" in the first line. Accordingly, it depicts aging as a ruthless state of siege in which a vibrant, active mind is trapped in and finally consumed by a decaying body. While frantically "signaling" its predicament to the outside world, the mind is powerless to do anything except "witness" its own gradual demise. Williams' choice of the verb "witness" is especially appropriate in this context since it connotes detachment and passive observation and thus underscores the disparity between the mind and body. The verb also suggests a distance between the author and subject of the statement, as if this impersonal voice were relating another's experience rather than his or her own. The phrase "old age, what it does, what it does to others" reinforces this separateness by insinuating that the narrator is somehow exempt from the tragic fate being discussed. This implicit denial of old age does not, however, provide any clues to the narrator's identity, since both Williams and Elena obstinately resisted their physical debilitation as long as possible.

Despite its stark, depersonalized tone, the passage does convey some information about the poet's relationship with his mother. The image underlying his description of a mind at the height of its cognitive powers, "better than ever—ripened," is that of a mature fruit. The choice is significant because it introduces the notions of inheritance and regeneration. Although ripeness is an ephemeral state followed rapidly by decomposition, the fruit bears within it the seeds of new life. Thus, Elena is a "seed" for Williams, not only in the obvious biological sense, but ethically as well; her example, in life and death, serves as a critical model for his own behavior. Watching her grow old was a source of both inspiration and despair for him, as he acknowledges a few pages later in the text:

> It is the limits that have made it possible, it is the awful finality of it that makes it uniform, universal, and beautiful—and dreadfully sad to witness. The return of a sort of pride—real enough. It has a reflection for the brave world—one should know it. Life isn't complete without having witnessed it. It is the end of a life that has a sort of bony flower to the end. (*YMW*, 54)

The fruit metaphor is her transformed into a "bony flower," an image which simultaneously evokes the withered understructure of a blossom like Queen Anne's lace and a human skeleton. Stripped of its sensuous petals, this ghostly flower signifies endurance rather than beauty or romance, and as such it is an appropriate emblem of old age. Williams, however, never specifically names old age in the passage, preferring to use the impersonal pronoun "it" throughout. The insistent repetition of this ambiguous referent (five times in the first sentence alone), in conjunction with the poet's rhythmic sentence patterns, makes the passage into a kind of litany praising the courage, resolution, and nobility of the elderly. Yet because of its comprehensive character, Williams' description can also be read as a tacit commentary on his own condition; like Elena's life, his too "has a sort of bony flower to the end."

This playful linguistic doubling, in which a single predicate is joined to an indeterminate, potentially multiple subject, is a crucial element in *Yes, Mrs. Williams*. The poet uses the device as a means of representing the intimate but uneasy bond which existed between himself and Elena and to demonstrate the myriad ways their lives and personalities were intertwined. At times the elusiveness of his rhetoric renders their identities virtually indistinguishable, as if mother and son comprised a single entity. Moreover, Williams' imaginative reconstitution of himself as Elena in old age is not merely an idiosyncracy confined to this particular text; the theme recurs in many of his later poems. "Tribute to Neruda the Collector of Seashells," for example, which was written in 1960 but not published until four years after Williams' death, illustrates the complex nature of his alliance with her:

> Now that I am all but blind,
> however it came about,
> though I can see as well
> as anyone—the imagination
>
> has turned inward as happened
> to my mother when she
> became old: dreams took the
> place of sight. Her native
>
> tongue was Spanish which,
> of course, she
> never forgot. It was the
> language also of Neruda the
>
> Chilean poet—who collected
> seashells on his
> native beaches, until he
> had by reputation, the second
>
> largest collection in the
> world. Be patient with
> him, darling mother, the
> changeless beauty of
>
> seashells, like the
> sea itself, gave
> his lines the variable pitch
> which modern verse requires.

(CLP, 267)

In the first three stanzas of this poem, Williams develops an elaborate network of interpersonal correspondences by linking himself with his blind, aged mother whom he then associates with Pablo Neruda by virtue of their common language. Yet after establishing this rather arbitrary linguistic tie, Williams does not pursue its logical implication—that through his identification with Elena, he is thereby linked to Neruda. Although the connection between the two men is never explicitly stated in the poem, Williams does in fact employ Neruda as a surrogate. He transforms the Chilean's habit of gathering seashells into a metaphor for writing poetry, and is thus able to draw a number of suggestive parallels between their lives and work. Like Neruda, Williams too was a collector of diverse organic forms which supplied the basis of many of his metrical innovations, most notably the variable foot. In Williams' case, however, these forms were intangible and ephemeral, consisting of the speech cadences and unusual colloquial phrases he encountered in his daily interaction with patients. Notwithstanding this obvious dissimilarity, both poets' collections are emphatically local in origin; Neruda's hobby therefore becomes a clever analogue to Williams' insistence that a writer make contact with the immediate conditions of his or her environment.

These correspondences culminate in the merging of the two writers' identities at the end of the poem. Thus, when Williams addresses his mother beginning in line 18, imploring her to "be patient" with Neruda for spending so much time engaged in a seemingly frivolous activity, he is actually seeking her indulgence for himself. By defending the intrinsic value of the Chilean's hobby, Williams is indirectly attempting to justify his own literary avocation in Elena's eyes. In this respect, the poem proves to be an intricate ruse—it is only peripherally a "tribute" to Neruda; its fundamental concern is rather Williams' problematic relationship with his mother.

This submerged biographical element places the details of the poet's address in a new light. The fact that he speaks to Elena in the present tense, for example, although she had been dead for more than a decade by the time the poem was written, attests to his profound emotional attachment to her; long after her demise, she remains a vital force in his imagination. Also, the muted tone of Williams' appeal suggests that Neruda's actions are those of an innocent but wayward child and therefore should not be dealt with too severely. This allusion, intended to elicit Elena's sympathy, implicitly relegates Williams to the position of son, locked in eternal subservience to his mother's authority.

The poet's evocation of Elena's presence and his own filial status is not a nostalgic attempt to recapture the past, but rather a symbolic declaration of the primacy of their relationship. The iconography of the situation Williams has created is also significant: by casting himself in the role of suppliant, he establishes his mother as a lofty, virtuous force akin to Dante's Beatrice. She serves as his audience, arbiter, and amour, guiding him along the path of a righteous and contemplative existence. Interestingly, the moral and spiritual elevation Williams ascribes to Elena here characterizes many of his other descriptions of her as well. In both his poetry and nonfiction, she is consistently represented as being "above" him, as the following passage from *I Wanted to Write a Poem* reveals: "I've always held [my mother] as a mythical figure, remote from me, detached, looking down on an area in which I happened to live" (*IW*, 16).

While this metaphorical distance typifies the conventional male attitude of reverence for the feminine, it also signifies alienation. Thus, in "Tribute to Neruda," the poet defines himself both in relation to and against his mother; the strong physical and psychological correspondences arising from their mutual loss of sight are modulated by an equally strong ideological disagreement about the appropriateness of writing poetry as an occupation. This tension between similarity and difference, intimacy and estrangement, and unity and duality illustrates the essentially ambivalent nature of Williams' relationship with Elena. Although their identities are closely allied and often border on convergence, a subtle dissonance always exists which preserves the individuality of mother and son. This paradoxical state of being "something else the same" (*P*, 32) underlies the structure and content of the entire poem. Williams' examination of his affiliation with Elena is embedded in a series of overt contradictions: that one can be blind but still able to see, that it is possible to be simultaneously dead and alive, and that fixed forms (e.g., "the changeless beauty of seashells") are capable of producing variation. These assertions, which fuse the literal and figurative dimensions of language, create a plausible context for the poet's intricate displacements of identity. In this ambiguous realm where both a statement and its contrary are true, the concept of selfhood is no longer fixed; identity becomes a dynamic, protean entity whose boundaries and attributes shift in relation to one's spiritual affinities. Hence, it is possible for Williams to "become" his mother as well as Pablo Neruda without abnegating his own personality.

In this respect, "Tribute to Neruda Collector of Seashells," is far more than a paradigm of Williams' relationship with Elena; the lyric also questions the fundamental nature of identity and the way in which language mediates experience. These issues, which were closely connected in the poet's mind, occupy a prominent place in his work. The highly autobiographical character of Williams' writing arises from an essentially solipsistic impulse—the need to understand and define the self. Ezra Pound acknowledged this aspect of his friend's personality in his 1928 review, "Doctor Williams' Position," describing him as an author deeply "concerned with his own insides."[9] Pound's comment, while typically astute, requires further elaboration since Williams' poetry demonstrates that his primary interest lay not exclusively within the self, but rather in the complex interaction between the mind and objective phenomena. Writing to a friend in 1926, Williams explains his relation to the external world this way: "I must look and digest, swallow and break up a situation in myself before it can get to me. It is due to my wanting to encircle too much. . . . As I exist, omnivorous, everything I touch seems incomplete until I can swallow, digest, and make it part of myself."[10] He echoes this same sentiment more than twenty years later in the opening lines of book 2 of *Paterson:*

Figure 2. Williams and His Mother in Rutherford, ca. 1918

Outside
                    outside myself
                                there is a world,
            he rumbled, subject to my incursions
            —a world
                        (to me) at rest,
                                which I approach
            concretely—

(P, 43)

These two passages are linked by the underlying violence of the poet's attitude towards the phenomenal world; he regards it as a thing to be devoured or plundered, a place which exists largely to enrich the self. His aggressive incorporation of the external world also transforms it into a potential source of art. If, as Williams claims in his essay on Emanuel Romano, "the artist is always and forever painting only one thing: a self-portrait,"[11] then an inherent part of that portrait is whatever he or she absorbs from the physical environment. The mundane sights and sounds of Williams' poetry constitute one facet of his integration of such material; more important, however, is his appropriation of other people's lives. The primary tropes in Williams' work are familial: he writes candidly about his parents (although far more about his mother than his father), wife, and children, as well as his extended family of patients and friends. The extraordinary degree of emotional detachment which allowed the poet to objectify events that intimately concerned him is perhaps best illustrated in the story "Danse Pseudomacabre," where an unidentified doctor, awakened in the middle of the night to attend a gravely ill patient, muses: "It is a dance. Everything that varies a hair's breadth from another is an invitation to the dance. Either dance or annihilation . . . And so I repeat the trouble of writing that which I have already written, and so drag another human being from oblivion to serve my music." (*FD*, 210) The physician's seemingly altruistic act thus has another, clandestine purpose—providing raw material for literature. His attitude, as the rhetoric of the passage indicates, is not at all selfless but domineering and egotistical; he will "drag" the patient back to wellbeing in order to "serve" his own aims.

In much the same way, Williams treats Elena as an aesthetic object, stating in the introduction to *Yes, Mrs. Williams:*

It is in complexities that appear finally as one person that the good of a life shows itself—bringing all together to return the world to simplicity again: this is her life. An interesting life because, I believe, in essence it is a good life as she has been a good woman—not good in a sense of being morally virtuous—because perhaps it was that too—but *good in the sense of being a valuable thing to me, when I think about it, a thing of value—like a good picture:* a sharp differentiation of good from evil—something to look at and to know with satisfaction, something alive—that has partaken of many things, welcoming them indiscriminately, if they seemed to have a value—a color—a sound to add still more to the intelligent, the colorful, the whole grasp of feeling and knowledge in the world. (*YMW*, 27–28: emphasis mine)

The poet depicts his mother in this passage as a microcosm; her character is so complex and diverse that it embraces "the whole grasp of feeling and knowledge in the world." This symbolic reduction of the universe to a single individual, an act he describes as "bringing all together to return the world to simplicity again," is on one level a device that renders the external environment more familiar and comprehensible. The generalized terms of his description, however, also suggest a recovery of the uroboric state of infancy in which a child is undifferentiated from its mother, so that she literally constitutes its world.

Moreover, this analogy transforms Williams' relationship with Elena into a metaphor for his relation with the phenomenal world. It is therefore befitting that he evaluates her life not on the basis of its own merit, but in terms of its usefulness to him. Although his discussion centers around the issues of good, evil, and virtuousness, Williams delimits the meaning of these concepts by personalizing them. If one pieces together the poet's trail of broken syntax, the import of his statement is extremely arrogant: Elena's life is adjudged both interesting and "good" solely because it serves as a "valuable thing" to him. Williams further emphasizes his mother's status as an object by likening her to "a good picture . . . something to look at and to know with satisfaction." She is thus converted into a work of art—static, beautiful, and eternal—which he, as maker and spectator, finds a source of pleasure and edification.

Williams subverts this image, however, by subsequently referring to Elena as "something alive," and in so doing, consigns her to a paradoxical state reminiscent of those described in "Tribute to Neruda." She is a living object, an animate painting which speaks the world to her son. As in the poem, this contradiction does not seem particularly bizarre or illogical in its original context. The passage is, in essence, a historical account of the way Elena acquired such immense significance for Williams; his insights, as announced in the opening line, are the product of lengthy observation and rumination: "It is in complexities that appear *finally* as one person that the good of a life shows itself. . . ." But rather than mimetically reproducing the progressive stages of his realization, the poet begins with his conclusion (i.e., mother as microcosm), then later cites evidence to support it.

He attributes Elena's metaphorical "worldliness" to her perpetual openness to new experience, which he describes in implicitly sexual terms—she "has *partaken* of many things, welcoming them *indiscriminately*. . . ." The erotic undercurrent in Williams' language is augmented by his equivocation about his mother's moral stance earlier in the passage: "she has been a good woman—not good in the sense of being morally virtuous—because perhaps [she] was that too. . . ." This statement is puzzling, especially since no historical documentation exists which would even remotely substantiate it. By all accounts, Elena was an extremely idealistic and ethical individual who steadfastly refused to compromise her principles for any person or goal. In an unpublished draft of *Yes, Mrs. Williams,* the poet illustrates this aspect of her character by recounting the story of a brief romance she had with a Spanish musician in Puerto Rico:

> She fell in love. He must have proposed. He was to finish his engagements when—by one means or another—she discovered that when he had left Spain to come to the islands and their prosperous merchants for his tour he had left a girl in Spain to whom he had promised that when he returned he would marry her. Elena found this out. She accused him. He said it was true. She flung him out of her life.[12]

While Williams admired the strength of his mother's moral conviction, he also believed it prevented her from wholly entering into and enjoying life. His remark in the memoir's introduction is therefore not so much an aspersion on her rectitude as an attempt to imaginatively liberate her from the repressive code she espoused. In suggesting that it is possible to be good without being morally virtuous, the poet implicitly projects his own values and behavioral norms onto Elena. This conflation of personal attributes broadens the meaning of the passage by demonstrating that the complexities Williams discovers and seeks to describe in his mother are ultimately his as well.

Interestingly, Elena's response to her broken engagement also provided a paradigm for the poet's own behavior under similar circumstances—namely, Charlotte Herman's rejection of his 1909 marriage proposal in favor of that of his younger brother, Edgar. As Williams relates in the biographical essay, "From My Notes about My Mother," Elena's brother Carlos had sent her to Paris in order to ease the pain of her recent heartbreak:

> There is no place in which to get over a love affair like Paris. She got over it, quick—or never. It is usually the intelligence which rallies first. Something is killed but the person we know, ourselves, is witnessed proceeding quite unaffected to the various points of vantage invented by the day—table and bed and in among the furniture and plants. Finally we are impressed and follow ourselves about, at first wanly, indifferent, but finally with a different kind of interest. The world comes up new. We begin to see it for the first time. It gets itself impressed on us. She found release in painting, in study, in the great world of Paris.[13]

Having personally experienced and survived a broken romance, Elena empathized with the plight of her eldest son who, upon receiving word of Charlotte's decision, promptly shut himself up in his bedroom and refused to eat for three days. It was his mother, bearing bowls of soup and the pragmatic advice that he would eventually "get over his grief" (*BU,* 261), who rescued him from self-pity and despondency. Like Elena, Williams also "rallied" and found release" in proposing to Charlotte's younger sister, Flossie, and travelling off to Leipzig, Germany for a year of postgraduate medical study.

This anecdote, along with Williams' compelling evocation of his mother in "Tribute to Neruda," suggests how central she was to his personal and artistic development. The poet's inscription of himself in the figure of Elena is, moreover, a subtle yet insistent feature of his work as a whole, from *Kora in Hell* through the last lyrics. This motif, which unifies many disparate aspects of his canon, also poses a significant hermeneutic problem for the reader: What is the nature and source of the strange textual symbiosis Williams proposes between himself and Elena? How can it be explained? Psychoanalysis provides a number of potential answers to these questions, but it alone cannot fully account for the phenomenon; the poet's preoccupation with his mother is far more than a fixation or identification.

In terms of actual experience, the notion that two people can be one is of course preposterous; it is only in the imagination that such a radical convergence can occur. Hence, the melding of mother's and son's identities takes place in the interstice between the real and the imaginary—on the hazy border between life and literature. Through his art, Williams converts Elena into a fiction which he can manipulate at will, much in the same way she molded his sensibilities as a child. This reversal of origins, in which the son becomes the creator of his own mother, subverts the historical chain of cause and effect, and places Williams and Elena in a timeless web of mutual influence. Their relationship, like that which exists between man and the city in *Paterson,* is "an interpenetration, both ways" (*P, 3*). Yet because the poet is dealing with a historical figure, a constant tension exists between his representation of his mother and the woman herself. The dynamic interplay of these two elements gives Williams' coalescence with Elena its undeniable force—through the agency of the imagination, even the impossible is rendered possible. Moreover, since the written word endures far beyond the lifetime of its author, the imaginative synthesis of mother and son eventually supplants their historical relationship and achieves a reality of its own.

Williams' textualization of Elena is also a process of conscious symbolization. He depicts her variously as his conscience, muse, and alter ego, associating her with creativity, the sublime, and the ethnic and cultural diversity of the New World. At the same time, however, he identifies her with negative qualities like rigidity, repression, and puritanical narrow-mindedness. Elena is a dualistic entity, serving as both generative source and scourge for her son. On a more abstract level, the antinomies Williams perceives in his mother's character reflect similar warring impulses within himself. The difficult, involuted nature of their relationship thus becomes an analogue for the poet's inner conflicts between artistic freedom and the moral strictures of his upbringing.

For these reasons, Elena—or more precisely, Williams' conception of her—is crucial to the development of his poetics. His complex fictive representations of Elena chronicle the evolution of his identity as a writer; she is the poet's grotesque double, the other through and against whom he defines himself. In this regard, *Yes, Mrs. Williams,* which has long been considered a weak addendum to his extensive canon, assumes a new centrality and significance. It is a highly problematic work, ragged in texture and filled with minor inconsistencies; nonetheless, since its composition spans Williams' most pro-ductive years as a writer, the book has strong stylistic and thematic links with *Kora in Hell, In the American Grain,* and *Paterson.*

The poet himself had grandiose notions about the importance of the memoir. Writing to Louis Untermeyer in 1939, for example, he stated: "I hope to make [my mother's] biography one of my major works—if not *the* major one."[14] And six years later, he issued the following progress report to Wallace Stevens:

> I'm working at my trade, of course, harder than ever, but also gradually maneuvering a mass of material I have been collecting for years into the introduction (all there will be of it) to the impossible poem *Paterson.* Then I'll do the biography of Mother, then either break loose to play for the rest of my days or die in the interim. (*SL,* 230–31)

Thus, even while he worked on *Paterson,* Elena's biography remained a dis-tinct priority for Williams; indeed, the passage implies that he considered the memoir his last word, the capstone to a long and varied career, after which he could settle into contented silence.

The poet's lofty ambitions for the work were never realized, however, due to his persistent problems with its form and the encroachment of old age. Shortly before the text appeared in 1959, Williams confessed his dissatisfaction with it to Winfield Townley Scott, saying: "I can't keep from telling you [it] will be far from a finished book when it is finally released—too many people have had a hand in its composition and I am powerless to do anything about it."[15] The pathos of this statement—the debilitated poet lamenting the loss of his artistic autonomy, stubbornly refusing to accept anything short of perfec-tion—is genuine, though somewhat misleading. Even under optimum condi-tions, it is unlikely that Williams could have successfully met his expectations for the work. In a sense, the memoir had to remain unfinished because, like *Paterson,* it too was an "impossible" text; to complete it would have been the symbolic acknowledgment of his own end.[16]

As the poet's failed magnum opus, *Yes, Mrs. Williams* comprises an es-sential counterpart to his greatest achievement, *Paterson.* It is the epic's pre-cursor and postscript, its underside and other half—the anima of this "white-hot man become a book" (*P,* 123).

2

Mimesis and the Mother:
The Formal Evolution of *Yes, Mrs. Williams*

If in a son one could live again! But it is impossible. And if you make it a work of the imagination, she might have said, it won't be me.
  I'll fool you, old girl. I won't make it a work of the imagination. I'll make it you.

Yes, Mrs. Williams

In "Two Pendants: for the Ears," one of the many poems Williams wrote about his mother shortly before her death in 1949, the following parenthetical directive appears:

>   (To make the language
> record it, facet to facet
> not bored out—
>
>   with an auger.
>
> —to give also the unshaven,
>   the rumblings of a
> catastrophic past, a delicate
> defeat—vivid simulations of
> the mystery   )

This statement, which momentarily interrupts the lyric's narrative progression, functions in much the same manner as a dramatic aside; the poet steps back from the emotional exigencies created by Elena's illness and announces, both to himself and the reader, a general aesthetic ambition. Moreover, the goal he articulates—to achieve a "vivid simulation" of the mystery of life through language—transcends the immediate context of the poem and applies to his work as a whole. As the imagery and diction of the passage suggest, Williams was not interested in an idealized representation of reality in which the sordid and

unhappy were "bored out" with a mental auger, but rather the coarse, "un-
shaven" actual wherein beauty was counterpointed, as in life itself, by disaster
and "delicate defeat." To attain this rigorously faithful mimesis, he recognized
that language had to be stripped of its accumulated associations; the hard, crys-
talline edges of words had to be restored, so that they would lie sparkling next
to one another "facet to facet." Only then could language accurately "record"
reality. In this respect, the specific problem of trying to recreate his mother in
words in "Two Pendants" (and, to a larger extent, in *Yes, Mrs. Williams* itself)
became for Williams a paradigm of the fundamental difficulties inherent in all
artistic representation. To make Elena a "work of the imagination," as he stated
in the memoir's introduction, was inadequate; instead, he strove to capture the
very essence of her being—in effect, to make the text "her." The poet's ability
to depict and preserve his mother in language was thus symbolically transformed into a consummate test of his artistic skill.

The mimetic potential of words was an issue that perplexed and intrigued
Williams throughout his literary career, beginning with his first significant
poem, "The Wanderer," in 1914. His query, "How shall I be a mirror to this
modernity?" (*CEP*, 3), is not merely rhetorical in character; rather, it articulates
both an aesthetic choice and a dilemma. The poet is, at this moment, renounc-
ing the lofty, neo-Keatsian subject matter of his first two books in favor of the
concrete realities of his local environment, while at the same time acknowledging the difficulty of finding a poetic technique which would accurately represent those realities. Williams believed the traditional verse forms of the past
were too inherently rigid to depict the modern experience, and that it was therefore necessary to invent new structures "intrinsic [to] the times" (*SL*, 130).
"The Wanderer" marks the beginning of his relentless search for such a form;
the poem is unrhymed and, aside from a few archaisms, characterized by fresh
colloquial language:

> And then for the first time
> I really saw her, really scented the sweat
> of her presence and—fell back sickened!
> Ominous, old, painted—
> With bright lips, and lewd Jew's eyes . . .

> (*CEP*, 5)

It was here, in the subtle cadence of common speech, that Williams discovered exactly what he was after—a diverse, energetic idiom which embodied
"all the advantageous jumps, swiftnesses, colors, [and] movements of the day"
(*SE*, 109). He used similarly kinetic terms in describing the vast poetic potential of oral language to Kay Boyle in 1932: "It is in the newness of a live
speech that the new line exists undiscovered. To go back is to deny the first
opportunity for invention which exists. Speech is the fountain of the line into
which the pollutions of a poetic manner and inverted phrasing should never

again be permitted to drain" (*SL,* 134). "Live speech," as heard daily from the mouths of Polish mothers and his countless other patients in Rutherford, represented a "fountain" to Williams, a pure, abundant, and as yet untapped source of new measures; one had only to listen closely in order to perceive its endless possibilities and permutations.

Williams' espousal of ordinary speech rhythms as an alternative to iambic pentameter and his adamant belief that a poem could "be made of anything" (*I,* 70) produced ground-breaking revisions in the nature of the genre itself. In conjunction with the stylistic experiments of other modernists such as Ezra Pound, these innovations transformed the poem from an essentially closed system—an elegant set piece or Wordsworthian expression of emotion recollected in tranquility—into a dynamic entity with and through which the poet could think.[1] Rather than conforming to any preconceived model, the structure of Williams' poems evolves out of the actual process of composition and is intimately connected to his engagement with the particulars of the subject under consideration. In this respect, his work anticipates Robert Creeley's famous dictum: "Form is never more than an extension of content."[2]

The poet's concern with vernacular speech and the interrelation of form and content is also reflected in much of the prose he wrote during the twenties. *In the American Grain,* for example, his landmark study of the founders and heroes of the new world, bears little resemblance to a standard historical narrative. Instead of constructing an objective, third-person account of these mythic individuals, he attempted to "get inside [their] heads" (*A,* 178) by examining whatever original records—letters, journals, autobiographies—they had left behind. By carefully editing and arranging these documents, Williams was able to present the heroes' stories largely in their own words. This technique made the past more readily accessible to the modern reader by converting remote, faceless figures like Columbus and Eric the Red into distinct individuals whose personalities were revealed by the idiosyncracies of their unique idioms. In sections of the text where, due to a lack of primary source material, Williams could not employ direct quotation, he effected a literary style which he felt was appropriate to the event or issue being discussed. As he states in the *Autobiography:*

> The Tenochtitlan chapter was written in big, square paragraphs like Inca masonry. Raleigh was written in what I conceived to be Elizabethan style; the Eric the Red chapter in the style of the Icelandic saga; Boone in the style of Daniel's autobiography. . . . *Thus I tried to make each chapter not only in content but in the style itself a close study of the theme.* (A, 183–84; emphasis mine)

This impulse to make the formal structure of a work consonant with its subject and theme is even more clearly demonstrated in Williams' improvisational writings. In texts like *Kora in Hell* and *The Great American Novel,* he challenges basic assumptions about plot, unity, and character by presenting a random series of subjective impressions in an ostensibly narrative format. His use of chapter headings, for example, to organize blocks of disparate, nonsequential material is not merely parodic, but an attempt to loosen the conventional strictures of the novel and thus enable it to accommodate a different kind of "story," namely, the gradual unfolding of individual consciousness.

Although he employs many of the techniques associated with stream-of-consciousness writing, Williams' improvisational prose differs from the work of Joyce and Woolf in that it lacks an overarching narrative frame. He denies the reader any preliminary knowledge of situation or context, plunging him directly into a chaotic miscellany of unrelated perceptions, as the opening lines of *January: A Novelette* reveal:

> Before, you could eat ice-cream out of it; after, you wouldn't spit in it. "Stride of Man." "Old Ireland." Collapse. End of first paragraph.
>
> Character, temperament, and desire would be the only cements of a new association. The trick is lost. Searching in the cloth the elastic band yielded before his fingers. The old fashioned trees were without a leaf. A chickadee made the pattern of three waves across the wall of the Congregational Church. . . . (*I*, 272)

This passage, which typifies the disjunctive style of all the improvisations, is too varied and diffuse to qualify as an interior monologue; rather, it appears to be a literal transcription of whatever enters the poet's mind—sensory data, fragments of conversation, memories of the day's trivial events. Since no formal logic governs the arrangement of these thoughts, it is only by indulging their idiosyncratic rhythm that the reader can begin to grasp some sense of the text's meaning.

Williams defended the hermetic character of his improvisations in *January* by maintaining that their apparent disorder was a truer, more "actual" representation of the flux of experience than any novel had ever achieved. In his opinion, it was smooth, consecutive narratives that were in fact "disjointed" because they bore "no relation to anything in the world or in the mind" (*I*, 275). This paradoxical inversion of the principles of order and disorder reveals the extent of Williams' commitment to faithfully reproducing the modernity in which he lived; for the sake of authenticity, he was willing to risk obscurity and even unintelligibility. But the primary significance of the poet's statement lies in his insistence on the referentiality, not of language, but of literary forms themselves. All *compositions,* he asserts, must correspond to something "in the world or in the mind."

This distinction between outer/inner, objective/subjective is helpful in assessing the nature of Williams' poetic achievement. "My whole intent, in my life," he told Kenneth Burke in 1947, "has been to find a basis . . . for the actual" (*SL*, 257). This remark, made more than thirty years after the publication of "The Wanderer," testifies to the consistency of the poet's aesthetic priorities; at the same time, however, it denotes a subtle refinement in his understanding of how to accomplish those goals. His youthful ambition to "be a mirror to this modernity" is implicitly grounded in the theory that art imitates life—indeed, the phrase itself is an updated version of the familiar aphorism in *Hamlet* about holding a mirror up to nature.[3] But in the early 1920s, Williams dismissed this notion as a serious misrepresentation of the creative process. Rather than slavishly copying nature, the artist creates an independent, coequal reality in his imagination and thus "rivals nature's composition with his own" (*I*, 121).

Williams' comment to Burke, which postulates a vaguer, more elliptical relationship between external phenomena and the perceiving eye than that expressed in "The Wanderer," reflects this change in attitude. Because the two statements are syntactically similar, their differences can be neatly summarized by a comparison of the four key terms. Whereas a mirror passively casts back a static image which is complete unto itself, a "basis" is a structure or foundation upon which something else is built; it implies the possibility of further construction, and is, in that respect, potentially active. "Modernity" and "the actual" prove more difficult to distinguish since they are virtually synonymous. In the context of "The Wanderer," "modernity" is a label applied to a broad spectrum of urban experience which is simultaneously intriguing and offensive to the poet. It is, in other words, a description imposed from without; once his immersion in the waters of the filthy Passaic is complete, this reality no longer appears ominous and impersonal. Thus, through a process of acceptance and gradual familiarization, "modernity" is translated into "the actual."

Like "imagination," "actual" is a word Williams frequently used but never explicitly defined. From a cursory examination of his writing one might be tempted to equate the term with the literal or physical because his poetry abounds with vivid images like the notorious red wheelbarrow, and the shapeless fetal form huddled on the international bridge between El Paso and Juarez in "The Desert Music." Yet "actual" also has a temporal sense: "in action or existence at the time; present, current."[4] Much of Williams' work, particularly the improvisations, attempts to capture the present moment, the instant at which the imagination engages and internalizes some person, object, or event in the material world. The term "actual" therefore refers to objective phenomena (things in and of themselves) as well as the subjective experience of that phenomena in the individual mind. These dual realities, as Hugh Kenner observes in *A Homemade World,* were inseparable for Williams:

> The imagination is the place where mental clarities occur, for you no more experience clarities in your head than you experience vision in your eye. Where is the seen world? It is behind the eye, in a space you have learned to create. And where, likewise, is the clarified world (where "so much depends [on a red wheel barrow"])? Ah, in the Imagination.
>
> Which, Williams meant, is where poems are, in a space you must likewise learn to create. "There is a 'special' place which poems, as all works of art, must occupy, but it is quite definitely the same as that where bricks or colored threads are handled": are handled, of course, by the intending mind that can reach through the fingers.[5]

The poet's preoccupation with finding a form capable of representing the actual is linked to a larger, more vexing issue—the nature of mimesis itself. As he told Kenneth Burke in that same 1947 letter, on a theoretical level, his task was relatively simple: "all one has to do is to discover the new laws of metric and use them" (*SL,* 257). The difficulty, of course, lay in their practical application. Despite his assertion in *Spring and All* that art equals and even surpasses nature, Williams understood that, in purely pragmatic terms, a poem was merely a verbal artifact, "a small (or large) machine made of words" (*CLP,* 5), which could approximate but never match the "real." This disparity between words and the "vague accuracies of events" (*P,* 23) troubled the poet and prompted him to continually test the mimetic capacities of language in his writing. Though he suspected his efforts were ultimately destined to failure, Williams believed that the challenge of trying to capture the elusive, "radiant gist" of life on paper was nonetheless worthwhile. As he states in "The Hard Core of Beauty":

> The most marvellous is not
> the beauty, deep as that is,
> but the classic attempt at beauty . . .

(*CLP,* 199)

This emphasis on process instead of outcome, endeavor instead of achievement, constitutes a pervasive ethos in Williams' life and work. The concept also appears in *Paterson,* in what at first seems to be a moral context, though it is finally as aesthetic imperative:

> Virtue is wholly
> in the effort to be virtuous.
> This takes connivance,
> takes convoluted forms, takes
> time!

(*P,* 189)

These three elements, "connivance . . . convoluted forms, [and] time," play a crucial role in Williams' lifelong search for accurate representation as well. The immensely complex nature of this mimetic undertaking is best demonstrated by the examination of a single text, *Yes, Mrs. Williams.* The memoir, which is his last published piece of prose, evolved over a thirty-year span from the mid-twenties to 1959, and is thus paradigmatic not only of Williams' complicated relationship with his mother but of his creative process as well. Drafts of the work in the Beinecke Library at Yale indicate that much of the raw material for the text had been assembled by the late thirties; what delayed its publication for two more decades was Williams' inability to find a form which he considered consonant with his subject. The published version of the memoir is in fact a palimpsest, bearing enigmatic traces of his earlier plans and organizational strategies; these clues, in conjunction with the Yale manuscripts, make it possible to reconstruct the various phases of the book's morphology as well as the motives which impelled that development. In this respect, *Yes, Mrs. Williams* resembles an archaeological site: through a careful excavation of its successive layers, the text yields a composite picture of Williams as artist.

The exact origin of *Yes, Mrs. Williams* cannot be located; its inception is inextricably entangled with Williams' own beginnings as a writer. He first formally declared his intention to write a book about Elena in the 1936 poem "Eve"; however, unpublished letters and manuscripts suggest the concept of the memoir predates the poem by at least twenty years. The promise Williams makes to his mother in "Eve" is nevertheless significant in that it sharply delineates the nature of their relationship:

> If you are not already too blind
> too deaf, too lost in the past
> to know or to care—
> I will write a book about you—
> making you live (in a book!)
> as you still desperately
> want to live—
> to live always—unforgiving

(*CEP*, 377)

This pledge to immortalize Elena in a text belongs to a time-honored poetic tradition. Yet, unlike his Elizabethan predecessors, Williams' intent is not to idealize and preserve the evanescent bloom on his youthful lover's cheek, but rather to create a realistic portrait of his mother's indomitable character. In the context of the poem, his vow is motivated by a desire to assuage the guilt he feels for keeping Elena, who lived with him at 9 Ridge Road for seventeen of the last twenty-five years of her life (1924–41), "imprisoned—in the name of protection" (*CEP*, 375). The melodramatic quality of Williams' language is misleading since his "guilt" arises more from a sense of frustration and helplessness than from any actual mistreatment. Because it is beyond his power as a physician to heal Elena's infirmities, in caring for her he becomes her captor, an inadvertent part of the dark conspiratorial force by which she feels surrounded. Only through his imaginative powers as a writer can Williams change his mother's situation; by documenting the intensity of her resistance to decrepitude and death, he makes her a symbol of the life principle:

> One would think
> you would be reconciled with Time
> instead of clawing at Him
> that way, terrified
> in the night—screaming out
> unwilling, unappeased
> and without shame—

Might He not take
that wasted carcass, crippled
and deformed, that ruined face
sightless, deafened—
the color gone—that seems
always listening, watching, waiting
ashamed only
of that single and last
degradation—
No. Never. Defenseless
still you would keep
every accoutrement
which He has loaned
till it shall be torn from
your grasp, a final grip
from those fingers
which cannot hold a knife
to cut the meat but which
in a hypnotic ecstasy
can so wrench a hand held out
to you that our bones
crack under the unwonted pressure—

(*CEP,* 378)

The contradictory images of Elena in these lines—her "wasted carcass" and arm-wrenching grip—convey the poet's simultaneous horror and admiration of her. Although her physical condition, "crippled and deformed, that ruined face sightless, deafened—the color gone," is devoid of dignity, her refusal to passively accept death is noble and compelling. Elena's plight has an undeniably allegorical dimension; her circumstance is a metaphor for the struggle of the human spirit against inevitable odds. Moreover, as the poem's title suggests, Williams considered this fierce will to live a particularly feminine trait. In a 1957 essay entitled "From My Notes about My Mother," he states:

So I say, in a life that continues there is a part that lives as there may be a part that dies. In her, though the part that was dying filled her with dread and resentment, for all that—call it cowardice if you will—there was a part that refused to die. *She never had in her any element of the suicide. That may be the female of it. I don't know. It was strong in her. She lived.*[6]

This same theme lies at the heart of the memoir; as the emphatic "yes" in its title implies, the text is a celebration of Elena's tough, life-affirming stance. The major difference between the two works is one of perspective: the poem, written when she was in her mid-eighties, is a direct, visceral response to the pathos of an ongoing condition, whereas the memoir, in its final form, is a requiem.

Yet the primary impulse underlying the genesis of *Yes, Mrs. Williams* was not the imminence of Elena's death, but the poet's persistent fascination with "her phraseology and way of thinking" (*YMW*, 37). A native of Puerto Rico who studied painting in Paris for three years before emigrating to the United States, she spoke a strange hybrid tongue which freely combined elements of Spanish, French, and English. Though Elena spent most of her adult life in Rutherford, New Jersey, she never mastered the nuances of English grammar, and thus her command of the language remained imperfect and thoroughly idiosyncratic. She was fond of popular colloquial expressions, but her attempts to use them often produced unintentionally comic results, as this 1904 letter, written when Williams was at the University of Pennsylvania, reveals:

> Now Mama I am going to tell you something funny. In your last letter you said you were "out of thoughts" and hoped I was in "good spirit." These are two very dangerous predicaments. I hope you will always have thoughts to fall back on. As for me, I am not ready to be "preserved" yet. You should have said "out of sorts" and "in good spirits." Never mind Mama, I love you all the more for such things as these.[7]

The obvious affection with which the twenty-one-year-old Williams treats his mother's linguistic blunders illustrates an intuitive recognition and appreciation of the vitality of her idiom. But the fact that he corrects her, albeit in the gentlest fashion, suggests that at this point he is still somewhat uneasy with any divergence from standardized forms. As the years passed, however, he grew to savor the ungrammaticality of Elena's utterances, discovering in them a unique source of new poetic measures.

Sometime around 1913 or 1914 Williams began jotting down his mother's remarks in a small red notebook along with other miscellaneous information relating to his position as the medical inspector of Rutherford's schools. These insignificant observations and unfinished phrases, like "Do you know what I did. I managed to get the cup and put my hand inside (gesture)" and "When Mrs. Thing comes—in the corner there—put away,"[8] while not specifically attributed to Elena, bear such a strong resemblance to statements in *Yes, Mrs. Williams* that there is little doubt as to their source. The closest the poet comes to identifying his mother in the notebook occurs in the following passage:

> Why you don't
> weigh more
> than a baby
> —carramba!
>
> She looked like
> a little old,
> old woman
>   with her
> little black
> screwed eyes
> just like her
> father—you

> couldn't see
> any of the whites
>
> ————
>
> she has never
> learned death—
>
> ————
>
> always new
> much to her
> embarrassment[9]

Several details—the Spanish exclamation "carramba," the references to "little black screwed eyes," old age (Elena was sixty-seven at the time the notebook was composed), and the denial of death—all point to Elena as the subject of the excerpt. Furthermore, Williams' technique of direct quotation ("Why you don't weigh more . . .") followed by an interpretive commentary prefigures the format he would adopt more than forty years later in the published memoir.

The poet continued recording his mother's anecdotes and sayings over the next ten years with no specific literary purpose in mind other than preserving "the flavor and accurate detail" (*YMW,* 23) of her words. According to the chronology he provides in the memoir's introduction, the idea of writing a book about Elena did not occur to him until the late twenties: "Once we translated a French novel together. . . . I enjoyed this contact with her and then, I think, conceived the idea of gathering her sayings which interested and amused me. . . . From this grew the idea of the biography . . . (*YMW,* 25–26). The French novel alluded to here is Philippe Soupault's *Last Nights of Paris,* which Williams and his mother translated during the winter of 1928–29. Williams undertook this project partly as a favor to Soupault, whom he had met in Paris four years earlier, but it was primarily a means of entertaining Elena. Another motivating factor, which Williams mentioned in a letter to Ezra Pound, was his admiration of the apparent artlessness and authenticity of the Frenchman's style:

> The first few pages of Soupault, by the way, are delightful reading. Easy, deceptive, accurate to the rules of conversation (which I am afraid Hem[ingway] doesn't at all understand, since it is rarely as expressive as he makes it and almost twice as succinct), just batting the air effectively and swimming in it—like an airplane. (*SL,* 104–5)

Interestingly, the "rules of conversation" play an important part in the collaborative act of translation as well. Soupault's text, while providing Elena with a considerable intellectual challenge, also engendered a flood of memories concerning her own student days in Paris. Throughout the course of their work, she told Williams countless stories of her teachers, friends, and the elegant soirées she had attended, fueling his curiosity to such a degree that he resolved to learn all he could about her past. Thus, by virtue of its language and setting, the novel served as a bridge between mother and son; as the immediate focus of their attention, it offered a ready-made topic of conversation, a false center around which valued personal information could be unself-consciously exchanged.

According to Dickran Tashjian, Williams' collaboration with Elena had an inherently reflexive dimension. "The very process of translation," he asserts, was "an act that replicated in language itself her own experience between two worlds."[10] The enterprise was, in addition, the outgrowth of a complex set of historical circumstances. Some years prior to the Soupault translation, the poet tried a similar experiment with his father, William George, an Englishman raised in the West Indies who spoke Spanish fluently. Together they translated a group of Spanish poems which appeared in the August 1916 issue of the little magazine *Others,* and a short story, "The Man Who Resembled a Horse," by Guatemalan writer Rafael Arévalo Martínez. The story was first published in the *Little Review* of December 1918, the same month in which the elder Williams died, and was later reprinted in the 1944 New Directions anthology. In a brief note appended to the story's second publication, Williams recounted the circumstances surrounding its translation. "In [my father's] last years when he was getting ready to die," Williams wrote, "I tried to invent ways to keep him entertained, one of them happened to be to help me translate Rafael Arévalo Martínez's story."[11]

This comment would not be at all remarkable but for the fact that Williams repeats it nearly verbatim in describing his subsequent work with Elena. Here, for example, is his account of their second collaboration from *Autobiography:*

> When Mother was in her eighties, and we looked about for something to do to amuse her, I hit upon an old book that Pound must have left here on one of his visits. We started to translate it, and we found ourselves richly entertained. *El Perro y la Calentura,* literally, *The Dog and the Fever,* it was the work of the famous Don Francisco Quevedo. . . . (*A,* 350)

Some obvious parallels exist between the two situations: in each case, the translation is undertaken as a creative diversion to help a severely ill, bedridden parent pass the time more pleasantly. These similarities indicate that not only was Williams' experience with his father a crucial precedent for his projects with Elena, but that the act of translation itself had become a trope for communicating with his progenitors. Williams chose this particular form of "entertainment" over other shared activities like chess or card-playing because it supplied him with a formal linguistic construct intimately connected with earlier phases of his mother's and father's lives. In addition to rendering the past accessible, the foreign texts became a vehicle for the retrieval and salvage of familial information which would otherwise have been irrevocably lost after their deaths. In this respect, the translations are a poignant, if somewhat circuitous, attempt by the poet to establish contact with his parents before it was too late.

There is, however, another equally important factor involved in these collaborations. Williams was, by his own admission, a late poetic bloomer, and the tardiness of both his first great lyrics (*Spring and All,* published when he was forty, in 1923) and any substantial public recognition instilled him with a deep sense of insecurity about his work. This feeling was exacerbated by the fact that his parents, who were generally supportive of his ambitions, regarded writing with a distinct ambivalence; the profession of writing poetry simply was neither pragmatic nor lucrative enough to suit their tastes. The task of convincing them of the validity and worth of his avocation therefore became one of Williams' major priorities, as if their approval constituted a fundamental prerequisite for his success.[12] In a curious way, the translations offered him an opportunity to do just that. By engaging his parents in a literary endeavor—an endeavor wherein the richness and subtlety of language had paramount importance—Williams was able to circumvent the constraints of filial submission and approach them on a more equitable basis. Within the parameters of the project, their familial bond yielded to a professional one; rather than relating as parent and child, they became colleagues united in pursuit of a common intellectual goal.

The collaborations involved a clear-cut division of labor. Because William George and Elena were extremely proficient in foreign languages, they did most of the actual deciphering of the texts. Williams served largely in the capacity of advisor, selecting words which he felt best conveyed the spirit of the original, and fashioning awkward phrases into graceful, idiomatic English. In this way, the poet used the process of translation as a performative space in which to demonstrate his facility as a writer. And, while entertaining his parents, he ingeniously induced them to "entertain" him in a different light—as a working artist.

Significantly, the translations Williams produced with his father and mother differ markedly in both character and style. This disparity can in part be attributed to the respective stages in the poet's career at which they were undertaken, but it is also directly related to the temperament of the individual with whom he was collaborating. The Spanish translations Williams did with his father in 1915–16, for example, closely resemble academic exercises—they are stilted, excessively literal, and full of strangely contorted diction. No imaginative risks were taken with the texts; instead, the two men concentrated on finding exact linguistic equivalents for each word and phrase. In his note on the Martínez story, Williams recalls how he and his father labored over the precise meaning of the verb in the title:

> For several days we just couldn't get the "Paresia." We had, the man who looked like a horse *or* the man who was like a horse *or* the man who appeared to be a horse. No good. Then one day I came to see him as he lay there ill and he said to me, I've got it. I could see how

happy it made him. Haven't you guessed it? he asked me. No. Why, you're supposed to be a writer, he smiled. No, I can't guess it, I said. It's the man who RESEMBLED a horse![13]

This anecdote is important for two reasons: it affords an instructive glimpse into the workings of the collaborative process and vividly underscores one of William George's salient character traits. On the surface, his resolution of this nagging textual dilemma represents an intellectual triumph as well as a source of personal pride and satisfaction. Yet the wry comment he makes to Williams, "You're supposed to be a writer," suggests that his pleasure derives not so much from the achievement itself, but in having beaten his son to it. The collaboration is thus undercut by a competitive impulse; rather than facilitating greater intimacy between the poet and his father, it proves to be the occasion for a struggle of wills. Although William George's remark is ostensibly made in jest, its implications are quite serious: by disparaging his son's resourcefulness and creativity, he mocks the young man's artistic aspirations and tacitly asserts his own superiority.

From a critical standpoint, the maneuver is unsuccessful since the father's interpretation of the word "paresia" belies any great imaginative or poetic power. A more daring translator would probably have chosen to omit the verb altogether and simply called the story "The Horse-Man," using the title's ambiguous connotations to accentuate the myriad equine qualities of the central character. But such a bold, impressionistic title was unthinkable to the elder Williams because it did not correspond to the syntax or structure of the original. It was risky, presumptuous, whereas his choice was undeniably safe. In this respect, the anecdote ironically illustrates the basic flaw underlying all of William George's translations: his conscientious commitment to literalism and detail was so strong that it impeded his sense of the work as a whole. This myopic tendency resulted, as the opening lines of the Martínez translation attest, in prose that, though strikingly faithful to the Spanish, was clumsy, insipid, and at its worst, painful to read:

> At the time we were presented he was at one end of the apartment, his head on one side, as horses are accustomed to stand, with an air of being unconscious of all going on around him. He had long, stiff, and dried-out limbs, like those of one of the characters in an English illustration of *Gulliver's Travels*. But my impression that the man in some mysterious way resembled a horse was not obtained then, except in a subconscious manner, which might have never have risen to the full life of consciousness had not my abnormal contact with the hero of this story been prolonged.[14]

The extremely formal, verbose language of this excerpt contrasts sharply with the incisive style of Williams' own prose, suggesting that his role in the translation was minimal. The poet's reluctance to colloquialize his father's heavily Anglicized diction bespeaks the tenuous nature of their relationship, yet ultimately remains an equivocal gesture which can be interpreted as an act either of deference to or defiance of the older man. In any event, the translations solidly corroborate his assessment of William George in the *Autobiography:*

> [Pop] was a stickler for fundamentals. I'll say that, and when he took hold of a thing insisted on going through with it to the bitter end to find out what it amounted to. If he couldn't understand a thing at last, he'd reject it, which was not Mother's saving way of facing the world. (*A*, 91)

The distinction Williams draws here between his father's steadfast pursuit of definitive meaning and his mother's willingness to accept things she did not understand leaves little doubt as to where his own predilections lay. His use of the adjective "saving" to characterize Elena's mode of interacting with the world implies a repudiation of William George's approach; if her way is redemptive, then his, by contrast, is harmful, perhaps even destructive, because it does not allow room for the imagination. Despite its moral overtones, this distinction helps to clarify the ways in which the poet's parents differed as translators. Williams' collaborations with Elena, though by no means exemplary, exhibit a sensitivity to the rhythm and flow of language that is generally lacking in those done with his father. They are freer, livelier, and more colloquial in style. Elena seems to have had a far more casual attitude towards the task than did her husband—she regarded the foreign text as something to be played with, lingered over, and enjoyed rather than a problem demanding immediate resolution. As a result, she was able to tease out nuances of meaning and tone which William George's rigid methodology did not permit.

Yet aside from these substantive dissimilarities, Elena's translations have one crucial feature in common with her spouse's: they are the locus of a powerful interpersonal dynamic. For both parents the act of collaborating was a highly cathectic experience and unconsciously became the occasion and vehicle for working out deeply rooted conflicts and insecurities. Rivalry, as we have already seen, is the predominant impetus underlying the father-son collaboration; in the mother's case, however, another equally potent force is involved. Because of a dramatic reversal in her family's fortunes, Elena had been unable to fulfill her youthful dream of becoming a great portraitist. She never fully recovered from the bitter disappointment of having to abandon her studies in Paris and return home to Puerto Rico; indeed, she dwelt on the memory of those brief, happy years in France throughout her life and frequently lamented the fate that had cruelly transformed her from a budding painter into a suburban New Jersey housewife. But rather than trying to reconcile the bizarrely disjunctive phases of her experience, Elena, the quintessential romantic, persisted in regarding herself as a failure, a hapless victim whose artistic goals had been thwarted by circumstance. "It is as if I were another person now—what I was then" (*YMW*, 60), she would sigh, frustrated yet simultaneously resigned to her plight.

Figure 3. Carte de Visite, Paris, 1876–79

"She was no more than an obscure art student from Puerto Rico, slaving away at her trade which she loved with her whole passionate soul, living it, drinking it down with her every breath."
(*YMW*, 5)

Figure 4. Williams and Elena, Chateau de Chillon, Switzerland, ca. 1897

In view of Elena's background, it is not surprising that she responded favorably to the idea of collaborating with her son. The translations offered an outlet for her long-repressed creative talents, albeit in a verbal rather than visual format. A subliminal process of identification thus takes place throughout the course of their endeavors. By working in conjunction with Williams, Elena felt that her artistic aspirations could be vicariously expressed and brought to fruition, and in the reflected glow of their literary achievement, her life would assume a new significance and value.[15] A number of intriguing statements which the poet makes in *Yes, Mrs. Williams,* such as "If in a son one could live again! But it is impossible" (*YMW,* 34) and "When she herself was unable to fulfill her desires for personal accomplishment, she transferred those ambitions to her children" (*YMW,* 140–41), indicate that he realized the profound importance his mother attached to their collaborations and used it to his own advantage in finding out more about her past. His comment on the Soupault translation in *I Wanted to Write a Poem* provides additional confirmation of this awareness: "My mother knew French well and *it pleased her to work with me. We worked and worked, intently*" (*IW,* 48; emphasis mine). In this respect, the outcome of Williams' collaborations with Elena was totally antithetical to that of his previous experiences with William George. The act of translation exposed a strong psychic bond between mother and son and a propensity towards convergence, whereas with his father it revealed distance, difference, and subtle antagonism. The divergence of the parents' responses to the same task thus serves as a metaphor for the larger, more fundamental nature of their different relationships to the poet himself.

Because the Soupault translation proved so mutually satisfying, Williams decided to try another collaboration with his mother several years later. The French novel had, as intended, generated a wealth of information about Elena's early adulthood, but now the poet sought to reach back into the more distant past—her youth in the provincial west Puerto Rican town of Mayagüez. Such a venture, as he noted in one of the unpublished drafts of the memoir, necessitated a cultural and linguistic shift:

> Growing old etc., etc. And so, some years ago, with the blindness and one thing and another—I thought it might be worth trying to translate something. I had just enjoyed Philippe Soupault's *Les Dernières Nuits de Paris* and she had read it too. So we did that. But now I thought of the Spanish. That seemed more like her childhood.[16]

The text Williams chose to accomplish this goal was an obscure seventeenth-century novella by Don Francisco Quevedo called *El Perro y la Calentura* [*The Dog and the Fever*]. His selection, given the vast range of Spanish literature, is decidedly peculiar, though not in the least arbitrary. First of all, the text, which had been gathering dust in the family bookcase ever since Pound left it there around 1910, possessed in the advantage of being close at hand. Because the translation was technically an "amusement," taken on in addition to Williams' full-time responsibilities as a writer-physician, convenience was an essential consideration. Of far greater consequence, however, was the fact that Quevedo had a tangential connection to Elena's childhood. He was apparently a rather colorful character, and stories of his scandalous exploits in the royal court had filtered down through the centuries, reaching even remote outposts of Spanish culture like Mayagüez, where she had heard them as a girl. In spite of her strong puritanical bent, Elena found the tales quite amusing, and later passed them along to her own children. In the introduction to the memoir, Williams reflects on the degree to which her familiarity with the writer's reputation influenced his choice:

> She has frequently in her life referred to Quevedo, telling one or another of the salty stories connected with his name, showing that she enjoyed them exceedingly well. Were it not for these stories she has told me, the old book would not have attracted me and nothing would have come of it—even the idea of the biography would not have taken form beyond the vague idea I had of it. (*YMW*, 36)

As the last line of this passage indicates, Quevedo was an integral component in the genesis of Elena's biography. Beyond the legendary resonance of his name, the text itself, which was written in archaic Spanish and filled with the kind of traditional proverbs she was fond of quoting, evoked other, more extensive memories of her island home. The novella also had a bawdy side which, according to Williams, "never discouraged Mother; she loved it" (*A*, 351). The translation thus served a dual purpose, linking the poet to the precise part of his mother's past he most wanted to explore, while at the same time revealing an intriguing, little-known facet of her personality.

The circumstances surrounding this collaboration, which began in 1935 and continued intermittently over the next three years, were adverse. Elena, who had broken her hip in the winter of 1930, was now permanently crippled and confined to her upstairs bedroom in Williams' home; to make matters worse, her vision was becoming increasingly clouded by cataracts. As the scope of her world diminished, Elena grew peevish and more demanding, straining the limits of the poet's patience as well as his capacity to find activities which would keep her occupied. The decision to undertake a second translation was therefore prompted, in large part, by an overwhelming sense of desperation—the project became a last-ditch effort to alleviate the misery of her predicament. The gravity of the situation is apparent from a passing remark Williams makes in the memoir's introduction:

> With her deafness and cataracts it was becoming difficult to find or make conversation by which to divert her. There is an incentive arising from the weak and defenseless that drives us devilishly to want to insult and even to kill them. It is bestial in a man to want to slaughter his old mother—so that he had better find an alternative.
> It took the form of an old book. . . . (*YMW*, 35–36)

This notion of the translation as an "alternative to slaughter," however shocking and ludicrous it seems, raises an important question about the nature of Williams' priorities. His reasons for taking on the task are essentially ambiguous: they can be interpreted as humane and altruistic (finding a constructive means of defusing his anger at Elena in order to protect her from the possibility of physical harm) or selfish (a necessary measure to insure his own sanity). The same can be said of his desire to document and preserve the details of his mother's past. Is the chief objective to immortalize her or himself by making use of her as an aesthetic object? These motives, while dissonant, are not mutually exclusive; in varying degrees, they all come into play during the collaboration, charging what would otherwise be a banal domestic scene with rich, unresolved tensions.

Moreover, this indeterminacy of purpose and priority constitutes one of the fundamental differences between the Soupault and Quevedo translations, and thus signals a critical development in the evolution of *Yes, Mrs. Williams*. The earlier collaboration, while demonstrating the efficacy of the poet's plan, was primarily intended as a means of amusing Elena; her needs, in this instance, took distinct precedence over his own. But by the mid-thirties, a subtle reversal had occurred: Williams began to view the act of translating as a ruse which would engage his mother's attention and provide him with an ideal opportunity to observe the intricacies of her character and discretely transcribe her words. With this shift in focus, the actual deciphering of the text assumed an ancillary importance; Quevedo's novella became more or less a prop, a contrivance essential to the achievement of Williams' larger goal. As the following excerpt from the memoir reveals, Elena herself was now the principal object of scrutiny, the human text whose mysteries he was determined to unlock:

> [*The Dog and the Fever*] is pretty hard for her, but we get along a few pages at a time. The thing isn't finished yet—we're about at page 65 out of a possible 96 and neither one of us had read it through—but it's interesting in spots. And it gives me a chance to listen to her now that she is extremely limited in what she can say; I get a chance to take her in, all, a sort of limited comprehensiveness in what is really an extreme limitation: her room, the few papers she can decipher, a word or two of conversation. (*YMW*, 54)

The rhythmic counterpoint Williams establishes here between limits ("the *few* papers," "a *word or two* of conversation") and comprehensiveness ("I *get . . . to take her in, all*") illustrates the manner in which his strategy broadens and transforms the interpretive possibilities of the situation. In his dual role as collaborator and observer, the poet enjoys the advantage of physical proximity to his mother while successfully maintaining the emotional detachment necessary to transcend the pathos of her plight and perceive its wider significance. And because his project, like Elena's, is ultimately an act of reading, there is an air of playful reflexivity about it: "As she would lean over, the large reading glass in her hand, studying some difficult word, the scheme of what I had in mind began to unfold and I could secretly, under guise of taking down the translation take down rather her own words" (*YMW*, 37).

Williams further underscores the similarity of their enterprises by drawing an analogy between his mother and the material text of Quevedo's novella; like the book, she too is a mysterious artifact—old, foreign, difficult to decipher— and must be approached with due caution and respect:

> I had held [the book] in my hands many times without ever having had the courage to dip into it. . . . Like her it is old, though far far older than she. It is an octavo of very much worn brown leather, with the title in crooked gilt letters, all but completely obliterated. The print is large, old fashioned, and irregularly spaced, and the punctuation is to say the least individual. (*YMW*, 36)

This superficial identification of Elena and the Spanish text deepened as their work on the translation progressed, becoming the basis of a much more complex entanglement. As the poet's stockpile of stories about his mother's childhood increased, the shape of her biography began to crystallize in his mind. He now understood that the novella furnished not only an occasion for eliciting these memories, but a potential means of arranging and unifying them into a coherent structure; it could, in other words, serve as a framework around which the story of Elena's life could be told.[17] Williams refers somewhat obliquely to this realization in the memoir's introduction, saying, "The book . . . gave me the clue to how my composition should be formed. A story turning about a story. I shall make it seem as if she told me her life while we were working over the translation, then as if we looked up from that work, speak as if she were telling me about herself" (*YMW*, 28).

The simple, straightforward diction of this statement belies its highly problematic meaning. Williams' idea of entwining the story of Elena's life with *The Dog and the Fever* can, in one sense, be construed as a logical extension of the self-reflexive character of his project: by recreating the context in which he originally heard and recorded her anecdotes, he could infuse them with a greater veracity. Yet the graceful, balletic image he uses to describe this composition, "a story turning about a story," produces just the opposite effect, collapsing the distinction between fiction and nonfiction, the imagination and objective reality, by placing his mother's words on a par with Quevedo's. Moreover, the litany of "as if" clauses in the concluding sentence indicates Williams' recognition of the artifice of his device. For though the scene he creates does not grossly distort or diverge from historical fact, it is nonetheless a deliberate exaggeration, as he admits several pages later in the text: "It is obvious that she could not have told me all that is to follow in that way—but she told me enough" (*YMW*, 37).

This lyrical assertion of pretense is complicated by the odd distinction which the poet makes between his mother's life and self in the same sentence: "I shall make it seem *as if she told me her life* while we were working over the translation, then as if we looked up from that work, speak *as if she were telling me about herself.*" The literal import of his statement appears to be that Elena spoke of her past (i.e., her "life" in a strictly historical sense) during the actual process of translation, but would only volunteer information about "herself"—her present condition and concerns—when diverted from the task. There is, however, an implicit conflation of her life and the novella in the first half of the sentence which disrupts that interpretation; the mother's story is an inextricable part of the translation, as if her personal reminiscences were somehow inscribed in the words of Quevedo's text. In addition, the bifurcation of "her life/herself" reinforces the emotional schism which already existed between Elena's mythic tropical past and her old age in Rutherford.

In 1938, after the bulk of the novella had been translated, Williams wrote a provisional introduction to his mother's biography which, with some emendations, later served as part 2 of the introduction to *Yes, Mrs. Williams.* This essay, published as "Raquel Helene Rose" in a 1941 issue of the little magazine *Twice-a-Year,* begins with the following statement: "A biography, gathered and roughly assembled from my mother's conversation, followed by a selection from her more recent letters, together with the translation of an early 17th century Spanish novel by Quevedo interpolated through the text: Qui n'entend qu'un cloche, n'entend qu'un son."[18]

In a single sentence, the poet conveys an abundance of information regarding the memoir's structure and content. He makes it clear, for example, that Elena's words—transcriptions of her conversation as well as actual letters—were to comprise the basis of the text. His own role, in contrast, was minimal; as scribe and editor, he simply "gathered and roughly assembled" the requisite raw data. The statement also clarifies the way in which Williams intended to incorporate the Quevedo translation into the memoir. The phrases "together with" and "interpolated through" suggest a thorough conjoining of the two works, the creation of a unique verbal tapestry through the deft insertion and interweaving of one story with another. The most helpful clue, however, is the French proverb, doubtlessly picked up from Elena, which Williams quotes: "He who only hears the striking of one clock, hears only one sound." In view of the casual, oral flavor of the memoir, this allusion to singular sound cannot be dismissed as a coincidence; rather, it implies that Williams planned to use Quevedo's text to amplify the resonance, texture, and meaning of his mother's words. By introducing a second voice (or "chime") distinct from yet complementary to the first, he could fabricate a context in which it was possible to read her stories as both fiction and biographical fact. The obliquity of Quevedo's style would also function as an analogue of the poet's own technique in the memoir. The "scheme" of the Spanish novella, as he notes in the *Autobiography,* "is a putting down of facts about the corrupt court, but not openly, which Quevedo couldn't afford. Instead we have a story told in terms of proverbs of the people, among the scene and sounds of the farm where he was then staying. It is all by implication, nothing is directly stated—very much as might be done today (*A*, 351).

Although the memoir is a completely apolitical work, it does rely heavily on intimation and allusion rather than direct exposition. Williams rigorously opposed the idea of writing a traditional biography about Elena in which he, as narrator, would strive to objectively assess the significance of her life, preferring instead to let the contours of her character emerge from the anecdotes themselves. Thus, like Quevedo's text, the memoir was also to be "a story told in terms of proverbs . . . all by implication"; the interpolation of the novella would form a structural and thematic counterpart of the work, mimicking its unorthodox organizing principle in a slightly different register.

In an unpublished draft of the text dating from this same period, Williams explains the reasons for his aversion to constructing a conventional narrative biography of his mother:

> How best to tell of her childhood is more than I can say. Let her own words sketch it, it seems more alive that way, sanguine still in spite of the years. Whereas to make a story of it seems disgusting, no matter how well-knit—something too delicate for nourishment—or anything but second-rate enjoyment. All I shall do, at the start at least, will be to arrange the sequences a little. Perhaps a note or two may be added now and again to hold the moments in place.[19]

The primacy which the poet accords Elena's words in this passage is crucial to understanding his aspirations for the memoir. The task of telling about her childhood is, in his estimation, beyond his capacity, something ineffably larger or "more" than he can say. Williams believed that a second-hand recounting of those events, no matter how skillfully wrought, would inevitably rob them of their essence and vitality, thereby reducing them to mere "stories." Although Elena herself is unable to recapture the immediacy of her childhood, she can, by virtue of being its experiential source and center, describe it in fuller, more realistic detail.

Moreover, the two adjectives Williams uses to characterize his mother's rendition of the past, "sanguine" and "more alive," have definite physiological connotations, suggesting that his concern with verisimilitude is not simply metaphorical. Throughout "Raquel Helene Rose," he insinuates that his intention is not to write a book *about* Elena (as he had earlier stated in "Eve") but to actually recreate her in the text. He relates an imaginary conversation in which she plays an adversarial role, pointing out the futility of his ambition:

> If you make it a work of the imagination, she might have said, it won't be me.
> I'll fool you, old girl. I won't make it a work of the imagination. I'll make it you. (*YMW*, 34)

The confident, resolute character of the assertion "I'll make it you" is modulated by the poet's fervent but tentative expression of his desire to preserve

Elena in other parts of the essay:

> She is about to pass out of the world; I want to hold her back a moment for her to be seen because—in many ways I think she is so lovely, for herself, that it would be a pity if she were lost without something of her—something impressed with her mind and her spirit—herself—remaining to perpetuate her—for our profit. (*YMW*, 24)

The series of subtle qualifications contained in the latter half of this passage recapitulate the direction in which both the memoir and Williams' theory of mimesis were evolving. Initially, he regards the text as a hazy tribute, a loving but inchoate attempt to preserve "something *of*" his mother's character; then, taking a slightly bolder step, it becomes "something impressed," indelibly stamped or marked, "with her mind and her spirit"; finally, it is metamorphosed into "herself." The syntactic structure of the sequence reveals that this equation of mother and memoir is not accidental: Williams uses dashes to visually isolate each alternative, thereby eliminating the possibility of reading "herself" as an extension of the preceding phrase. He further reinforces this disjuncture by employing the vague term "something" to describe the memoir in the first two instances, then omitting it in the third. The radicality of the poet's proposal is undercut by the wistful, yearning manner in which he articulates it: "I *want to hold* her back," he declares, because "*it would be a pity*" if she were lost," yet he seems uncertain of his ability to achieve that aim.

Williams vacillates between such expressions of confidence and self-doubt about re-presenting his mother throughout the essay, but remains steadfast in his commitment to the goal itself: "If I speak of the good, not a single word of truth is presumed here—nothing but the words I know and set down for what they may be worth: it is from being myself sure that if they are worth anything it will be in how closely they are able to approach all that which she, in herself, was and lived (*YMW*, 301–31). This statement reveals the extent to which Williams' ego is involved in the endeavor—he believes his words will be false and absolutely worthless if he cannot somehow approximate or encompass "all" that Elena "was and lived." In the manuscript of "Raquel Helene Rose," however, he makes a much different claim: "if [these words] are worth anything, it will be how closely they are able to approach a veracity which they can never assume."[20] The poet's recasting of this remark indicates that while he privately acknowledged the infeasibility of his ambition, he was unwilling to accept this failure, and thus persisted in his attempt to transcend the mimetic limitations of language. In this respect, the memoir became an emblematic challenge for Williams, a test not only of his own capabilities as a writer, but of the power of art to catch Elena's "fragrance": "If I can catch enough of it to make it seem—then it will have been proved to be! And one will have partaken of it, lived by it. Lived" (*YMW*, 33).

Williams' sole concession to the conventions of literary biography, made in order to bolster the coherence of the experimental form he had chosen, was to include a brief sketch of the "exterior details" (*YMW*, 32) of his mother's life in the memoir's introduction. This skeletal outline would contextualize what he termed the "proofs" of her existence—the anecdotes he so assiduously collected—by providing a historical framework against which they could be read; in addition, it would help prevent her stories from melding into Quevedo's text.

Unfortunately, no manuscripts have survived which document how Williams intended to incorporate the novella into his memoir; there are, however, several "writing plans" for the biography among his papers at Yale that supply a number of fascinating, if contradictory, clues. His most explicit statement, dated March 8, 1941, reads:

> Writing Plan for the Biography:
>
> 1. The introduction stands as it is—possibly with a cut or two here and there.
>
> 2. Section I—in Mother's own words with 3 or 4 rather long interpolations by "the author," independently and freely written (in the style of the Introduction) of comment and explanation of the child's general circumstances—parents etc.
>
> 3. Her student life in Paris. Again—comments and a word or two of explanation. The account must move smoothly, not jerkily but more freely than in the first section, the text and the comments more blended (?)
>
> 4. Married Life: these headings to be definitely stated—bringing the focus to a sharp point on what is being spoken of. Now autobiographical interpolations of "the author" (her son) are permitted.
>
> 5. A word or two and then the translation, perhaps cut a little where it drags—the cuts to be indicated by . . . A note on Quevedo might not be out of place, Q. and his times, Cervantes, Lope and Gongora—their significance for us.
>
> 6. Her letters: Note—their *imagery* and their *language*. Not English but a new start from a new base. Old age.[21]

At least five variants of this plan exist, attesting to the poet's nagging dissatisfaction with the structure he had devised. Several features remain unchanged throughout the revisions, such as the fact that the text, which was to be largely quoted from Elena, would be divided into chapters and chronologically arranged. What troubled Williams was the constellation of material into specific units, prompting him to continually amend both the number and organization of chapters, and more importantly, the placement of the Quevedo translation. He entertained a wide range of possibilities regarding the latter issue: alluding to the translation but not including it, appending it to the memoir as a separate chapter, or interpolating bits of it throughout the entire text.[22]

Williams never successfully resolved this dilemma, however, because a larger, more fundamental problem arose with the memoir. As his elliptical references to "the author" in the above writing plan indicate, he was uncomfortable with the degree of his own presence and visibility in the text. When he began assembling the story of Elena's life in the early forties, he discovered that his knowledge of her, while extensive, was riddled with lacunae. Consequently, in attempting to string her anecdotes together and "hold the [fragmentary] moments in place," he found himself lapsing into an increasingly narrative mode, equivocating about times, places, and events. Manuscripts of the memoir dating from this period demonstrate the nature of his quandry:

> I was never sure of the chronology of her movings about after her mother's death. I don't even know whether or not the mother dies before the doctor son's return, or if she lived it was not for long. . . . At any rate, her mother and father had died, her brother had returned from Paris a physician and set up his office. She, a girl of sixteen, lived with him, still I think, in Mayagüez, and took care of him.[23]

When Williams realized the text was becoming precisely the kind of biography he wished to avoid, he set it aside in frustration, and began focusing all his energies on writing *Paterson,* a poem whose heterogeneous form was closely tied to *Yes, Mrs. Williams* in that he originally envisaged it as a series of letters from various individuals.[24] In the maelstrom of activity surrounding the epic's creation, the memoir was all but forgotten, though Elena herself would become a pervasive subtext in the poem. It was not until after his mother's death in 1949, when the sayings he had been collecting for decades suddenly became all that was left of her, that he began seriously to rethink the memoir.

Over the course of the next decade, Williams discarded his previous schemes for the text, seeking a new, less convoluted means of highlighting the unique qualities of Elena's language. *The Dog and the Fever* was published as a separate volume in 1954, becoming a historical adjunct to the memoir rather than an integral facet of it. In a note written during the summer of 1958, Williams instructed his typist to simply transcribe Elena's anecdotes and number them sequentially, since "they are generally unconnected in time or place."[25] He continued: "Most important of all . . . the check marks and erasures, made at some previous period, are to be completely ignored. That is the principal reason for the present text. I want to forget what I have done in the past and to return to my Mother's unadorned words."[26] The poet's desire to return to and highlight the hard-edged clarity of Elena's language was the predominant factor in determining the memoir's final form. The technique he adopted to realize this ambition is rooted in one of the basic tenets of his early improvisational prose, "conversation as design." Williams' resolution of the formal dilemma posed by the text is thus an exemplary instance of his attempt to reconcile art with the "actual" and achieve accurate representation in his work.

3

Conversation as Design

Do we not see that we are inarticulate? That is what defeats us. It is our inability to communicate to another how we are locked within ourselves, unable to say the simplest thing of importance to one another, any of us, even the most valuable, that makes our lives like those of a litter of kittens in a wood-pile.

Autobiography

It takes writing such as unrelated passing on the street to rescue us for a design that alone affords conversation.

January: A Novelette

Yes, Mrs. Williams, published in 1959, is a paradoxical work, a simultaneous inversion and outgrowth of the book Williams originally intended to write about his mother. Though its scope is biographical, the text's structure defies the formal conventions of that genre, making it in effect an anti-biography. It contains no continuous narrative or chronological ordering of events, but consists rather of discrete fragments: Elena's proverbs, anecdotes, and letters. Contrary to all the poet's previous plans, the memoir is neither divided into chapters nor arranged in any discernibly systematic fashion; it is more an aggregate of miscellaneous parts than a unified whole. What little coherence the work has derives from Williams' italicized commentary which is irregularly interspersed between his mother's remarks and provides a loose contextual web for them.

This apparently random assemblage is preceded by a discursive two-part introduction wherein Williams presents basic biographical data about Elena and an informal history of the text's genesis. While such information is vital to understanding the nature of his idiosyncratic project, the introduction also poses a serious exegetical problem in that it was not composed expressly for *Yes, Mrs. Williams,* but is rather a pastiche of earlier prose. The first part (*YMW,* 3–20), in which Williams reminisces about his parents and a number of childhood incidents, is a variant of the opening chapters of his *Autobiography,* published in 1951. Two explicit references to Elena's death occur in the narrative (*YMW*, 5, 20), indicating that it was written sometime after October 1949. The second section (*YMW*, 21–38), on the other hand, is a nearly verbatim reprint of the introduction to Quevedo's *The Dog and the Fever,* published in 1954 by the Shoe String Press. This essay, in turn, proves to be another amalgam, since embedded within it is the 1941 piece "Raquel Helene Rose."[1]

The memoir's introduction thus combines assessments of Elena's character from three crucial phases in the poet's emotional life: 1949–50, immediately following the trauma of her death; 1954, amidst his own struggle with depression and life-threatening illness; and 1941, just prior to experiencing the first birth pangs of *Paterson.* The conjunction of the three narratives is, moreover, far from seamless; though each account overlaps slightly, the redundancies— for example, the stories of Casey Wright (*YMW*, 4, 35) and Elena's unhappy return to Puerto Rico from Paris (*YMW*, 5, 33)—have not been edited out. These gratuitous repetitions are puzzling, but ultimately nonproblematic since they offer consistent interpretations of a given event or situation. What is much more disconcerting about the introduction's composite structure is the strangely skewed time frame it creates and the distorted image of the memoir which emerges as a result. The first part is written entirely from a retrospective vantage point. Elena, now dead and buried, becomes the object of a highly sentimentalized encomium. "Our mother was an angel" (*YMW*, 14), Williams gushes at one point, and extols her stoic, uncomplaining attitude in the face of death: "With her, Ai! Ai! Ai! which I can still hear in the night, as much as to say, give me a drink—of water! that's all she would ever touch to relieve her of her pain except, on rare occasions, a swallow of whiskey in the night to put her to sleep again: it meant nothing more to her" (*YMW*, 20).

In part 2, however, she is imaginatively revivified by authorial fiat; after briefly discussing Quevedo's life and the circumstances surrounding their translation of his novella, Williams abruptly announces:

> So much for Quevedo. I might have gone on writing a scholarly thesis upon his name or upon the occasion of his composition of *The Dog and the Fever,* what he meant by such a title in relation to the times in which we wrote. But what do I know of those times? Nothing. I am not a student of Spanish history, and what I should write would be at best second-hand. . . . But what I can write about is the woman who did, in effect, most of the translation: my mother. *So that for the balance of this book, counting on her natural sympathy for Quevedo to bridge the gap, I shall speak from now on about my mother, as if my mother were still living.* (*YMW*, 23; emphasis mine)

In strictly pragmatic terms, this awkward transition[2] allows the poet to dovetail "Raquel Helene Rose" into his text with a minimum of effort—no changing of verb tenses or nostalgic recasting of unfavorable descriptions is necessary. Instead, he simply pretends that his mother's death has not yet occurred. By openly acknowledging his strategy, Williams cannily invites the reader to join him in this fantasy, so that it is actually the reader's indulgence rather than Elena's "natural sympathy for Quevedo" which bridges the hiatus in his prose. The pretense becomes, in other words, a kind of game, played with the audience's tacit complicity.

Yet this "game" has far-ranging consequences in that it subverts and unravels the linear progression of time in the introduction. Williams fashions an ahistorical context in which his mother's factual existence is irrelevant since she is relentlessly alive both in his mind and on the page. He depicts Elena as old, decrepit, and hovering on the brink of death, but refuses to let her succumb. Instead, at the conclusion of the essay, he hints at an imminent rejuvenescence which will take place in the memoir proper: "So we began [to translate Quevedo]. It served its purpose which was to draw out her comments. Let her come first, her childhood and early years exactly as she told it" (*YMW*, 38).

This statement, which is a palimpsestic vestige of the poet's earlier schema for the memoir, fundamentally misrepresents *Yes, Mrs. Williams* by implying that its structure is chronological and that it incorporates the Quevedo translation as an addendum to Elena's life story ("Let *her* come first," thereby inferring that Quevedo will come afterward). The introduction, in this respect, performs an ironic function: rather than preparing the reader for what follows, it misleads him by establishing expectations which the text subsequently denies. But though these particulars are indeed deceptive, the piece as a whole is faithful to Williams' larger ambition of recreating his mother in words.

In the last paragraph of the introduction he shifts back into the present moment but deftly maintains the ambiguity of Elena's state: "Very seldom does a man get a chance to speak intimately of what has concerned him most in the past. This is about an old woman who had been young and to a degree beautiful a short number of years ago—this is as good a way as any to pay her my respects and to reassure her that she has not been forgotten" (*YMW*, 38). The phrase "what has concerned him most *in the past*" effectively signals this transition, insinuating that with the publication of the memoir, Elena's powerful hold on Williams' psyche is finally broken. The obsession now exorcised, he can safely relegate her to a dusty compartment of memory and move on to other concerns. The fact that he refers to both himself and his mother in the third person here suggests he is trying to achieve some emotional and aesthetic distance from her; suddenly, they are metamorphosed from individuals into generic figures, a "man" and an "old woman" between whom no specific kinship or ties are postulated.

Despite the impersonal quality of his language, Williams has still not escaped the bonds of filial devotion and deference, as his desire to "pay . . . respects" to Elena and "reassure her that she has not been forgotten" attests. Significantly, neither of these phrases appears in the introduction to *The Dog and the Fever* or "Raquel Helene Rose," both of which end the following way:

"Very seldom does a man get a chance to speak to his sons intimately so take this book—about an old woman who had been young and beautiful a surprisingly short number of years ago—this is as good an occasion as any to inform you of a number of things you might not have picked up otherwise."[3]

Although the conclusion of the memoir's introduction closely resembles the earlier version in style and syntax, its dramatic focus is substantially different. Rather than addressing his two sons, Williams now seems to be speaking to Elena herself. This change in intended audience reflects the predominant trend in the text's evolution: the poet no longer regards the work as an archival document designed to augment his children's knowledge of their ancestry, but as a private tribute to his mother. By excising the reference to William Eric and Paul, he breaks the thread of intergenerational continuity and collapses the sphere of the memoir into a timeless world of two.[4]

In contrast to the forthright manner Williams adopts with his sons ("So take this book . . ."), his address to Elena is subtle, meek, and indirect. His diction thus complicates rather than clarifies the already perplexing issue of her status in the text. The expression, "to pay respects," for example, which is often used in relation to the dead, broadly denotes the discharging of an obligation. The sense of terminus and completion inherent in the phrase reinforces with the poet's description of his preoccupation with Elena a few lines earlier as a topic that "concerned him most in the past." Yet the remainder of the sentence refutes these intimations of pastness and death by claiming that the memoir is intended to "reassure her that she has not been forgotten." Williams' use of the verb "reassure" is extremely important here because it evokes associations of presence, proximity, and communication, and thereby implies that his mother is still alive. The paradoxical nature of his assertion effectively seals the indeterminacy of her status; in the context of the memoir, she is both dead and alive, old and young, literal and symbolic.

Beyond creating a powerful, mysterious aura around the figure of his mother, Williams' revision of this passage confirms the integrity and authority of the introduction as a whole. First of all, the very existence of the emendations proves that the earlier essays were closely scrutinized before being incorporated into the memoir. A line-by-line comparison of the introductions to *The Dog and the Fever* and *Yes, Mrs. Williams* reveals several other differences, mostly of a minor, technical nature: certain paragraphs have been reshaped, sentences conflated, qualifiers dropped. Such modifications do not alter the text's basic meaning, but are nonetheless significant because they suggest that the material left intact was done so by choice rather than oversight or impotence. If Williams, in his enervated condition, was capable of making these changes in the text, why not others as well? Why, in particular, continue the pretense that Elena was still alive? It appears that the poet, far from being an incompetent editor of his own work, recognized the bizarre effect produced by the composite introduction and used it to his advantage. The suspension of linear time became a crucial tool in achieving the memoir's principal objective—making Elena live again.

Considering the aberrant style of both the introduction and the memoir itself, it is not surprising that *Yes, Mrs. Williams* met with a distinctly lukewarm critical reception. Because it was the work of an aging major writer, reviewers apparently felt obliged not to dismiss the text entirely; however, they uniformly complained about its lack of coherent structure. Phoebe Adams, for example, commented in the *Atlantic Monthly:* "Nothing holds [the book] together. Like bits of glass in a kaleidoscope, odd events and inexplicable details form patterns which suddenly fall into pieces."[5] Others, like Reed Whittemore, felt the memoir was "merely the raw material for an as yet unwritten biography" and thus of primary interest to those who had "faith . . . in such artless immediacy."[6] Even Babette Deutsch, whose critique in the *Herald Tribune Book Review* is arguably the most astute contemporary response to the text, characterized it as "haphazard," "casual," and full of "meager and confused biographical details [which] the reader must labor to assemble."[7]

John Ciardi's discussion of the memoir in *Saturday Review* also centers on the question of form, but situates it within the larger problem of mimesis itself. He emphasizes the intimate, highly emotive character of the work, asserting that it was Williams' fascination with the "brilliance of [his mother's] flame" which prompted his "effort to record the living fact of her spirit."[8] According to Ciardi, this fervor comprises the text's greatest liability because it clouded the poet's judgement about the efficacy of the work's structure:

> The trouble is—and Williams as a master of fiction as well as of poetry certainly realizes it with that other side of himself—that simple recording will never capture that *experienceable illusion of personality* which is the essence of achieved writing. In art, the thing-itself cannot simply be stated: it must be created into form. As it stands, this memoir consists of not much more than a series of disconnected jottings, many of them actually scribbled on the backs of envelopes. What the reader finds is this remark and that remark, and always that glimpse of a personality he hungers to know, but never the full dimension of that personality, and never the recreated scene of the happening. To be sure, the process of recreating the scene of the happening would inevitably involve some minimal fictionalization, and it is exactly such fictionalization Williams insists on avoiding. But the price is a certain dullness: the reader cannot be brought to be as interested in the material as was the author.[9]

The dichotomy Ciardi proposes at the beginning of the passage between Williams the sentimental, pietistic son and Williams the dispassionate writer has a certain validity, though not in the particular context he claims. His assessment of the memoir is founded on the false assumption that the poet subscribed to the same traditional theory of mimesis as Ciardi did, and therefore believed "that simple recording will never capture the experienceable illusion of personality." Williams, however, was not at all concerned with the "illusion" of personality, but rather with its concrete manifestations; moreover, he would have violently disputed the statement that "in art, the thing-itself cannot simply be stated; it must be created into form." Ciardi's concept of literary form is much more rigid than Williams'; to his mind, it was impossible that the "disconnected jottings" of the memoir represented anything but the absence of structure. The critic's charge that the text neither recreates the "scene of the happening" nor reveals the "full dimension" of Elena's personality offers additional evidence of his conservative stance. The memoir fails, in his estimation, precisely because it lacks the accoutrements of conventional biography—setting, plot, and above all, narrative structure.

Ciardi's review is especially curious in that his conclusions about the book are remarkably accurate, although the reasons he cites to support them are not. Williams was indeed adamant about avoiding fictionalization in the memoir, but Ciardi views this as a sign of obstinacy rather than as a deliberate aesthetic strategy. Since he refuses to accept the text's fragmentary form as a purposeful design, Ciardi fundamentally misdiagnoses the cause of its failure. Williams chose the technique of "simple recording" not out of sentimentality, but because he believed it was the truest, most mimetically faithful means of capturing the "full dimension" of his mother's personality. His inability to totally engage the reader in the material stems more from its commonplace content than from the unorthodox mode of presentation. Many of Elena's remarks, such as, "Son, will you see there in the writing desk if there's a piece of chewing gum there. Right there . . ." (*YMW*, 142), are admittedly trivial; however, their inclusion in the memoir affirms Williams' zealous commitment to delineating all aspects of her character—the banality as well as the wisdom, the strict probity along with the coarseness.

Contrary to what Ciardi and other contemporary reviewers believed, *Yes, Mrs. Williams* is not an artless, aleatoric work. It has a very definite, if subtle, structure based on one of the commonest forms of human interaction: conversation. The text is essentially a dialogue between mother and son, the synthetic representation of a lifetime of intimate discourse. In this respect, the memoir has an implicitly dramatic form; indeed, Williams himself described the work in an unpublished manuscript at Yale as "a play opening, two talk at considerable length, quietly, telling a thing interesting for itself, creating suspense—such as a doctor listening to a patient's account of herself. . . ."[10]

The poet's rhythmic alternation of Elena's words with his own, accentuated by the use of contrasting typeface, constitutes his most radical departure from the norms of traditional biography in that it violates the singularity of subject and focus. Unlike the classic biographer, he makes no attempt to efface himself or achieve any semblance of objectivity in the memoir; instead, he openly declares his bias at the outset. Although Elena occupies the foreground of the work, Williams remains a necessary and discernible presence throughout, since it is the filter of his consciousness which orders and unifies her random observations.

The success of this dialogic strategy depends largely on the memoir's introduction which supplies both the backdrop and dramatic context for the disjunctive exchanges that follow. Rather than depicting his mother as an aloof, solitary figure in these prefatory pages, Williams presents a familiar domestic tableau—the two of them sitting together, quietly conversing. The attendant details of this configuration—Elena's debility and extensive dependence on her son, the diversionary nature of their translations—implicitly draw him further towards the memoir's center. As his mother's collaborator, confidant, and primary caregiver, he becomes her complement; together they comprise the substantive core of the work. In this respect, the text's focus is social and interpersonal rather than purely personal; it not only illustrates specific traits of Elena's character, but enacts the involutions of the mother-son relationship itself. Because conversation is based on the mutual exchange of ideas and information, it creates an informal bond between people, making them, within the limited confines of its duration, metaphorically one. Thus, by virtue of its dialogic form, the book raises broader, more philosophical questions about identity, individuality, and the nature of interpersonal influence.

Williams' use of colloquy as a stylistic device is by no means restricted to the memoir; it also plays an important role in parts of *In the American Grain* (notably the chapters "De Soto and the New World" and "The Founding of Quebec") and *Paterson* (particularly the He/She passage in book 2).[11] The dialogue in these works, however, is embedded within and subordinate to a larger governing structure, whereas in *Yes, Mrs. Williams* it constitutes the very foundation of that structure. In this regard, the text which most closely parallels the shape and style of the memoir is Williams' 1929 improvisation, *January: A Novelette*. Significantly, the composition of this piece coincides exactly with the project he claimed was the major impetus to writing Elena's biography— their joint translation of Soupault's *Last Nights of Paris*. As such, the work reflects many of the same issues and aesthetic concerns that underlie the memoir and also offers important clues to the source and significance of its idiosyncratic form.

Like all of Williams' improvisational prose, *January* is a miscellany, a commodious ragbag of random observations and details. Though fragmented and highly allusive in character, the "novelette" is considerably less opaque than some of his other experiments with this genre (e.g., *Kora in Hell*, to cite the most extreme example) in that it possesses a self-reflexive dimension which allows the poet to articulate and assess his intentions while engaged in the process of trying to realize them. On one level, the text concerns Williams' wife Flossie and the changes wrought in their marriage by the rigors of the 1929 influenza epidemic; its larger subject, however, is the disparity which exists between words and the things they are supposed to represent. In an attempt to bridge this gap between signifier and signified, Williams devised a technique called "conversation as design," which appropriated the distinctive features of oral discourse—colloquial language, incomplete sentences, implied connectives, rapid shifts in subject matter—as the basis of a new literary form. Curiously, he did not attribute the inspiration for this concept to his daily interaction with patients (although *January* is filled with bits of such diagnostic dialogue), but instead linked it to a visual source, namely, the paintings of Juan Gris:

> There is no conversation in novels, the novel soaks it all up. There is the story, the timbre.
> There is no conversation in the papers, one must always convey the timbre of the news.
> Always the one thing in Juan Gris. Conversation as design. Were it not so—it is less than actual, it is covered, dull, a makeshift. I have always admired and partaken of Juan Gris. Singly he says that the actual is the drawing of the face—and so the face borrowing of the drawing—by lack of copying and lack of a burden to the story—is real. (*I*, 286)

Williams' usage of the term "conversation" in this passage is somewhat unconventional; as the first two paragraphs make emphatically clear, it is not synonymous with either dialogue or direct quotation. The crucial difference, to the poet's mind, is one of context rather than content. Once conversation is incorporated into a story (whether fictional or nonfictional), its freshness and authenticity are invariably lost, "soaked up" by the surrounding text. Williams extends this metaphor of engulfment by referring to the "timbre" of novels and newspaper articles, thereby implying that their orchestrated narrative form drowns out the singular instrument of conversation—the human voice. In order to retain its actuality, conversation must be isolated and totally autonomous, its shape determined by nothing other than the rough, unpolished edges of the participants' own words. Williams' tacit insistence on conversation as an independent, organic entity significantly broadens the term's meaning by making it applicable to other, nonverbal modes of expression, and thus provides the basis for his cryptic allusion to Juan Gris in the latter half of the passage.

Williams' declaration that Gris' work typifies the principle of "conversation as design" is rooted in an abiding fascination with the artist's distinctive Cubist style. In *Spring and All*, for example, he describes at greath length the Spaniard's 1921 painting, "The Open Window," which he had seen a black-and-white reproduction of in the little magazine *Broom*, calling it a paradigm of "the modern trend" (*I*, 107):

> Here is a shutter, a bunch of grapes, a sheet of music, a picture of sea and mountains (particularly fine) which the onlooker is not for a moment permitted to witness as an "illusion." One thing laps over on the other, the cloud laps over on the shutter, the bunch of grapes is part of the handle of the guitar, and the mountain and sea are obviously not "the mountain and sea," but a picture of the mountain and the sea. All drawn with admirable simplicity and excellent design—all a unity— (*I*, 110–11)

From this description, it can be inferred that the quality Williams deemed "conversational" in Gris' art was his arrangement of elements on the canvas so that they overlap and intersect (thereby creating a unified "design"), yet still maintain their integrity as individual forms. He mentions "The Open Window" in *January* as well, but focuses on a single detail of the composition rather than the entire work:

To be conversation, it must have only the effect of itself, not on him to whom it has a special meaning but as a dog or a store window.

For this we must be alone.

It must have no other purpose than the roundness and the color and the repetition of grapes in a bunch, such grapes as those of Juan Gris which are related more to a ship at sea than to the human tongue. As they are. (*I*, 287)

By drawing what initially appears to be an absurd analogy between conversation and a cluster of grapes, the poet underscores the sensuous, palpable, and altogether familiar nature of oral discourse. Like the fruit—round, richly colored, arranged in a neat geometric pattern on its stem—words too are objects, the lustrous components of an organic whole. The parallels, however, do not stop there. Williams extends the scope and complexity of his comparison by shifting referents in midsentence, replacing what the reader assumes is a literal bunch of grapes with those in Gris' painting. Though the fruit's physical characteristics are the same in both instances, he differentiates between their purpose and context by noting that Gris' grapes "are related more to a ship at sea than to the human tongue." Whereas real grapes are to be eaten (and so are related, in an obvious manner, to the tongue), the artist's two-dimensional representation can only be taken in with the eyes, and hence must be appreciated purely as a shape, a visual form, "a ship at sea." Williams seems to have selected this nautical image at random as a means of hyperbolizing the unreality of Gris' grapes; however, it may in fact derive from a subliminal association he makes between the angular shape of the fruitbowl in "The Open Window" and a boat's prow. But regardless of its source, the image evokes an unmistakable sense of isolation and self-containment, and thus strengthens the link between Gris' painting and Williams' notion of conversation, which, as he states at the beginning of the excerpt, "must have only the effect of itself."

Moreover, the poet's allusion to the grapes compounds and reinforces the distinction he draws between the literal mountains and sea and Gris' "particularly fine" picture thereof in *Spring and All*. These disparate physical details epitomize the trait he admired most in the Spaniard's work: the representation of common forms which are simultaneously related to, yet separate from, the material world:

Things with which he is familiar, simple things—at the same time to detach them from ordinary experience to the imagination. Thus they are still "real," they are the same things they would be if photographed or painted by Monet, they are recognizable as the things touched by the hands during the day, but in this painting they are seen to be in some peculiar way—detached. . . . (*I*, 110)

The obvious parallel between Williams' description of Gris' technique and his own poetic style suggests that his affinity for the painter derived in large part from the compatibility of their aesthetic views. This recognition, prompted by his intuitive response to "The Open Window," was confirmed later in the

1920s by the appearance of Gris' theoretical writings on art. Although no incontrovertible evidence exists indicating that the poet actually read these works, it is virtually certain he did. Gris' essay, "On the Possibilities of Painting," for example, was published in the July and August 1924 issues of the *transatlantic review*, a journal Williams was following closely at the time since his own work was featured in the March, May, and August numbers.[12] The essay, moreover, contains several assertions that bear directly on his appraisal of the relationship between life and art in *January*. Gris, like Williams, believed strongly in the transformative power of the imagination, and was thus similarly convinced that art did not merely copy nature, but created what Williams termed "a thing advanced and apart from it" (*A,* 241). Gris states:

> A picture with no representational purpose is to my mind always an incomplete technical exercise, for the only purpose of any picture is to achieve representation. Nor is a painting which is merely a faithful copy of an object a picture, for even supposing that it fulfills the conditions of colored architecture, it still has no aesthetic, no selection of the elements of the reality it expresses. It will only be the copy of an object and never a subject.[13]

According to Gris, the selection of elements from reality constitutes the essence of art; representation, in other words, is not an indiscriminate, mimetic process, but rather a system of subjective choices, displacements, and exclusions. And while the artist is solely responsible for these decisions, he does not proceed with a specific, predetermined outcome in mind; instead, Gris declares,

> Until the work is completed, he must remain ignorant of its appearance as a whole. To copy a preconceived appearance is like copying the appearance of a model.
> From this it is clear that the subject does not materialize in the appearance of the picture, but that the subject, in materializing, gives the picture its appearance.[14]

This strange, quasi-mystical notion of materialization unlocks the meaning of Williams' comment in *January* that "singly [Gris] says . . . the actual is the drawing of the face—and so the face borrowing of the drawing—by lack of copying and lack of a burden to the story—is real" (*I,* 286). The dynamic exchange which both men describe between the model's face and the artist's drawing of that face becomes a metaphor for the harmonious interplay of objective and subjective realities in the creation of art. Rather than simply imitating nature, art represents a dialogue that extends beyond the limited surface of the painter's canvas to the unconsciousness of the viewer, challenging and enlarging his perceptual construct. It is in this respect that Gris' work most powerfully illustrates the principle of "conversation as design."

But how does Williams' assessment of the Cubist painter relate to his memoir about Elena? Is there some intrinsic connection between his treatment of the two figures? These questions are answered in part by the opening of the "Juan Gris" chapter in *January:*

Because he was not Picasso—nor discouraged by him—but a Spaniard full of admiration
for French painting and lived in Paris where he worked: like you. This is exceptional praise.
I am the Paris of your eyes: it is not in what you say but that you say it.
If I am indifferent to the extraneous: so little does it matter what we wear.
—faults of patients, I should have said.
That singleness I see in everything—actual—which has been my life, because of the haste
due to the epidemic, I see in you and so you become beautiful partly because you are so but
partly because of other women. (*I*, 283)

The insistent pattern of direct address evident in these lines pervades the
entire improvisation. Although Williams never directly names the "you" he
speaks to in the text, critics have tended to assume the pronoun refers to Flossie, since she is one of its principal subjects. This supposition, while generally
true, clearly does not apply to the above passage; Floss, unlike the woman
being compared with Gris, was not Spanish, she did not paint, and she never
lived and worked in Paris. These details correspond rather to the life of another
of Williams' female intimates—his mother. Moreover, the ambiguity produced
by this unannounced "shifting of category" (*I*, 286) from wife to mother is conscious, deliberate. Throughout the text, the poet plays with the notion of a
female archetype, asserting that Flossie, "as a wife," represents "the freshness
of all women" (*I*, 286) to him. This dualistic perspective creates an aesthetic
distance which enables him to recognize and extract the generic essence of her
individual attributes: "So she—building of all excellence is, in her single body,
beautiful; enforcing the mind by imperfections to a height. Born again, Venus
from the confused sea. Summing all virtues. Single. Excellence. Female" (*I*,
282).

Considering the strong archetypal element present in Williams' depiction
of Floss, his failure to distinguish between her and Elena in *January* acquires
even greater significance. Both are avatars of the eternal female principle and,
as such, one. The conflation thus implicitly illustrates his perception of woman
as "other," the sense that all females, despite their diverse, multiplex characteristics, are part of a larger "composite necessity" (*I*, 282).

Because the structure and logic of the passage are highly associative, Williams is able to manipulate the ambiguity between his mother and spouse in a
variety of ways. The chapter begins, as it were, *in medias res:* the poet's first
fragmentary statement is a direct response to a query which, though not included in the text, appears to be something on the order of "Why do you like
Juan Gris?" Although neither the question nor the identity of the questioner is
divulged, the ingenuous extravagance of Williams' reply leaves little doubt as
to his intended audience. While the parallels he draws between Elena and Gris
are more circumstantial than substantive, the comparison is in itself immensely
flattering; indeed, Williams seems to be openly flirting with his mother, courting her favor as one would a beloved's. But what is most adulatory about the
comparison is the implicit suggestion that if Elena had only been given the op-

portunity to fully develop her artistic talent, her work would have rivalled that of her compatriot. The veracity of this inference is inconsequential; its significance lies rather in a personal, emotive sphere, as testimony of Williams' confidence, devotion, and love for his mother.

In the space between the first and second paragraphs, Williams substitutes himself for Gris as a point of comparison with Elena, thereby signaling a shift between the fantasy of what might have been and the sober reality of her present condition. His declaration, "I am the Paris of your eyes," is a complex double entendre: by identifying himself with the city which symbolized the essence of art, creativity, and passion to his mother, he implies that he is the locus where her thwarted ambitions can be vicariously realized. The statement also has mythological connotations, since Paris was the husband of Helen of Troy, whose name is echoed by Elena's own. The incestuous marriage of a mother and son evokes still another mythological figure, Oedipus. Shortly before his death in 1918, William George bequeathed Elena to his eldest son, saying: "The one thing I regret in going is that I have to leave her to you. You'll find her difficult" (*A, 159*). As his father's surrogate, the poet did perform many of a spouse's traditional functions, acting as Elena's protector, provider, and steadfast companion.

There is also an undeniably erotic undercurrent in both Williams' claim of being his mother's "Paris" and their relationship in general. From youth upwards, he regarded her as a feminine ideal, writing to her from the University of Pennsylvania in 1904,

> Today I spent part of the afternoon at Uncle's [Irving Wellcome's]. He had a big pile of old photographs which he had just taken out of a trunk and I was looking them over. As I was glancing from one picture to another I came upon a young girl of about twenty leaning on some old book. She was a beauty in fact she was such a girl as I have often dreamed of but never seen. I fell in love right away. She was not only beautiful for anyone could read her fine character through and through by looking into her eyes. She is as near my ideal as I have ever gotten. Mama it was you. . . . How coarse all the girls I know seem beside you. . . . (*YMW*, x)

The poet's perception of Elena as an unattainable object of desire is reaffirmed by the tacit sense of Oedipal rivalry in his account of William George's bequest in the *Autobiography*. The tone of the elder Williams' statement is highly equivocal; his admonition, "You'll find her difficult," can be interpreted as a mixture of regret at having to burden his son with the responsibility of caring for Elena and skepticism that perhaps the young man is incapable of meeting its demands. The remark is thus simultaneously an apology and an aspersion, a curious amalgam of concern, anxiety, and competition which typifies all Williams' interactions with his male parent.

In terms of the passage from *January,* this erotic element is manifested in the nature of Williams' praise for his mother. Like a lover, he commends her beauty, though his use of the term is more metaphysical than physical. He also expresses a profound admiration for Elena's language, stating: "It is not in what you say but that you say it." This avowal, on the one hand, intensifies the romantic associations between mother and son by placing him in the classic pose of suitor, cherishing each of his beloved's words, not for their content or signification, but simply because of their source. Its full implications, however, run much deeper. The poet's ascription of this vague but awesome power to the maternal logos constitutes the fundamental raison d'etre of *Yes, Mrs. Williams.* The literal fact of Elena's speech (i.e., that she "says it") is inextricably entangled with its *sui generis* style; thus, Williams is actually lauding her *manner* of speaking as well. In his estimation, her ungrammatical, trilingual utterances possessed a clarity, freshness, and poetic intensity that standard English lacked. These qualities are illustrated by the following excerpt from a letter quoted in the memoir's introduction wherein Elena describes the circumstances surrounding her father's death:

> My father was from Holland extraction, he was a merchant associated with two Germans in Mayagüez. . . . I was only eight years old when I lost [him], I didn't know much; a fierce dog was put at night to guard the cargo newly arrived, the name of the dog was Moro. One night he came home like a demon dragging his long chain. It had rained much and the earth was mud, he went to my father's room howl and howl went all over, the house was in mourning the master was gone. Wasn't that strange? (*YMW*, 28–29)

Elena's disregard for the conventions of written English is amply demonstrated by the wrenched syntax, lack of punctuation, and use of nonparallel structures in the passage. Yet, as the penultimate sentence reveals, these grammatical distortions greatly enhance the vividness and immediacy of her account. In particular, her rapid conjunction of the phrases "he went to my father's room howl and howl went all over, the house was in mourning the master was gone," creates a strong impression of simultaneity; actions and details overlap, but their outlines remain crisp, unblurred. Hence, it is in the way Elena wields words rather than a paintbrush that she most resembles Juan Gris; she achieves with language the same innovative effect he produced with color, line, and mass. Through the unusual juxtaposition and emphasis of elements, both artists revivify the thing being represented and "make it new."

Williams' affirmation of his mother's linguistic power assumes an entirely different tenor, however, when examined in light of the statement immediately preceding it: "I am the Paris of your eyes: it is not in what you say but that you say it." According to the Greek myth, Paris was a seducer and thief; his bold abduction of Helen from her husband Menelaus was the principal cause for the Achaean expedition against Troy. Like Paris, the poet also engages in thievery, albeit of a more subtle, abstract variety—appropriating Elena's words for his own literary purposes. His statement can thus be read as an assertion of dominance as well as aesthetic appreciation; moreover, it contains a smug in-

timation of arrogance stemming from an awareness that his actions are the vehicle of Elena/Helen's immortality.

The rich, ambiguous resonances of this passage rehearse many of the
themes found in *Yes, Mrs. Williams;* as such, it—and indeed the entire text of
January—serves as a template for the structure and content of the later work.
Perhaps even more than the novelette itself, *Yes, Mrs. Williams* succeeds in
realizing the poet's ambition of creating a literary style akin to "unrelated passing on the street [which would] rescue us for a design that alone affords conversation" (*I,* 287). The dialogue in the memoir is not a continuum but a series
of discrete vignettes varying in length from a few lines to several pages which
are juxtaposed like the geometric shapes in Juan Gris' canvases. The text is
nevertheless more cohesive and accessible than *January* because its focus is
confined to two primary speakers. Consequently, details which at first seem
confusing or extraneous gradually fall into place as the work progresses and the
complex dimensions of mother's and son's personalities unfold.

But the preeminent link between "conversation as design" and the memoir
is that Williams' stylistic technique, like the painter's, is grounded in a "selection of elements from reality." Although he attempts to minimize his role in the
text by characterizing himself merely as a scribe who records Elena's anecdotes
"exactly as she told [them]" (*YMW,* 38), the poet is actually the "author" of the
image the reader formulates of her. He not only chooses which of his mother's
remarks are to be included in the book, but determines the order of their arrangement, and frames them with his own interpretive commentary. Thus, despite Williams' rigorous claims about the artlessness and verisimilitude of his
portrait, the memoir ultimately proves to be a fictive work, detached "from ordinary experience to the imagination" (*I,* 110) in the same way as Gris' art.

The degree to which Williams shapes Elena's image in the text is demonstrated by his elaborate narration of the translation ruse in the introduction. According to an unpublished draft of the memoir now in the Beinecke Library at
Yale, the poet found it necessary to conceal from his mother the fact that he
was writing a book about her because of her reluctance to provide him with any
specific information about her past. "These notes," he states, "have been collected surreptitiously. Whenever I have come straight out with a question she
either cannot remember or avoids giving a straight answer."[15] The translations
were, in large measure, an ingenious "cover," a ploy designed to absorb
Elena's attention so that Williams could maneuver his queries into their conversation without her noticing. This subterfuge ironizes the mother/son relationship by transforming it into a game: Williams assumes the guise of a typically
naughty child who delights in doing something his elder has forbidden, yet
simultaneously fears being caught at it. The comic dimension of his scheme is
illustrated in the following passage:

> [Sometimes] she would catch sight of me out of the corner of her eye putting down some-
> thing she had just said on the back of an envelope.

What are you writing there, she would say accusingly.

Oh, just something I want to remember.

Are you writing down what I say because if you are . . .

Well, Mother, after all. I like to remember those proverbs you tell me. I think they are worth preserving. She wasn't fooled.

I don't want you to write my biography, she said. My life is too mixed up.

So much the more reason, my dear, I answered her. For here you are.

Very unhappy . . .

Very happily, my mother! I made a bow. She smiled. (*YMW*, 26–27)

Here, as in *January*, Williams seems to be flirting with Elena, adroitly mollifying her displeasure with him through a combination of flattery and mock obeisance. When she questions him about his actions, he initially feigns innocence, then invents a feeble excuse ("Well, Mother, after all. I like to remember those proverbs you tell me. I think they are worth preserving") which understandably fails to satisfy her. The poet's apparent ingenuousness is counterpointed by Elena's shrewd, incisive demeanor; clearly, she is not an individual who is easily deceived. She articulates her suspicions about Williams' activities in a stern, forthright manner, phrasing her questions "accusingly" and even threatening him at one point ("Are you writing down what I say, because if you are . . ."). The fact that Elena's statement is incomplete, however, makes its exact meaning uncertain; the ellipsis can be read either as an intensification of her threat (by leaving it unnamed) or its attenuation (by allowing her words to trail off unfinished).

This ambiguity is noteworthy because it reveals the underlying duplicity of the entire passage. The superficial traits Williams assigns to himself and Elena here belie their actual roles in the memoir's composition; his representation thus distorts historical circumstances rather than faithfully reproducing them. A close analysis of their dialogue, which is constructed in such a way that the connotations of mother and son's words subvert their literal meaning, illustrates the tension between these real and purported roles. Despite his meek, deferential stance, Williams is the master of this situation; the control he exerts over Elena becomes especially evident towards the end of the anecdote when she protests that he shouldn't write her biography because her life is "too mixed up." His response, "So much the more reason, my dear. . . . For here you are," is ostensibly intended to cajole his mother into reconsidering her position; yet in graciously overriding her objections, he asserts his own authority. The poet implicitly claims the ability to perform a deed which Elena herself cannot accomplish—sorting through the confused details of her life and arranging them in a coherent fashion. This imposition of order and meaning from without, particularly while she is still alive, is an aggressive act, a declaration of Williams' power as both writer and son.

Furthermore, the brief exchange following this remark suggests that he will not only arrange the events of Elena's life, but revise them according to his perceptions of her. Thus, when she describes her plight as "very unhappy," Williams immediately counters with "very happily, my mother!" This emphatic rejoinder initially seems to refute her assessment; however, in substituting an adverb (happily) for her adjective (unhappy), he obliquely shifts the referent of his statement and significantly alters its meaning. The poet's comment does not pertain to his mother's condition at all, but rather the fortuitous literary opportunity which her presence affords him. He will "read" her character in the same manner that she reads Soupault and Quevedo, carefully deciphering and teasing out the meaning of her words.

The forcefulness of Williams' pronouncement brings their discussion about his actions to an abrupt close; instead of disputing his claim, Elena simply acquiesces with a smile. Yet even this gesture is equivocal; it can be read as either a credulous response to her son's flattery or a wan admission of defeat. The remainder of their conversation favors the latter interpretation since the poet's blandishments become noticeably more exaggerated after his mother smiles, as though he were anxiously attempting to dispel some doubt or resentment she is feeling:

> Why even Captain Stousland, I went on, who looks the picture of Ibsen and is in fact his second cousin, admired you.
> I don't remember him.
> Just this morning, in the post office, he asked after you again. He has never forgotten how you recited that speech from *Phedre* that night . . . "*Rome enfin que je hais!*" Do you remember?
> Yes, I remember. (*YMW*, 27)

The introduction of a mysterious admirer, none other than Henrik Ibsen's second cousin, is an ingenious move on Williams' part. The esteem of this distinguished personage constitutes a seemingly irresistible appeal to his mother's vanity, particularly because it is based not on her faded physical beauty but on an inner, performative power which she still retains—the ability to infuse words with energy and raw emotion. The occasion of Elena's recitation, as Williams relates in section 1 of the introduction, was a meeting of the Rutherford Polytopic Club:

> At one time I was elected president of the [club's] entertainment committee. I developed the curious idea to have a reading of poems from the masters, but the feature of this dramatic reading was to be that it would be in the original language in every case. . . .
> Then, the meeting at our house, it came my mother's turn to do her bit. . . . Taking her time she delivered, in French, a speech from Corneille ending in the famous curse, "*Rome enfin que je hais!*" which left us speechless. All her contempt and even hatred that we had earned in this benighted country through the years was contained in that anathema. She finished and from the depth of her soul it came out, but good. She sat back, her cheeks aflame, her audience was spellbound. (*YMW*, 17–18)

The vibrant, dramatic flair which attracts Captain Stousland to Elena is the same quality that prompted Williams' own interest in collecting her sayings; thus, the stranger's admiration provides indirect confirmation of the legitimacy and value of the poet's undertaking. But in spite of its cleverness, Williams' ploy utterly fails to beguile his mother. She says little in response to his disclosure, and though the text gives no indication of the tone of her comments, it is extremely difficult to hear any warmth or enthusiasm in them. Their terse, perfunctory character, which is accentuated by the poet's unctuousness, suggests rather a mood of sullenness and recalcitrance. Moreover, Elena's wooden replies represent the antithesis of the poetic power both men admire in her speech; hence, in refusing to conform to that style, she expresses dissatisfaction with her present condition.

Although Williams' ruse does not achieve the desired result, it nonetheless provides a crucial insight into his relationship with Elena. In relaying Captain Stousland's regards to her, the poet serves as an intermediary, a liaison between his mother and the outside world. This configuration typifies their interaction during the last two decades of Elena's life, when, as a result of her physical debilitation, she was almost totally dependent on her son. What the scenario suppresses, however, is the adversity and inevitable frustration of coping, year after year, with the small but relentless demands of an aging parent. Williams conceals these difficulties behind a thin facade of pleasantries; Elena's feisty exterior masks her helplessness, while his gallantry disguises selfish, manipulative intentions.

Despite the deceptiveness of his characterization, the poet's inclusion of this disagreement about whether or not he should write his mother's biography in the introduction is significant because it transforms Elena from a passive, unwitting subject into an agent of sorts. Her awareness of his plans, evinced in the assertion "She wasn't fooled," suggests that some degree of complicity exists between them, even though she is not an especially eager participant in the project. Just as she collaborates with her son on the translations, so too she is a partner in this venture. Moreover, Elena's cognizance of Williams' intent provides her with a crucial source of leverage: by refusing to cooperate with him, she is able to achieve a modicum of power and negotiate for the recognition of her own preferences and needs. Her strategy, however, is no match for the poet's. He generally ignores her threats and interdictions, and even flaunts his authority by incorporating one of them into the text:

> In the French school where I went when I was a little girl, there was an old servant, Avriette. She was so old that when she would lean over some wind would come out and she would make a noise brrrrrp! So we would make fun of her: *Avriette! tirez nous petez BOOM! le navire est arrive!* (Avriette! Fire us BOOM! the ship has come to port!)
> Now don't you go put that into your book—or I won't tell you *anything*. (*YMW*, 115)

The content of Elena's anecdote is innocuous and irrelevant; what matters is that Williams has deliberately gone against her wishes in recording it. As in the introduction, his actions appear playful, but the stakes of the game are political (and implicitly sexual) power.

A strange symbiotic exchange is thus at work in the memoir. Williams and his mother stand in enantiomorphic relation to one another: both are cut off from information they greatly desire (in his case, stories about the past; in hers, news of the present), and each looks to the other as the primary way to attain it. Their reciprocal desires function as a magnet, drawing them into close, but highly manipulative contact, since each is determined to extract this coveted knowledge from the other. Because of her infirmities, Elena's situation is more patently desperate than the poet's. As the following passage from the 1957 article "From My Notes about My Mother" illustrates, he is her lifeline; without his contact, she would exist in a void akin to death itself:

> Poor soul, when sometimes I'd be tired and short with her, exasperated at her continual complaining about her "pains" which were eternally worse than any she had ever had in the past, she'd say, "If I don't speak to you, then I don't speak at all." She would get her way and I'd say no more. So that, rather than see her sit wooden-faced and silent at table, I'd deliberately give her a glass of vermouth or anything we had, if she'd take it. It was like fishing, was fishing in fact, for more often than not she'd come up with a story.[16]

In assuaging Elena's unhappy isolation, Williams simultaneously satisfies his own craving for information about the past. Mother and son, as this anecdote suggests, form two links in a dynamic human chain: sitting together in the eternal present of the memoir, they imaginatively move back and forth in time, each joining the other to facts, phenomena, and worlds which would otherwise be unavailable to them. This nexus deepens and perpetuates the already complicated bond between Williams and Elena; in depending exclusively on one another to fulfill these potentially insatiable demands, they become caught in an insidious circuit of desire and frustration. They progress towards their goals, obtaining brief, tantalizing glimpses of the past or present through the shadowy filter of the other's experience, but are unable to ever fully achieve them.[17]

The underside of this warm, intensive familial bond that Williams presents in the memoir is revealed by an unpublished fragment from the early forties entitled "Conversation between an Old Woman and Her Son":

> (He, screaming, in a harsh voice.)
> If you will TURN your head *side*ways so a person can talk INTO your ear and not try to LOOK at him that way all the time you'll HEAR better. You need a *trumpet*, something like this and HOLD it toward the person who is talking.
> (She makes a sound of despair and irritation and begins to cry)
> (He, trying to make conversation to relieve his embarrassment)
> Did you heard any voices last night?
> I hear lots of things.

Figure 5. Elena in the Late 1920s

"His Mother, stonedeaf, her face a wizened talon,
her hair the burnt-out ash of lush Puerto Rican grass;
her black, blind, bituminous eye inquisitorial."
                    (Robert Lowell, "William Carlos Williams")

(She half fills her empty coffee cup with sugar, both lump and granulated. She removes her heavy glasses and wipes her eyes. Drinks her orange juice, puts down the glass and begins to take some of the sugar out of her cup and put it back into the bowl. He sits embarrassed on the side of her bed, finally gets up and leaves.)[18]

Nothing even vaguely approaching the harshness and grim reality of this exchange appears in the memoir. Here, the attempt at conversation is an exercise in futility; rather than drawing mother and son closer together, it simply reinforces the barriers of their isolation and unhappiness. In the published text, Williams strives to keep such bitter emotions in check, though he does on occasion vent mild frustration at Elena's "infantile tactics" (*YMW, 55*), "bad temper, fears, and vindictiveness" (*YMW,* 130). Yet because these complaints are woven into the texture of an overwhelmingly positive portrait, they lose their sting and become additional confirmation of the intimate association between mother and son.

Another aspect of Elena's character which Williams consciously minimizes in the memoir is her fascination with the supernatural. Throughout her life she was deeply involved with spiritualism and periodically fell into mediumistic trances; one particularly striking incident, related in the introduction to the text, occurred in the poet's early childhood:

Out of the blue about seventy years ago, at the supper table, something happened to Mother. It was a seizure of some sort, but she did not lose consciousness, her alertness was rather quickened, concentrated, brought to a point—or so it seemed. I myself was too young the first time to make any proper estimate of it. I got to hate the things as they recurred from time to time in the following years. They scared me.

Ed and I were just children, but we realized at once the seriousness of the situation. We cooperated with Father when he told us what to do. She indicated that she wanted us, her children, to come on either side of her, which we did. She placed her hands on our heads.

So these are the children. How they have grown.

Then she caressed us, patted our heads and kissed me.

And who is this? said Pop.

Don't you know me? answered my mother. Lou Payne.

And with that the occasion ended. Mother relaxed and went on with her supper. The sequel is interesting. For Father at once sent a telegram to Jessie, Lou's husband, living with his wife in Los Angeles. Has anything happened to Lou?

For two weeks no reply came, then there was an answer apologizing for the delay: When I received your telegram Lou was on the operating table. We thought she had died. But under artificial respiration she started to breathe again. When I had your telegram I couldn't think of anything else but her care. (*YMW,* 18–19)

Williams' narration of this event is perhaps more telling than he himself realized. Amid the most mundane of circumstances—at home, the family assembled for the evening meal—Elena undergoes a radical transformation, momentarily becoming someone else. There is no stimulus or perceptible outward cause for this sudden change in identity; we witness only the distinctive effect, a quickening of Elena's "alertness" and "consciousness." The poet depicts his mother as a passive victim; "something" inexplicable "happened *to*" her that she has no power to control. The sense of emotional withdrawal and estrangement implied in Elena's bizarre metamorphosis from the familiar, nurturing presence who had cared for her two sons all day long (and presumably cooked the dinner they were engaged in eating) into Lou Payne, a distant but affectionate acquaintance, who exclaims, as if after long absence, "So these are the children. How they have grown" seems to have made a profound impression on the poet. He was more frightened than intrigued by this unusual aspect of his mother's character because in such moments she became an entirely alien figure, cut off from the objective world of reality which he inhabited. And despite the eerily calm lucidity with which Lou Payne "speaks" through Elena, on other occasions Elena's mediumistic trances seemed more deranged than oracular. As the following excerpt from the *Autobiography* reveals, both Williams and his brother Edgar were mortified by these occurrences:

> Mother would be possessed at such times—and it went on for years—by an uncontrollable shaking of the head. It would happen anywhere and at any time. I even saw it happen once while she was playing the piano at Sunday school. Ed and I were horribly embarrassed. But most often it would be at home primarily under strained circumstances as after the death of some friend or intimate, but not necessarily involving the appearance of that particular person.
>
> We'd all know at once what was about to take place—Mother's look would become fixed, her face would flush, and she'd reach out her hand and grasp the hand of one of us. Sometimes she'd indicate that she wanted Ed or me or anyone. Then someone would say, Is it this one? or that one? and she would try against heavy restraints to put her hand forward, but it would be impossible for her to do it. She'd struggle to try to clasp the hand offered to her, but if this were not the one she wanted, she'd recoil, violently, unable to seize it. Her face would be red, contorted, she couldn't talk, her whole body seized by some inscrutable violence.
>
> A name would be offered. No. Then another. She would shake her head violently, her cheeks flaming, her eyes like those of a person in violent effort of any sort. Finally Pop might say, "Is it Carlos?", meaning her brother, and she'd grasp the hand offered in both hers, and the presence would leave her.
>
> How Ed and I dreaded these occasions! Pop believed literally, I think, in their authenticity: that the spirits of the dead did materialize through her and did try to reach us. But why they should want to come I never could understand. (*A*, 17)

This account is much more detailed and disturbing than the Lou Payne incident recounted in *Yes, Mrs. Williams.* The poet here outlines the basic pattern of his mother's possessions, although it is clear that the predictability of the sequence (fixed gaze, flushed countenance, the grasping of various hands, etc.) does not in any way diminish its horror. He decries the "inscrutable violence" and futility of these episodes, giving particular emphasis to Elena's inability to communicate, which reduces those present to players in a macabre guessing game. After acknowledging the dread which these trances inspired in him and his brother, Williams tries to defuse their unsettling emotive power by denying their authenticity. He counters his father's superstitious belief, doubtlessly bred of his West Indian childhood, that the spirits of the dead can and do, in fact, return to earth through individual mediums with a pragmatic skepticism, stating, "But why they should want to I never could understand."

The supernatural anecdote in the memoir's introduction is characterized by a similar tone of denial. In reporting Elena's mysterious transformation into Lou Payne, Williams assumes the objective stance of a scientist, the rationalist attempting to empirically explain the uncanny, and describes the event in medical terms as a type of "seizure" which abated with his mother's advancing age. He distances himself from this "curious phenomenon" by relegating it to the past and assigning a logical cause for its later, more subtle, manifestations:

> These seizures finally changed to an occupation with dreams. She had her favorites about whom to dream. This was when she was almost blind, when in my opinion it was a compensation for her failing vision. In her dreams she could see perfectly well. Mr. Luce, now many years dead, often stood beside her, occupied with whatever he had to do. She loved to have him about.
>
> Once she described him with the minutest accuracy with a piece of knitting in his hands. She was fully aware of the humor of the situation. Luce, a man, at a woman's occupation! She was fascinated. To hear her tell it, she watched him with greatest admiration, the minute stitches hour after hour. Beautiful! She didn't dare disturb him or he might stop. What a wonderful experience. (*YMW,* 19–20)

Williams recounts this same anecdote in the *Autobiography,* but does not identify it as a dream. Instead, he simply quotes Elena's matter-of-fact assertion that "a man who had been dead for twenty or more years came to visit her one day," and adds, "Who was I to contradict her?" (*A,* 306). This discrepancy underscores the poet's desire to mitigate the threatening aspect of his mother's visions in the memoir; rather than labelling Mr. Luce's appearance a delusion or hallucination, he situates it in the realm of the unconscious. As a dream, the story seems tame, humorous; it is no longer an aberration or possible sign of madness, but a creative response to the plight of old age.

Spiritualism is also mentioned several times in the memoir proper, though Williams treats it in a cursory, almost contemptuous manner. When, for example, Elena says, "Someone is with me today and I don't know who it is. (Wringing her hands convulsively)," his response is gruff and unsympathetic: "Never mind, you'll find out later" (*YMW,* 95). In other instances, such as her narration of an especially frightening seance that took place in the poet's youth during which she "went completely out of [her] head" (*YMW,* 113), he does not reply at all. His silence is implicitly damning, a voiceless expression of disfavor and unbelief.

Despite these curt nods in the direction of the paranormal, Williams refused to acknowledge in either the memoir or the *Autobiography* that Elena's visions actually grew more intense and bizarre in the last few years of her life. Because she could no longer apprehend the physical world through her senses, she fabricated an extensive cast of characters and events which functioned as an alternative. In a letter to Louis Zukofsky on November 18, 1948, Williams offers this picture of his mother's mental state:

> Decided this morning with fog outside the bedroom window that I might as well believe in a future life. Why not if it makes the mind lively?
>
> Me ma is wonderful on the subject, the only difficulty being that all her revenants are such nasty bastards. I don't know why she had to pick such skunks. She says they want to "hurt people" but she can't say why. Poor soul, being unable to see or hear or walk she has invented the most marvelous assembly of witches and whore-masters to entertain her. The other day it was an endless column of Mexican cavalry riding bareback "to show us how they ride." There's a war on between Mexico and the U.S. . . . you know. She tells you all about it.[19]

The brashness and extremity of Elena's ravings, particularly her story about the "war" with Mexico, profoundly disturbed the poet. Two days after writing to Zukofsky, he began a play called "No Love, or What Use to Grow Old" which centered around his mother. The dramatis personae were several family members (Edgar, Flossie, Young Dr. Bill, et al.) as well as "characters from the old woman's 'illusions': the Princess, the Count of Miramar, Various Young Men—all with half-told secrets, and many others."[20] The "Argument" for the play was as follows:

> Approaching her 92nd birthday the old woman wants to see young Dr. Bill married, Ingrid [Edgar's daughter] as well. She is virtually blind and deaf and cannot walk: but she is relentlessly alive.
>
> She does not scheme. She believes she is being deceived and that the truth is being kept from her. She believes Dr. Bill is married and that a man has asked Ingrid—and cannot understand why, why, why these things go on.
>
> Incidentally she has been "told" of a war between Mexico and the U.S.
>
> So she fills her life . . . with drink and sleep and dreams.[21]

Though the play never developed beyond this one-page draft, its essence was distilled into the poem "Another Old Woman," which also dates from late 1948:

> If I could keep her
> here, near me
> I'd fill her mind
> with my thoughts
>
> She would get
> their complexion
> and live again. But
> I could not live
>
> along with her
> she would drain me
> as sand drains
> water. Visions pos-

sess her. Dreams
unblooded walk
her mind. Her mind
does not faint.

Throngs visit her:
We are at war
with Mexico—to
please her fancy—

A cavalry column
is deploying
over a lifeless terrain
—to impress us!

She describes it
her face bemused—
alert to details. They
ride without saddles

tho' she is ig-
norant of the word
"bareback," but knows
accurately that I

am not her son, now,
but a stranger
listening. She
breaks off, her looks

intent, bent
inward, with a curious
glint to her eyes:
They say that

when the fish comes!
(gesture of getting
a strike) it
is a great joy.

(*CLP,* 205–6)

The poem begins with a rather odd fantasy: Williams imagines giving his mother a mental transfusion—placing his thoughts in her mind—as a means of making her "live again." The poet's desire to revitalize Elena implies that she is already dead, not in a literal sense, but so caught up in a world of private phantasms that she herself has become a specter. His depiction of her is indeed reminiscent of a ghost or zombie: "Visions *pos-* / *sess* her. Dreams / *unblooded* walk her mind" (emphasis mine). In order to rescue Elena and "keep her here" in the physical world, Williams offers himself as a sacrificial victim: "I could not live / along with her / she would drain me / as sand drains / water." The act which he contemplates is, on the one hand, selfless and destructive, a fantasy of martyrdom. Yet, conversely, it also represents an ecstatic union, a consummate merging of mother and son. The poet would, in this respect, not die at all, but continue to live in and through Elena.

Williams' description of his mother's delusions in the lyric helps explain why he both found them so threatening and chose to downplay their existence in the memoir. For example, the visual doubling of "her mind. Her mind," produced by his enjambment of two sentences in line 15, accentuates a split he perceived in Elena's condition. Though her apparitions denote some form of dementia, she remains outwardly lucid and "alert to details." She is also, according to the poet, aware of the gaping emotional distance these visions create between them. The "lifeless terrain" across which the phantom cavalry rides is an interior landscape which Williams can never see or hope to share, regardless of the power of his mother's evocations. Thus, in listening to her tales, he is no longer "her son . . . but a stranger," alien, aloof, detached. Elena's withdrawal into this fantasy world causes a breakdown of intimacy and communication; she slips elusively beyond Williams' grasp, as his concluding image of her powerfully conveys: "She / breaks off, her looks / intent, bent / inward, with a curious / glint to her eyes."

Throughout his life, Williams sought to achieve with Elena the spiritual closeness and familiarity that he had never been able to develop with his father. This desire grew more urgent during her last years as he helplessly watched her dwindle and fade slowly into a corpse. Elena's visions constituted a serious obstacle to the poet's ambition in that they estranged him from her; hence, he felt it was necessary to deflate them as best he could in the memoir. The earnestness of his desire for intimacy with Elena is poignantly illustrated in a 1949 poem entitled "The Horse Show":

> Constantly near you, I never in my entire
> sixty-four years knew you so well as yesterday
> or half so well. We talked. You were never
> so lucid, so disengaged from all exigencies
> of place and time. We talked of ourselves,
> intimately, a thing never heard of between us.
> How long have we waited? almost a hundred years.
>
> You said, Unless there is some spark, some
> spirit we keep within ourselves, life, a
> continuing life's impossible—and it is all
> we have. There is no other life, only the one.
> The world of the spirits that comes afterward
> is the same as our own, just like you sitting
> there they come and talk to me, just the same.

They come to bother us. Why? I said. I don't
know. Perhaps to find out what we are doing.
Jealous do you think? I don't know. I
don't know why they should want to come back.
I was reading about some men who had been
buried under a mountain, I said to her, and
one of them came back after two months,

digging himself out. It was in Switzerland,
you remember? Of course I remember. The
villagers tho't it was a ghost coming down
to complain. They were frightened. They
do come, she said, what you call
my "visions." I talk to them just as I
am talking to you. I see them plainly.

Oh if I could only read! You don't know
what adjustments I have made. All
I can do is to try to live over again
what I knew when your brother and you
were children—but I can't always succeed.
Tell me about the horse show. I have
been waiting all week to hear about it.

Mother darling, I wasn't able to get away.
Oh that's too bad. It was just a show;
they make the horses walk up and down
to judge them by their form. Oh is that
all? I tho't it was something else. Oh
they jump and run too. I wish you had been
there, I was so interested to hear about it.

(*CLP*, 185–86)

The mood of this poem, in sharp contrast to "Another Old Woman," is tranquil, quiet. Elena's gaze is not "bent inward," but focused intently upon her son. She speaks in a controlled, philosophic manner about her "visions," attempting to rationally explain their occurrence in terms of her belief that "the world of the spirits . . . is the same as our own." In addition, she tacitly corroborates Williams' speculation that the apparitions are a compensation for her diminished physical capacities by asserting, "You don't know what adjustments I have made." In spare, monosyllabic language, Elena describes the desperation of her circumstances, identifying only two outlets through which she can alleviate her isolation—memory and her son. The paucity of her resources makes the poem's conclusion all the more heart-rending. Although the horse show is in itself a trivial, mundane event ("they make the horses walk up and down / to judge them by their form"), Elena has invested it with a tremendous importance. Williams' inability to attend and report back to her about it is thus a major disappointment which painfully reinforces her loneliness and insularity.

The dialogue which takes place between mother and son in both "Another Old Woman" and "The Horse Show" is, to all appearances, of the same general character as that recorded in the memoir. Yet Williams' decision to translate these particular incidents into individual poems rather than incorporate them into his larger tapestry provides further confirmation of the text's scrupulous selectivity. The two lyrics concern moments when Williams fails to reconnect Elena to the substantive reality of her immediate environs, either by not infusing her mind with his thoughts or by not attending a horse show. Communication between them falters as a result, and the bonds of intimacy are weakened. The memoir, in contrast, documents only the poet's successes, the occasions on which he was able to genuinely make contact with his mother and imbibe the rich fragrance of her character. Thus, the true "design" of conversation, as a close look at the text's dialogue reveals, extends beyond the friendship and familiarity of social discourse to a radical merging of selves.

4

Mother Tongue, Mother Muse

I do not come to you
            save that I confess
                    to being
                    half man and half
woman.
                    "For Eleanor and Bill Monahan"

In his 1942 review of Anaïs Nin's *The Winter of Artifice,* Williams discusses a delicate and highly controversial issue, namely, the role that gender plays in artistic creation. There is, he asserts, "an authentic female approach to the arts";[1] however, in order to define it, he resorts to a comparative strategy—setting this "female approach" in relation to its dominant male counterpart:

> The male scatters his element recklessly as if there were no end to it. Balzac is a case in point. That profusion you do not find in the female but the equal infinity of the single cell. This at her best she harbors, warms and implants that it may proliferate. Curie in her sphere was the perfect example of the principle. Naturally some men write like women and some women like men, proving the point; two phases with a reciprocal relationship.[2]

The literary distinction Williams draws here has its origin in biological difference: male "style" is phallic and profuse, characterized by a reckless scattering of his seminal "element" into the outer environment, whereas that of the female is internalized and womblike, symbolized by the harboring and eventual implantation of a "single cell." Yet, as the last sentence of the passage implies, these traits do not typically exist in pure, independent states, but are instead androgenetically mixed. The male and female elements together comprise two reciprocal "phases" of the artist's creative impulse. For this reason, Williams states, the best writing occurs when a dynamic interplay exists between these disparate elements: "Maximum vigor lies in two strong poles between which a spark shall leap to produce an equilibrium in the end. When we get a piling up at one pole without relief the feeling is transitional. . . . This is the mood and the background, a stasis, an absolute arrest."[3]

Jerome Mazzaro, in his book, *William Carlos Williams: The Later Poems,* uses these theoretical assertions about gender and writing as the basis of a provocative comparison between the poet's incorporation of Marcia Nardi's letters into *Paterson* and his direct recording of Elena's remarks in *Yes, Mrs. Williams.* Both, he declares, are attempts to create a "stasis" or balance of male and female psyches:

> What Williams may have wanted to produce by including the letters was a "stasis" . . . which would prove his ability to present a female psyche. If any "marriage" of Paterson with "C." is to evolve from this stasis, he may want it to occur not on the page but in the minds of his readers. A similar feature of balance occurs in his biography of his mother. After a series of biographical sketches, Williams again tries to let the woman present her character through scraps of conversation, notes, letters, proverbs, and asides. . . . The book's improvised nature reaffirms the sense that the lack of design is intentional, a harking back to his old definition of woman as the concrete thinker whose failure when she fails is that of design not of detail. By emphasizing detail to the detriment of design, the book pretends to approximate a female way of thinking; yet the very imitative fallacy behind both presentations—a mirroring of mental processes rather than objects in order to achieve an inner Geist—throws Williams' theory of art as imitation into question.[4]

This analogy is purely stylistic: Mazzaro draws a specific connection between Williams' use of counterpoint in *Paterson* and *Yes, Mrs. Williams,* but does not pursue an analysis of the overall relationship between the two works. Beyond the texts' formal similarities, numerous personal parallels exist between Nardi (or "Cress") and the poet's mother which help to clarify Williams' imaginative perception of women in general. Like Cress, Elena is "a woman dying of loneliness" (*P,* 87), isolated, unhappy, oppressed by circumstances, and thwarted in her artistic aspirations. Alienated from the mainstream of patriarchal society, the two women turn to the poet for companionship and emotional support. Their appeals to him are characterized by an underlying urgency and despair, since both have difficulty in communicating with others, and believe that he alone can help them. In "From My Notes about My Mother," Williams quotes Elena as saying, "If I don't speak to you, then I don't speak at all";[5] similarly, Cress states in book 2 of *Paterson:*

> There are people—especially among women—who can speak only to one person. And I am one of those women. I do not come easily to confidences (though it cannot but seem otherwise to you). I could not possibly convey to anyone of those people who have crossed my path in these few months, those particular phases of my life which I made the subject of my letters to you. I must let myself be entirely misunderstood and misjudged in all my economic and social maladjustments, rather than ever attempt to communicate to anyone else what I wrote to you about. (*P,* 64)

This attitude augments the desperation of both women's plights—if they fail to make contact with Williams, they are cut off from the world and confined in utter solitude. Moreover, the extremity of their emotional needs places Elena and Cress on distinctly unequal footing with the poet; he is dominant, autonomous, and powerful, while they, in varying degrees, are helpless and dependent.

Yet despite the similarities in their situations, the two women differ markedly in their individual response to him. Elena, who had forsaken her ambition of becoming a great portraitist when she emigrated to the United States and married, is more tractable and outwardly submissive than Cress. She is totally resigned to "woman's wretched position in society" (*P*, 86), a position which, in her case, is exacerbated by the substantive barriers of language and culture. Because she is no longer actively engaged in a creative endeavor, Elena views Williams' appropriation of her words not as an exploitive act, but as a means of vicarious recognition and success.

Cress, on the other hand, is immersed in a seemingly endless struggle to eke out an existence as a writer; in this respect, she represents a possible version of Elena's fate had she persisted in her artistic career. She shares the older woman's idealism and steadfast refusal to compromise her principles, telling Williams in the long letter which concludes book 2, "It's *writing* that I want to do—not operating a machine or lathe, because with literature more and more tied up with the social problems . . . any contribution I might be able to make to the welfare of humanity . . . would have to be as a writer, and not as a factory worker" (*P*, 90). The earnestness of this frustrated ambition causes Cress to regard Williams as much a rival as a colleague. She bitterly resents the relative ease and security of his position, his established poetic reputation, and violently resists his attempts to usurp her thoughts and transform them into literature. In sharp contrast to Elena's mild protests that Williams should not write her biography, Cress lambastes the hypocritical split in his consciousness which allows him to separate the potential aesthetic value of her ideas from the painful human context that spawned them. Though both women's remonstrations are, in the final assessment, equally ineffectual, Cress' strident criticism, embedded within the body of *Paterson,* remains a serious indictment of Williams' poetic practices, whereas his mother's anger is neutralized and defused by the warm, affectionate tone of the memoir.

The male/female balance that Mazzaro observes in *Paterson* and *Yes, Mrs. Williams* is therefore not fixed or uniform, but diverse, protean. The balance between the poet and Cress, for example, is antagonistic, the result of mutual misapprehension and foiled expectations. The failure of their communication is underscored by the fact that only her side of the correspondence (or more accurately, Williams' selections thereof) is included in the text. No direct dialogue takes place between them; Williams in no way responds to or attempts to shield himself from the steady stream of invectives Cress hurls at him. His silence intensifies the shrill, neurotic energy of her accusations by serving as a blank screen upon which she projects her own highly subjective interpretations of recent events. Cress' letters contain only two objective bits of information regarding the poet's actions—that after she initiated a correspondence with him, he ignored several of her letters, and that he then sent a note asking her to refrain from writing him any further.

The violent explosion of anger provoked by this breach of epistolary etiquette is vastly disproportionate to the actual infraction. Having imaginatively cast Williams in the role of father and literary arbiter, Cress endows him with a tremendous power and simultaneously renders herself extremely vulnerable; his approbation becomes the prime measure of her own self-worth. For this reason, she views his standoffishness as a devastating personal rejection: "I am forced, psychologically, to feel that what I wrote you about, was sufficiently trivial and unimportant and absurd to merit your evasion" (*P*, 48). As the sequence of letters progresses, her description of the effects of Williams' attitude grow increasingly melodramatic. His (in)action, Cress claims, has caused "the complete damming up of all my creative capacities" (*P*, 45) and "destroy[ed] the validity for me myself *of* myself" by inducing an emotional schism, "an exiling of one's self from one's self" (*P*, 45) in which "that whole side of life connected with those letters . . . took on for my own self that same kind of unreality and inaccessibility which the inner lives of other people often have for us" (*P*, 48). With each rearticulation of her predicament, Cress aggrandizes the poet's power and diminishes her own, until he acquires for her the distant, almost mythical status of a potentate before whom she is totally abject: "The one thing that I still wish more than any other is that I could see you . . . but *even if you should grant it* I wouldn't want to see you unless with some little warmth of friendliness and friendship on your part" (*P*, 75–76; emphasis mine).

The pathos of Cress' position, as evinced by the above statement, arises from her misguided belief that Williams is both the source of her problems and the vehicle of her salvation. She is thus unable to break out of the desperate, self-defeating circuit of need in which she finds herself and assert her independence. Instead, she paradoxically persists in blaming the poet for events and circumstances over which he has no jurisdiction, while courting his favor at the same time:

> I have been feeling   that I shall never again be able to recapture any sense of my own personal identity (without which I cannot write, of course—but in itself far more important than the writing) until I can recapture some faith in the reality of my own thoughts and ideas and problem which were turned into dry sand by your attitude toward those letters and by that note of yours later. That is why I cannot throw off my desire to see you. . . . (*P*, 76)

The extent of Cress' impotence is reflected in the second postscript to her last letter in *Paterson;* after pouring out her deepest emotions to Williams page after page, trying to make him understand the difficulties inherent in being a female artist, she realizes with horror that he may cursorily dismiss her text without even glancing at its contents. All she can do in hope of averting this situation is append a plea that he read the letter in its entirety "carefully, because it's about you, as a writer . . . [and also] out of fairness to me—much time and much thought and much unhappiness having gone into those pages" (*P,* 92). Williams' incorporation of the letter into his poem tacitly suggests that he heeded Cress' advice; indeed, its presence can be interpreted as a response of sorts to her. There is, in addition, a certain poignance about the letter in that it marks the bleak denouement of their relationship. Williams and Cress do not make contact: he remains locked inside the "glass-walled conditions" (*P,* 87) of his own safe life, while she, as the result of her efforts, sinks "a million fathoms deeper" (*P,* 89) in her loneliness and despair. The letter's inclusion also ironically confirms one of Cress's chief complaints about the poet ("my ideas . . . were interesting to you, weren't they, in so far as they made for literature?" (*P,* 86) and thus provides a tangible example of the vast but nebulous power she repeatedly ascribes to him. Without uttering a word, he nevertheless manages to have the final say by ignoring her protestations and placing her within his text where her achievements do, in a sense, "serve as a flower in his buttonhole" (*P,* 91).

Because Cress' letters recapitulate many of the themes in books 1 and 2 of *Paterson,* she is generally regarded as the poet's feminine counterpart. In Taoist terms, she represents the primary manifestation of yin in a predominantly yang structure. According to Paul Mariani, Williams felt that in Cress he had found "the exact monstrous female voice to complement his own."[6] The nature of this complement is, however, primarily antagonistic. Cress functions as the poet's guilty conscience, perpetually chiding and berating him for his selfishness, insularity, and egotism. No "marriage" takes place between them either on the page or, as Mazzaro proposes, in the minds of individual readers. Their voices are sharp, dissonant, and highly distinct; their tale is not one of harmonious union, but rather of blockage and divorce, the tragedy of failed communication.

By comparison, the male/female balance in *Yes, Mrs. Williams* is far more amicable and euphonic. This difference can be attributed in part to the fact that an intimate bond of kinship exists between the parties in the memoir, whereas Williams and Cress are complete strangers whose encounter, conducted principally through the mail rather than face to face, is abrupt, intense, rife with insecurities, and hence even more prone to misunderstandings. Moreover, the balance of male and female psyches in the memoir is not limited, as Mazzaro suggests, to the relationship between the poet's prefatory "series of biographical sketches" and Elena's "scraps of conversation, notes, letters, proverbs, and asides." The italicized commentary which is interpolated between her remarks throughout the body of the text itself comprises an ongoing dialogue between mother and son and thus achieves a more pervasive sense of equilibrium. Unlike *Paterson,* where the futility of attempted communication between the sexes is symbolized by the juxtaposition of monolithic blocks of words, the memoir records numerous instances of casual, direct conversation, as illustrated by the following passage:

I think I'll close that window.

Yes, do. It's very funny, any change affects me. I may even be sleeping and if it gets very hot, I wake up right away. Or, if it gets cold, it's the same thing. I suppose my nerves are very sensitive, anything affects me. I am not a person anymore, but I still have some use as a barometer—when it is cold my pains are much worse.

Won't you have a cigarette, Mother. Really, you ought to learn to smoke, it would do you good, it would quiet you down . . .

No. I don't want to. Once when I was a girl they told me that if I cleaned my teeth with a cigar it would make them strong and white. So I took a cigar and rubbed them with it. Well, before breakfast. Chah! I was sick as a dog after. (*YMW*, 89–90)

It is here, in these brief and often banal exchanges, that the "stasis" of male and female voices actually occurs. While the diverse scope of Elena's remarks does reveal a great deal about her temperament and mental processes, the memoir does not "pretend to approximate a female way of thinking." Williams' intention is much more radical: to subtly intertwine his words with those of his mother as a means of blurring the boundaries of their individual identities and imaginatively fusing them. The text thus explores a type of "balance" which is only obliquely hinted at in *Paterson*—the androgynous character of the artist. Williams had been fascinated with this subject ever since the beginning of his career, as the 1914 poem "Transitional" indicates:

First he said:
It is the woman in us
That makes us write—
Let us acknowledge it—
Men would be silent.
We are not men
Therefore we can speak
And be conscious
(of the two sides)
Unbent by the sensual
as befits accuracy.

I then said:
Dare you make this
Your propaganda?

And he answered:
Am I not I—here?

(*CEP*, 34)

Part of the poet's abiding preoccupation with Elena stems from a curiosity about the nature and origins of his own artistic impulse. *Yes, Mrs. Williams* in a sense represents the culmination of that curiosity; it is simultaneously two books in one, a biography and a spiritual autobiography. As early as 1937–38, when Williams was composing "Raquel Helene Rose," the essay that eventually became the latter half of the memoir's introduction, he realized that the actual subject of his investigation was not his mother, but rather himself:

> There it is. Let that be the scaffolding. I'll speak of all these things as if she told them to me while we were translating [Quevedo's *The Dog and the Fever*]—only the pretext: the real story is how all the complexities finally came to play one tune, today—to me—what I find good in my own life. She has lived through—and stands as an example of that. (*YMW*, 26)

It was not until the fifties, however, that Williams devised a stylistic strategy which would allow him to present the "real story" in all its complexity while still preserving the primacy of Elena's language. By alternating his remarks with hers, the poet tacitly establishes an extensive network of emotional, linguistic, and ideological correspondences between himself and his mother. These parallels echo and reverberate in the reader's mind, drawing the two figures closer together through the gradual accretion of internal evidence rather than the intrusive assertion of an omniscient narratorial voice. The rhythm of their words thus blends and merges, forming a single "tune."

The memoir's structure is, in this respect, antiphonal. Williams' interpolations are direct responses to Elena's comments, though they vary considerably in length, diction, and tone. There appear to be three distinct types of interpolations in the text, broadly characterized by a progressively elliptical relationship to the remarks which prompt them. The first group, illustrated by a fragment of dialogue quoted several pages earlier ("I think I'll close that window . . ."), consists of literal answers to his mother's statements and/or actions. These conversations, which range in topic from the poet's spilling of her breakfast tray (*YMW*, 99) to a family discussion about the virtues of brown rice (*YMW*, 53), offer instructive glimpses of the comfortable domestic milieu—the manners, habits, and daily rituals that form the ground of their interaction.

In the second type of interpolation, direct dialogue is replaced by analysis and critical commentary. Williams now speaks *about* Elena rather than specifically to her, and attempts to objectively assess various aspects of her personality. Generally, these interpolations elucidate and expatiate on a particular anecdote, providing additional information about her background where necessary to clarify the text's meaning. He pushes beyond the obvious denotative meaning of his mother's statements, treating them instead as valuable clues to her attitudes and beliefs. The following passage typifies the detached perspective inherent in the poet's commentary:

> *She's an intelligent woman, but when she gets those bilious attacks she goes to bed in her own room.* Yo prefiero morirse antes que tomar esas remedios de la botica! (*I would prefer to die than to take those drugstore remedies*)
> *Her son sends for the doctor, but she won't do anything. She prefers to take her own remedies, camomile and—You don't have those things here, she says.*
> *That sounds like the old Puerto Rico!* (*YMW*, 55)

Williams uses the third-person point of view in this passage as a distancing device, referring to Elena not by name, but with the generic pronoun "she," and designating himself simply as "her son." The resulting sense of detachment and defamiliarization, which is characteristic of the second group of interpolations as a whole, is amplified in this instance by a fundamental disagreement between the two parties. Elena's harangue about "drugstore remedies" illustrates a number of her salient personal traits: that she is old-fashioned, feisty, childish, and extremely reactive. Williams skillfully avoids placing himself in direct opposition to his mother's traditional ideas by not acting as her physician here. He implicitly denies and displaces that role, projecting it outward onto another individual, and thereby becomes an agent who, in "send[ing] for the doctor," defers to the authority of modern medicine, but does not incarnate it. In thus distancing himself from the immediate target of Elena's "bilious attack," Williams is able to view her position with a combination of admiration, wry amusement, and tolerance which would be impossible in a professional capacity.

It is apparent from these representative excerpts that the identities of mother and son remain separate and inviolate in the first two groups of interpolations. It is in the third category, those sequences which have only a marginal connection to the anecdotes and statements directly preceding them, that the blurring of ego boundaries takes place. The first two groups are nonetheless vital to the poet's project since they help prepare the reader for the radical merging he attempts in the third. Their subtle stylistic differences, namely, the shift in perspective from first to third person and gradual movement away from dramatic dialogue, reflect essential stages in Williams' evolving conception of his mother.

Because the memoir has a totally nonlinear structure, it is somewhat misleading to describe the interpolations as "evolving" in a particular direction. Williams does not segregate the three groups, but freely intermingles them throughout the text. Hence, they do not record an unswerving progression towards a much-coveted goal, but rather a delicate oscillation or, to use one of the poet's favorite metaphors, a dance between singularity and coalescence.

The third group of interpolations, where this mysterious fusion takes place, is distinguished from the others by their length and snarled syntax. In addition, the tone of these passages tends to be more abstract and poetic than that of the preceding groups; here, Elena's words serve as the springboard and occasion for private meditations on larger subjects, like the difficulties of aging, which are equally applicable to both son and mother. In strictly technical terms, Williams accomplishes the merging of their identities in two fundamental ways. He deliberately mimics Elena's unusual style of discourse in the interpolations, using short, broken phrases and incomplete thoughts which are strung together by a series of dashes. The following illustrates her characteristically fragmented syntax: "When I was a child—children are very foolish you know, and it can be dangerous. They wouldn't let me go—I don't know any more where it was—with them. I took a little piece of candle—(*YMW*, 49).

And here, by the way of comparison, are two statements by Williams:

> Begins with a attack upon old age, what it does, what it does to others—sclerosis—faces expressionless—the mumbled word—and the mind, as if enclosed, signaling alive from within—better than ever—ripened—every fault exaggerated, witnessed and unable to check it. (*YMW*, 49)

> Here by the watertank and the stone, mottled granite, big as a rhinoceros head—cracked on one side—damn families. (*YMW*, 101)

These two passages also demonstrate the poet's second strategy for conflating his identity with his mother's—the elimination of personal pronouns. Neither the speaker nor subject is clearly identified in the above statements, creating an indeterminacy which pluralizes and, to some extent, confounds their semantic resonance. This lack of substantive referents and gender indicators makes both Williams and Elena the potential and equally plausible authors (and/or subjects) of the comments. For a moment, mother's and son's voices are indistinguishable, thoroughly interchangeable, one.

The poet's syntactic maneuvers assume even greater significance when considered in light of this excerpt from "From My Notes about My Mother," an essay which Edith Heal culled from the jumbled drafts of *Yes, Mrs. Williams* in 1957:[7]

> Perhaps my way of telling you this isn't exactly what you might prefer or expect, but in this family *you are expected to understand what is said and interpret, as essential to the telling, the way in which it is told—for some reason which you will know is of the matter itself.* That is to picture it. "Figure to yourself," as my mother would often say—obviously translated directly from the French. (emphasis mine)[8]

Williams' defense of the aberrant, nonnarrative style of his "notes" is that the method of telling is inextricably connected to "the matter itself." The ramifications of such a notion are extensive: in writing about his mother, he writes *like* her as well, and thereby implicitly enlarges the scope of his inquiry to include himself. The subject or "matter itself" is no longer solely Elena, but the complex dynamic of Elena and Williams.

Moreover, as his allusion to the French proverb, "Figure to yourself," suggests, much of the memoir's meaning is veiled and indirect, and therefore requires the reader to dig beyond its superficial content. Many of Elena's stories, for example, have proverbs or aphoristic bits of folk wisdom at their center, which, as Williams remarks in an unpublished version of the work, are "from her life—*use them in the text as revealing hints, also to the composition as to what is said*" (emphasis mine).[9] This statement infers that the proverbs serve a dual purpose in the memoir, providing insight into Elena's cultural heritage and value system as well as intriguing "hints" about the nature and import of "what is said." In this regard, two of her anecdotes add an intriguing self-reflexive dimension to the text. Both stories, recalled from her youth in Puerto Rico, concern two people between whom a certain degree of intimacy exists or has existed in the past. In speaking to one another, they say very nearly the same thing; it is only a slight linguistic variation (in the first instance, gender tags; in the second, word order) which differentiates them:

> How would you say in English? How would you translate it?
> Y esta es aquella? (And this is she?)
> Y esto es aquel? (And that is he?)
> It was two who used to be lovers. They were going each with a friend and they passed the one they had been in love with years before. And he said to his friend: Y esta es aquella? He couldn't believe it. And she said too: Y esto es aquel? You couldn't translate that into English without a long sentence explaining what it was. (*YMW*, 72)

> There were two old men, very old, and half asleep that were talking together and one of them said to the other—
> Pues, yo ya. (Well, here am I) and the other answers him—
> Pues, ya yo. (Well, I am here) (*YMW*, 135)

The imperfect verbal mirroring contained in these vignettes is not simply a coincidence; rather, it serves as an indicator of familiarity, psychic attunement, and the haziness of interpersonal boundaries. As such, the anecdotes are variants on a single suggestive theme: the subtle interplay of voice and identity. In the first, a chance meeting between former lovers—two individuals who, as a couple, were previously considered one—momentarily revives that bond, as their simultaneous queries reveal. Elena's remark, "You couldn't translate that into English without a long sentence explaining what it was," refers specifically to the ambiguous resonance of the demonstrative pronoun "aquel, aquella" (literally meaning "that one, the former") which is an acknowledgment of both similarity and difference.

In the case of the two old men, however, the merging of self and other is prompted not by an unexpected encounter, but by a physiological condition—drowsiness. Sitting together, wavering between sleep and consciousness, they are in a liminal state where objects lose their crisp contours and borders imperceptibly begin to yield. Thus, in responding to the first man's comment, the second repeats his words but modifies their order. This echoing blurs, but does not fully dissolve the distinctions between them, leaving them instead on the threshold of an imminent merging.

An implicit correlation exists between these anecdotes and Williams' larger intention in the memoir. Often, as a result of his playful linguistic manipulations, the only solid clue to the speaker of a particular passage comes from the typeface in which it is set. If the statement is italicized, the reader can generally assume that Williams himself is speaking. Yet according to David

Figure 6. The Poet and His Mother, mid-1930s

"one unlike the other, twin
of the other, conversant with eccentricities
side by side"

(*Paterson*)

McDowell, the publisher of *Yes, Mrs. Williams* and a number of the poet's other works during the fifties, the implementation of contrasting type in the memoir was his idea rather than Williams' own.[10] Because of the text's non-narrative form, he felt it was necessary to supply a visual cue that would help the reader differentiate Elena's words from those of her son. Williams approved McDowell's suggestion, although he did not share the publisher's concern about the possible confusion of identity.[11] His only specification for the phys-ical layout of the work—that each anecdote be separated by an area of white space—was intended to emphasize its disjunctive character. Each space signals a pause, a brief interval of silence before the conversation resumes. This struc-tural device is in itself a tacit concession to the principles of order and clarity since early portions of the memoir printed in *The Descent of Winter* (1928) make no distinction at all between mother's and son's statements. Their words are simply dovetailed together in the same paragraph as if spoken by a single person:

> I remember, she said, we had little silver plaques with a chain on it to hang over the necks of the bottles, whiskey, brandy, or whatever it was. And a box of some kind of wood, not for the kitchen but a pretty box. Inside it was lined with something like yes, pewter, all in-side and there was a cover of metal too with a little knob on it, all inside the wooden box. You would open the outer cover and inside was the lid. When you would take that off you would see the tea with a silver spoon for taking it out. But now here are the roses—three opening. Out of love. For she loves them and so they are there. They are not a picture. Hol-bein never saw pink thorns in such a light. Nor did Masaccio. The petals are delicate. It is a question if they will open at all and not drop, loosing at one edge and falling to-morrow all in a heap. All around the roses there is today, machinery leaning upon the stem, an aeroplane is upon one leaf where a worm lies curled. Happy it seems and enormous, it seems to hold up the sky for it has no size at all. We eat beside it—beside the three roses that she loves. And an oak tree grows out of my shoulders. Its roots are my arms and legs. The air is a field. Yellow and red grass are writing their signatures everywhere. (*I*, 240–41)[12]

This passage appears verbatim in the memoir, though arranged much dif-ferently on the page. The paragraph has been divided into two separate sec-tions, the latter of which (beginning "But now . . .") is italicized. These typo-graphical changes effectively signal a shift in speakers to the reader, while pre-serving the rich conceptual interplay between the two voices. Williams' inter-polation, which functions as both a counterpoint and a corollary to Elena's statement, illustrates the meditative quality typical of this third group. His de-scription of the three roses rhymes with her vivid reminiscence of the teabox in its exacting attention to physical detail and appreciation for things of this world. Moreover, by focusing on a common object which his mother holds as dear as her memory of the box, the poet establishes a thread of thematic con-tinuity between their remarks, and thereby links the remote past with the pres-ent moment of his composition.

There are, however, a number of important differences between the two descriptions as well. Elena is so totally absorbed in the act of remembering that the context and significance of the teabox are eclipsed by the minute particulars of its external appearance. The object undoubtedly has a powerful resonance for her, perhaps as a symbol of the material prosperity her family enjoyed in her early youth, yet its import is never discussed in the text. Rather, the anecdote stands, isolate, mysterious, incomplete—a luminous but enigmatic detail from Elena's past.

Williams, in contrast to his mother, has an intellectual distance from his subject that allows him to perceive it in a larger, more abstract framework. He views the three roses not merely as beautiful forms, but as a metaphor for the evanescence of the moment. He thus accentuates their fragile materiality, insisting, "They are not a picture. Holbein never saw pink thorns in such a light. Nor did Masaccio." This allusion underscores the disparity between the immutability of roses depicted in art and their literal counterparts, whose petals may not "open at all . . . but drop, loosing at one edge and falling tomorrow all in a heap." Poised tenuously on the verge of imminent fruition and death, the roses become the axis of the poet's perceptual construct: "All around the roses is today, machinery leaning upon the stem, an aeroplane is on one leaf where a worm lies curled." The fanciful juxtaposition of opposites in this statement—the large and small, the ponderous and infinitesimally light, the technological and organic—illustrates the paradoxical nature of the roses and the moment of perception itself. Despite their delicate ephemerality, both comprise the center of a subjective reality, and are thus capable of holding up the entire sky. Williams' description of how the physical world impinges on the roses echoes his cubist poem "The Rose" in *Spring and All,* where the flower is depicted projecting outward into space, its petals "cementing the grooved / columns of air" (*I,* 109). Also, in a less obvious manner, his treatment of the three roses parallels the famous red wheelbarrow poem in that both images crystallize the power of the present moment; "so much depends" on the forgotten, rain-glazed implement in exactly the same way the nameless machinery and airplane "lean upon" the roses.

As the passage continues, it moves into an increasingly private sphere, ending with the poet's imaginative metamorphosis into an oak tree: "Its roots are my arms and legs. The air is a field. Yellow and red grass are writing their signatures everywhere." All semblance of the objective physical world with which the paragraph began ("But now, here are the roses, three opening") has disappeared, replaced by an inner visionary reality where bizarrely colored grasses inscribe their "signatures" as if in some blank cosmic text. The precise meaning of this transformation is unclear, open to conjecture; since the oak is a traditional symbol of permanence, longevity, and strength, it can possibly be interpreted as an allegory of Williams' power to capture and preserve the ephemeral roses (and Raquel Helene Rose) in words. But the primary significance of the passage is the gradual shift in focus from mother to son, achieved through a series of subjective associations and leaps in logic.

A more extreme, hermetic example of this same associative technique occurs in an interpolation a few pages later in the memoir. Elena, reminiscing about the scarcity of water one winter shortly after arriving in the United States, says:

> —there are no rivers. I remember one winter all the water was frozen. The only place we could get water was at Demarest's, he had a cistern in the yard.
>
> I wonder how they do now. They had nothing, but well water. They had big cisterns. Where else could they get it? (*YMW,* 105)

And Williams' "response" is this:

> I like Chopin because he was honest and good and he was a genius and he could play the profound, and tremendous states of being cannot exist here—that is the ultimate felicities of understanding, we rise to our occasions like starved trout to a flake of tobacco leaf, therefore, our staccato verse and fragmentary prose. To stay on a point is huge work not possible when one is inevitably opposed by many, the one must go down the scale to succeed or be content to touch understanding only by flashes. Mammie look at the little flowers they are growing. The greater swallows the rest: If my legs were tougher I'd play baseball tomorrow which proves that muscles are of no importance, but that weakness is excessively to the point. He did not know it, but he was born to be smothered in ammonia. I'll bend the God damned parallels until they meet O elm before their bedroom windows blossoming. (*YMW,* 105–6)

If any connection exists between Elena's comment and the poet's, it is too remote and obscure for the reader to grasp. The subject of his interpolation is the artist's plight in America, specifically the way in which the country thwarts creative genius by refusing to recognize it. "Tremendous states of being cannot exist here," he asserts, because the cultural milieu is inimical to nurturing artists who, like Chopin, are "honest and good . . . and [can] play the profound." Instead, the American artist must continually compromise his or her principles in order to survive under these improverished circumstances: "that is the ultimate felicities of understanding, we rise to our occasions like starved trout to a flake of tobacco leaf, therefore, our staccato verse and fragmented prose." Williams is clearly writing from his own experience here, although his use of the plural pronoun "we" and allusion to "fragmentary prose" (à la the style of his mother's anecdotes) suggests he may be thinking of Elena as well. In "From My Notes about My Mother," he recounts a poignant story about her hopes of pursuing an artistic career in the United States:

> When she left Paris it was to join her brother and his family in Puerto Plata, Santo Domingo. There her fate awaited her among the low tin roofed and thatched houses in the person of her future husband, a young Englishman who left the island to go to the United States.

So she came to America and was married. Before the ceremony, she lived for a time with a professor's family in Jersey City. I once had a card of hers, though I cannot find it now, on which was printed: *Instruction in Spanish, French, Piano, Singing and Painting.* I couldn't help smiling. Poor mother. I suppose by sheer weight of potentialities she hoped to make a go of it—in Jersey City, 1881. I wonder if she ever had a pupil.[13]

Mother and son thus typify the two options which Williams claims are available to American artists: she survives by forsaking her ambition and becoming a housewife (i.e., going "down the scale to succeed") whereas he must combine the rigorous careers of doctor and poet and "be content to touch understanding only by flashes." At this point in the passage, however, Williams abruptly changes the focus of his discussion, enjoining Elena to "look at the little flowers they are growing." The direct address is significant in that it provides further evidence of the subliminal connection the poet makes between his mother and art, and also mitigates the harshness of his criticism. Despite the spiritual aridity of the United States, its landscape is not entirely bereft of beauty; the soil is at least capable of sustaining "little flowers," and that in itself is cause for hope.

The paragraph's conclusion follows the same general pattern as the earlier interpolation, moving closer to the realm of the unconscious and becoming increasingly involuted and unintelligible. But while the former passage describes a unified "vision," this one ends with three rather cryptic nonsequiturs: "The greater swallows the rest: If my legs were tougher I'd play baseball tomorrow which proves that muscles are of no importance, but that weakness is excessively to the point. He did not know it, but he was born to be smothered in ammonia. I'll bend the God damned parallels until they meet O elm before their bedroom windows blossoming" (*YMW*, 106).

Williams does not supply sufficient background information for the reader to decipher the exact meaning of these statements. (Who for example, was "born to be smothered in ammonia"? More exasperatingly, "God damned parallels" between what or whom?) His assertions are deliberately elusive, evoking a tantalizing constellation of possible interpretations, but no single or definitive meaning. An implicit parodic element can be detected here as well, since the content of the poet's sentences belies their coherent, seemingly rational structure. This is nonsense masquerading as logic, or more accurately, the manifestation of an intensely private, and therefore inaccessible, logic.

Williams seems to be engaging in something akin to automatic writing in these two interpolations, invoking a state of mind wherein the rigidities of consciousness are loosened and free association of ideas takes place. Interestingly, certain images (flowers, trees, leaves) and themes (the nature of art, the actual versus the ideal, the polarities of weakness and strength) recur in both passages, indicating that the questions raised therein are the focus of an ongoing meditation. Also, the latter interpolation is the only place in the memoir where

Williams alludes to his own declining health ("If my legs were tougher I'd play baseball tomorrow"), yet this admission of infirmity is counterbalanced and ultimately subverted by his forceful expression of determination, imaginative vigor, and will in the concluding sentence. Although the poet's mind, like Elena's, is trapped within a decaying body, this does not prevent him from exercising his creative faculty. As with his metamorphosis into an oak tree, the declaration "I'll bend the God damn parallels until they meet O elm before their bedroom windows blossoming" bespeaks a magical or godlike power that derives from the imagination itself. Through the agency of his mind and pen, Williams can effect radical transformations, creating and destroying whole universes; in this manner, he is able to slyly bend the parallels between himself and Elena in the memoir, making them meet, blossom, and finally merge.

The highly esoteric nature of this third group of interpolations links the memoir with Williams' early improvisational work, *Kora in Hell*. In fact, the strong stylistic resemblances between the two texts may have been what prompted David McDowell's decision to use italics in *Yes, Mrs. Williams* since *Kora* itself is comprised of brief paragraphs followed by an italicized commentary. In *I Wanted to Write a Poem,* Williams explains that the source of this anomalous structure was

> a book [Ezra] Pound had left in the house, *Varie Poesie* dell' Abate Pietro Metastasio, Venice, 1795. I took the method used by the Abbot of drawing a line to separate my material. First came the Improvisations, those more or less incomprehensible statements, then the dividing line and, in italics, my interpretations of the Improvisations. . . . The copy above the line represents my day-to-day notations, off the cuff, thoughts put down like a diary in a year of my life. The remarks below the line are a clarification of the notation. (*IW,* 27)

This unusual combination of "incomprehensible statements" and interpretive "clarification" exemplifies, as Rod Townley convincingly argues, the two primary stylistic tendencies in Williams' writing:

> The non-italicized paragraphs are the impassioned expostulations of "Carlos," the inspired Spanish peasant. Their very bluntness is a kind of obscurity, deriving, one suspects, from the fools in Shakespeare's plays, from *El Romancero* and other folk literature, and especially from Williams' mother, "a creature of great imagination," who always sees "the thing itself without forethought or afterthought but with great intensity of perception" [*I*, 8]. But Williams was also the son of a cultured Englishman, and in the italicized paragraphs all his suppressed gentility surfaces in a pure form. . . .[14]

Although Townley does not specifically mention this, Williams actually quotes Elena several times in the improvisations; thus, the voice he identifies as that of "Carlos" literally belongs, in certain instances, to the poet's mother. Her comments are easily identifiable, since they usually begin with some Spanish phrase or proverb, like "Ay dio!" (*I,* 33) and "Baaaa! Ba-ha-ha-ha-ha-ha-ha-ha! Bebe esa purga. It is the goats of Santo Domingo talking. Bebe esa purga!" (*I,*

75). There is, however, one sequence which contains no Spanish that is especially relevant to *Yes, Mrs. Williams* because it reveals that *Kora* is an essential precedent for the later text:

> This that I have struggled against is the very thing I should have chosen—but all's right now. They said I could not put the flower back into the stem nor win roses upon dead briars and I like a fool believed them. But all's right now. Weave away, dead fingers, the darkies are dancing in Mayagüez—all but the one with the sore heel and sugar cane will soon be high enough to romp through. Haia! leading over ditches, with your skirts flying and the devil in the wind back of you—no one else. Weave away and the bitter tongue of an old woman is eating, eating, eating venomous words with thirty years' mould on them and all shall be eaten back to honeymoon's end. Weave and pangs of agony and pangs of loneliness are beaten backward into the love kiss, weave and kiss recedes into kiss and kisses into looks and looks into the heart's dark—and over again and over again and time's pushed ahead in spite of all that. The petals that fell bearing me under are lifted one by one. That which kissed my flesh for priest's lace so that I could not touch it—weave and you have lifted it and I am glimpsing light chinks among the notes! Backward, and my hair is crisp with purple sap and the last crust's broken.

> *A woman on the verge of growing old kindles in the mind of her son a certain curiosity which spinning upon itself catches the woman herself in its wheel, stripping from her the accumulation of many harsh years and shows her at last full of an old time suppleness hardly to have been guessed by the stiffened exterior which had held her fast till that time. (I, 62–63)*

This passage concerns a process of imaginative restoration and rejuvenation—putting "the flower back into the stem" and "win[ning] roses upon dead briars." Williams attempts to strip away from Elena's character the deadening "accumulation of many harsh years" and so reveal her "old time suppleness" and true self. The metaphors he uses to describe this undertaking—weaving, spinning, unraveling—suggest the traditional activities of the three Fates, with the crucial difference that the poet is "weaving *away*," moving backward in time through the trajectory of his mother's misfortunes, to get back to the "heart's dark," the secret core of her identity. According to the italicized interpretation, Williams' endeavor is motivated by a "certain curiosity" about Elena's past, yet another, much different reason emerges from the improvisation itself.

It returning to Elena's "heart's dark," a dramatic change occurs in Williams. He is suddenly liberated from a delicate, but stiflingly oppressive burden: "The petals which fell bearing me under are lifted one by one." This image of a dying flower dropping its petals signifies, on one level, Elena's loss of beauty, youth, and vitality, yet it also can be read as a metaphor for the religious and ethical values she passed on to her children. What is most striking about Williams' statement, however, is its insinuation that his destiny is inextricably enmeshed with his mother's. Although he does not identify the exact nature of the "petals" which have buried him, the remainder of the passage suggests he is referring to Elena's rigid moral standards. The phrase, "That which kissed my flesh for priest's lace so that I could not touch it," evokes the spiritual legacy of her strict Roman Catholic upbringing in its insistence on the sanctity and chasteness of the body and absolute denial of sensuality. As Williams told his friend John Thirlwall in 1953, "My poor mother always taught me the highest ideals: to be an artist—to be pure—to be sexless—and that almost tore me apart."[15] It is only by "weaving" backward and imaginatively recreating the vagaries of Elena's own sexual experience ("kiss recedes into kiss and kisses into looks . . .") that the poet can escape the bonds of her repressive influence and acknowledge his own physicality. The improvisation ends with a strange mythological image reminiscent of those in the two interpolations discussed above. Williams is here metamorphosed into a Dionysian figure whose "hair is crisp with purple sap," in other words, a satyr. He has thus broken through the "last crust" of his own "stiffened exterior" by rejecting the strictures of his mother's puritanical morality.

Despite the fascinating glimpse this passage provides into the mother/son relationship, it is at once infuriating and problematic since it does not adequately explain what Williams discovers in the secret recesses of Elena's heart that could engender such a profound change in his character. The reader is instead presented with a baffling tale of conflated identity wherein the poet's investigation of his mother's past somehow becomes a vehicle for introspective analysis. His opening remarks in the prologue to *Kora in Hell* offer some potential, albeit vague, clues as to what this mysterious discovery might be; however, it is not until the appearance of *Yes, Mrs. Williams* nearly four decades later that the matter is fully examined and resolved. *Kora* and the memoir, which are respectively his first and last published pieces of prose, thus form distant, interlocking halves of the same puzzle—namely, what does Elena ultimately signify for Williams?

The answer to this question lies in the intimate connection Williams perceived between his mother and his writing. The prologue to *Kora*, his first formal statement on poetics, begins, not at all coincidentally, with a long story about her rather than himself:

> The sole precedent I can find for the broken style of my prologue is *Longinus on the Sublime* and that one farfetched.
>
> When my mother was in Rome on that rare journey forever to be remembered, she lived in a small pension near the Pincio Gardens. The place had been chosen by my brother as one notably easy of access, being in a quarter free from confusion of traffic, on a street close to the park, and furthermore the tram to the American Academy passed at the corner. Yet never did my mother go out but she was in fear of being lost. By turning to the left when she should have turned right, actually she did once manage to go so far astray that it was nearly an hour before she extricated herself from the strangeness of every new vista and found a landmark.

There has always been a disreputable man of picturesque personality associated with this lady. Their relations have been marked by the most rollicking spirit of comradeship. Now it has been William, former sailor in Admiral Dewey's fleet at Manila, then Tom O'Rourck who has come to her to do odd jobs and to be cared for more or less when drunk or ill, their Penelope. William would fall from the grape arbor much to my mother's discomfiture or he would stagger to the back door nearly unconscious from bad whiskey. There she would serve him with very hot and very strong coffee, then put him to scrubbing the kitchen floor, into his suddy-pail pouring half a bottle of ammonia which would make the man gasp and water at the eyes as he worked and became sober.

She has always been incapable of learning from benefit or disaster. If a man cheats her she will remember that man with a violence that I have seldom seen equaled, but so far as that could have an influence on her judgement of the next man or woman, she might be living in Eden. And indeed she is, an impoverished, ravished Eden but one indestructible as the imagination itself. Whatever is before her is sufficient to itself and so to be valued. (*I*, 6–7)

On the basis of two rather mundane traits, her tendency to get lost and inability to learn from previous experience, Williams establishes Elena as his muse, an embodiment of the intensity of poetic perception and the imagination itself. He thus implicitly places himself in the company of the various "disreputable" men who perennially surround his mother and are supported and nurtured by her. Yet these dual facets of Elena's character are not the genuine reasons she occupies this lofty position in the poet's mind; rather, they are convenient metaphors for a more intangible quality he observes in her language:

My mother is given over to frequent periods of great depression being as I believe by nature the most light-hearted thing in the world. But there comes a grotesque turn to her talk, a macabre anecdote concerning some dream, a passionate statement about death, which elevates her mood without marring it, sometimes in a most startling way.

Looking out at our parlor window one day I said to her: "We see all the shows from here, don't we, all the weddings and funerals?" (They had been preparing a funeral across the street, the undertaker was just putting on his overcoat.) She replied: "Funny profession that, burying the dead people. I should think they wouldn't have any delusions of life left." W.— Oh yes, it's merely a profession. M.—Hm. And how they study it! They say sometimes the people look terrible and they come and make them look fine. They push things into their mouths! (Realistic gesture) W.—Mama! M.—Yes, when they haven't any teeth.

By some such dark turn at the end she raises her story out of the commonplace: "Look at that chair, look at it!" (The plasterers had just left.) "If Mrs. J. or Mrs. D. saw that they would have a fit." W.—Call them in, maybe it will kill them. M.—But they're not near as bad as that woman, you know, her husband was in the chorus—has a little daughter Helen. Mrs. B., yes. She once wanted to take rooms here. I didn't want her. They told me: "Mrs. Williams, I heard you're going to have Mrs. B. *She* is particular." She said so herself. Oh no! Once she burnt all her face painting under the sink.

Thus seeing the thing itself without forethought or afterthought but with great intensity of perception, my mother loses her bearings or associates with some disreputable person or translates a dark mood. She is a creature of great imagination. I might say this is her sole remaining quality. She is a despoiled, molted castaway but by this power she still breaks life between her fingers. (*I*, 7–8)

The reference to Longinus which opens the prologue is not nearly as "far-fetched" or inconsequential as Williams leads the reader to believe; on the contrary, it has a crucial, if somewhat oblique, bearing on the nature of his comments about Elena. Curiously, the one overt parallel the poet draws between his "broken style" and that of Longinus' treatise is essentially inaccurate, since the disjunctiveness of the ancient text stems from lacunae in the manuscript rather than the author's conscious intent. Williams' prologue does, however, have several other features in common with Longinus's work. It is, first of all, a polemical document, written in response to the poetic practices of expatriates Ezra Pound and T. S. Eliot, whose "Love Song of J. Alfred Prufrock" had recently appeared in *Poetry,* just as Longinus' book is a refutation of a contemporary monograph by Caecilius, *On Sublimity,* which he felt was "inadequate to its high subject and failed to touch the essential points."[16] Both writers thus articulate and define their aesthetic positions in opposition to a particular adversary, although the tone of Williams' essay is much more contentious than that of his classical counterpart. In addition, both texts focus on language and are, in varying degrees, prescriptive, offering advice and rhetorical examples on how to achieve (or avoid) certain literary effects.

But the most important link between the prologue and Longinus's work is Williams' tacit—and perhaps even unconscious—association of Elena with the notion of the sublime. According to his accounts in both the *Autobiography* and *I Wanted to Write a Poem,* Williams read Longinus early in his career at the behest of Ezra Pound, but confessed that it "meant little" (*IW,* 6) to him. He does not indicate what, if any, his objections to the text were, yet it can be safely assumed that Longinus's strict guidelines as to what can and cannot be considered sublime seemed too remote to be of use in his own work. The strongest influences on the young poet's developments were not books, but rather individuals—among the most important of them, his mother. As James E. B. Breslin notes in his study *William Carlos Williams: An American Artist:* "Into a largely sterile environment, Mrs. Williams introduced an early and important impetus toward artistic activity. Because of her Williams was at first interested in painting. But the direction of her influence was not immediately creative, since it inspired a sense of beauty that was dreamily nostalgic; it was she who led him to Keats."[17]

Elena's aesthetic sensibility was firmly rooted in nineteenth-century romanticism: she believed that art should be the lofty, ethereal expression of all that was noble in man's soul. Indeed, in describing her views on art to others, she made frequent use of the term "sublime." Writing to Marianne Moore's mother in 1937, for instance, to commiserate about the strange poems their children were producing, Elena says: "The little I have read of modern poetry I don't like it. I always look for the spiritual and the symbols, the sublime. When I see the bride all in white I don't think of the flowers nor the quality of them but of the symbol of purity. I say the same for poetry."[18]

The degree to which Williams assimilated these beliefs as a young man, as well as the grounds for his eventual rejection of them, are illustrated by an essay written between 1910 and 1915 with the Keatsian title of "Beauty and Truth." This piece, which the poet said reflected "a struggle . . . to be at peace in his own mind" (*EK,* 153), is a fanciful parable about the rigors of the artistic process; in it, he makes numerous references to his "sublime search" for absolute beauty, a search he ultimately realized was futile. Williams pokes fun at his idealistic desire to collect "all the scattered parts of beauty . . . into one perfect whole" by ironically envisioning his achievement as a pathetic taxidermic prize—something "for men to stare at as if it were a stuffed bird" (*EK,* 163). The crucial breakthrough in the poet's development comes in "at last forgetting all about my sublime search and in fact of beauty altogether. Thus the search being forgotten I am at last truly started in the trail of beauty" (*EK,* 162). This recognition marks the genesis of Williams' mature aesthetic stance. Rather than vainly pursuing a distant, unattainable beauty, he chooses to concentrate on the details of the actual world around him and unlock the beauty hidden therein. Perhaps the most concise articulation of his relation to the sublime is the following statement made by Dev Evans in *A Voyage to Pagany:* "I do not run from fineness, but small doses of it suffice. I soon tire. I feel a real need for the vulgar. I have been accused before of running away. Well, I want to plant it, IT; to see if it grows. Fineness, too much of it, narcotizes me. It drives me wild. I do not want that" (*VP,* 213).

This radical change in Williams' aesthetic outlook utterly mystified Elena, whose commitment to the "sublime search" remained constant throughout her lifetime. Over the years, he made numerous attempts to explain his position to her, in hopes of receiving the benediction of her approval. The 1923 poem "The Drunkard," prefaced in *The Collected Earlier Poems* by a letter to Elena, typifies the nature of his undertaking:

Dearest Mother: Here is a poem to set beside some of my "incomprehensible" latter work. I think you will like this one. It seems the sort of thing that I am going to do. Art is a curious command. We must do what we are bidden to do and can go so far as the light permits. I am always earnest as you, if anyone, must know. But no doubt I puzzle you—as I do myself. Plenty of love from your son. W.

You drunken
tottering
bum

by Christ
in spite of all
your filth

and sordidness
I envy
you

> It is the very face
> of love
> itself
>
> abandoned
> in that powerless
> committal
>
> to despair
>
> (*CEP,* 437)

The tentative tone of the letter ("It seems the sort of thing that I am going to do") is dramatically counterpointed by the direct, explosive energy of the poem itself. Although Williams' praise of a "drunken, tottering bum" was almost certainly guaranteed to shock his proprietous mother, the statement, "I think you will like this one," is not intended facetiously. In the last three stanzas of the lyric, the depravity of the bum's plight becomes a metaphor for the abandonment and destruction of "love itself" through despair, a phenomenon Elena could identify with since it paralleled the experiences of bitter disappointment and necessary psychological readjustment in her own life. If the poem's diction was objectionable, the emotional signification of its content was nonetheless something she could understand and accept.

Nor was this the only occasion on which Williams submitted his writing to his mother for comment and approval. Until Elena's cataracts made it impossible for her to read, the poet continued to share his work with her and invite her critical response. As the following letter, written shortly after the publication of *A Voyage to Pagany* in 1928, reveals, that response was often unfavorable:

> Son:
>
> I wanted to read your book again to find out my real feeling or opinion. ¾ part of the book is fine, but the beginning, the first quarter, is all sex, sensual, no *love* of the sublime—in human nature—you would have more success with another story than the one chosen.
>
> I am sure if you had daughters at the imprecionable [*sic*] age you would not give them books of that sort to read—
>
> Too much damns and hells, I am sure you were not brought up in that coarse language. I hate it; beside[s], the nature of a poet is more refine[d]—or it should be.
>
> Before I die I would like you to write a book following your noble character and intellect, a book to pick up once in a while as a solace and enjoy the fine elevating spirit of the author.[19]

In evaluating this somewhat comical letter, it is necessary to remember that it is not addressed to a young, fledgling writer, but to a man approaching fifty who had already published nine books. Elena's critical mode is clearly more parental than professional; indeed, her remarks constitute the verbal equivalent of a smart slap on the hand of a disobedient child. She chides Williams for betraying the moral principles of his upbringing and using coarse language, but the major thrust of her critique is that, in writing such an "immoral" book, he has deviated from the true, refined nature of a poet. Williams' response to this letter unfortunately has not been preserved; yet, judging from the wealth of available information about their relationship in general, it is unlikely that he dismissed or blatantly ignored her comments. In fact, another letter Elena wrote to Williams concerning an unidentified collection of his poems suggests that he was genuinely wounded by her expressions of critical disapproval. The tone of this missive is gentler and more conciliatory than the one quoted above, as if she were attempting to assuage some residual tension or antagonism between them:

Dear Son,

You say that I don't like the things you write, and it is a great mistake; however, I want to speak with sincerity if I can make myself understood.

Your book of poems is like a garden of flowers to pick and choose and the mind to enjoy [*sic*], it is in the earthly plain [*sic*]. I am more inclined on the other feeling, and soar to the lofty strain of the heart and soul. A poet to me is transfigured to the ideal when the soul is touched and bring [*sic*] to us the beautiful emotion to our sensitive inner soul that craves for a brother feeling [*sic*]. . . .

Now don't misunderstand me, for I do enjoy what you write.[20]

The distinction Elena makes in this letter between Williams' attraction to "the earthly plain" and her own rarified preference for the "lofty strain of the heart and soul" is indirectly challenged by his remarks about her in the prologue to *Kora in Hell*. As Linda Wagner notes in *The Prose of William Carlos Williams,* the poet admired his mother "not for what she knew but for what she was: clairvoyant, rash, foreign, and always womanly."[21] This observation can be extended a bit further: Williams admired Elena not for the ideals and beliefs she espoused, but rather for the qualities she unconsciously embodied, such as toughness, adaptability, and earthiness, which were generally antithetical to those beliefs. His description of her discourse in the prologue offers a good example of this rift between knowing and being: "There comes a grotesque turn to her talk, a macabre anecdote concerning some dream, a passionate statement about death, which elevates her mood without marring it, sometimes in a most startling way. . . . By some such dark turn she raises her story out of the commonplace . . ." (*I,* 7–8).

The effects of Elena's speech—a startling "elevation" of mood and raising of narrative "out of the commonplace"—are characteristics traditionally associated with the sublime.[22] Yet the way in which she achieves these effects, via "grotesque," "macabre," and "passionate" turns of thought, are obviously not. Moreover, the particular examples Williams cites of her conversation seem quite ordinary (e.g., "Look at that chair, look at it!"), though they do possess an undeniable candor, freshness, and emotional intensity. Of the five sources of sublimity described by Longinus (the power to conceive great thoughts, strong and inspired emotion, figures of both thought and speech, noble diction, dignified and elevated word arrangement),[23] only the second—strong and inspired emotion—is directly applicable here. Towards the end of Longinus's treatise, however, there is a brief discussion of the literary "use of everyday words" which expands the range of "noble diction" to include certain kinds of colloquial expressions and thus puts the poet's comments in a different perspective:

> An idiomatic phrase is sometimes much more vivid than an ornament of speech, for it is immediately recognized from everyday experience, and the familiar is inevitably easier to credit. [The phrase] "To stomach facts" is thus used vividly of a man who endures unpleasantness and squalor patiently, and indeed with pleasure, for the sake of gain. There are similar things in Herodotus: "Cleomenes in his madness cut his own flesh into little pieces with a knife till he had sliced himself to death," "Pythes continued fighting on the ship until he was cut into joints." These phrases come within an inch of being vulgar but they are so expressive that they avoid vulgarity.[24]

Similarly, Elena's comment about undertakers "pushing things" into the mouths of corpses to enhance their appearance comes "within an inch of being vulgar," but successfully avoids that dubious distinction through its strange, expressive power. In this regard, she represents two radically divergent aspects of sublimity to her son: the sterile, repressive idealism of her conscious values on the one hand, and the vibrant, fecund energy of her language on the other. Furthermore, the tension generated by these dissonant impulses is the spark which ignites the poet's own creativity. As Williams explained in a 1935 letter to Marianne Moore:

> There is a good deal of rebellion still in what I write, rebellion against stereotyped poetic process—the too meticulous choice among other things. In too much refinement there lurks a sterility that wishes to pass too often for purity when it is anything but that. Coarseness for its own sake is inexcusable, but a Rabelaisian sanity requires that the rare and the fine be exhibited as coming like everything else from the dirt. There is no incompatibility between them.
>
> My dear Mother is perhaps my example. Cruel to blame anything on her and through her to blame a certain Latin influence. She exasperates me too but there are times when I see her eye light with a curious fire and I know what is coming. It comes from the manure heap sometimes. It clears the atmosphere. In any case I am made up of heavens and hells which constitute a truer me than my face-to-face appearance could possible suggest. (*SL*, 155–56)

Yes, Mrs. Williams records the working out and eventual reconciliation of the poet's "hells and heavens" by demonstrating that coarseness and "the rare and the fine" spring from a single source. The project of the memoir is thus an extension of the improvisation from *Kora* discussed above to strip away the refined facade Elena had constructed in dealing with the world and expose the

"Rabelaisian sanity" lying beneath it. Her mythos of the "defeated romantic," as he claims in the introduction, "is not by any means a true picture. Despondency, discouragement, despair were violent periodic factors in her life. Under it lies the true life, undefeated if embittered, hard as nails, little loving, easily mistaken for animal selfishness. Unexcavated from her own consciousness, the good that is in her—crying for release, release from herself, a most difficult animal" (*YMW,* 33–34).

Like an archaeologist, Williams "excavates" the various layers of his mother's personality in the text, documenting its diverse features and phases through the meticulous collection of verbal artifacts. Through the kaleidoscopic juxtaposition of this fragmentary evidence, he presents glimpses of the formal, decorous, and modest Elena ("We never went bathing in the sea. What! take off our clothes where men could see us!" [*YMW,* 101]) as well as the woman who was enamoured of the gracious style and accoutrements of aristocratic society: "For this dinner, [Mme. Keratry] bought me the materials for a dress and had it made too, beautifully. It was pongee silk with little ruffles of lace all over. Very finely made. It was beautiful the way they lived" (*YMW,* 88).

Elena's lofty aesthetic sensibility is also illustrated in the memoir, perhaps most compellingly, by her sole literary endeavor—a poem—which Williams translates from the original Spanish:

From My Window

Look, look how they fall
They are the dried leaves
   of the inexorable Autumn
No need to be sorrowful
   they will relive
In the radiant Springtime
Alas, for lost illusions
They are leaves falling from
   the tree of the heart
   these will not relive
But they are dead in the
Winter of human life.

(*YMW,* 1, 2, 3)

The title of this piece obliquely alludes to Elena's debilitated physical condition during the later years of her life when she was crippled and confined to bed. Her contact with nature, and the outside world in general, was therefore restricted to the view from her upstairs bedroom window at 9 Ridge Road. The poem itself is structured on a simple, albeit heavy-handed, analogy between autumnal leaves and the lost illusions which fall from "the tree of the [human] heart." Though the literal tree will be rejuvenated in the spring, the innocent ideals of one's youth bloom only once, then remain forever dead. The lyric's exaggerated, elegiac tone reaffirms the romantic image that Elena perpetuated about her past, that of the artist thwarted and made helpless by circumstance. Moreover, the piece exemplifies the sort of poetry she wished her son would write—symbolic, edifying, noble.

Elena's air of suffering and despondency, along with her prim fastidiousness, is, however, dramatically counterpointed by the large number of rather off-color anecdotes she relates in the text. These remarks concern a variety of bodily functions and all manner of excreting—spitting, belching, vomiting, farting, and defecating.[25] They range from quick aphorisms, such as "He's little, but he shits big!" (*YMW*, 97) and "Yes, she married a man called le Merdet!" (*YMW*, 120) to more involved narratives like

> There there was a man, what was his name? They were afraid to invite him because he shocked the people. He would say anything that came into his mind. He liked it. He would come with all his [war] decorations on his chest. "Je viens avec toute ma ferblanterie" (I have so many holes all through me), he would say, "sans counter le trou de mon cul" (without counting my asshole). Then everyone would hide his face or look away. (*YMW*, 114)

and

> I'll tell you a story, it is true—not very clean but—one time there were a lot of men at supper I suppose and they were pulling corks from bottles of beer—or wine, I don't know. Poor Toledo was pulling hard at a cork when a little wind escaped him. Blup! Don Sebastian Sedo quickly turned to him and offered him a cork on the end of a corkscrew. That is a true story. (*YMW*, 98)

By modern standards, these anecdotes seem quaintly crude at worst, more naughty than genuinely obscene. The two most offensive stories Elena tells in the memoir illustrate her penchant for the gross and morbid which Williams had noted decades earlier in the prologue to *Kora in Hell:* "I knew a black man, he was a shoemaker and he burst his eye with a needle, pulling it. You can never tell about such things" (*YMW*, 121) and "I remember one of the girls in Puerto Rico she was already married, one day she was eating guava paste and that cheese, what do you call it? Cottage cheese, when druup! She vomited pure blood, they were all laughing and eating around in a little circle when she vomited pure blood" (*YMW*, 111).

The graphic images Elena creates of an eye bursting like a pricked balloon and a woman unexpectedly vomiting a revolting combination of blood, cottage cheese, and guave paste have a stark, poetic quality that Williams marveled at. Moreover, he recognized that the anecdotes' shocking content was intensified by the simplicity and dispassionate directness of his mother's reporting; their forceful effect was produced by a unique marriage of subject and style. For these reasons, Williams considered his mother's stories a rich literary resource, a treasury of models to be analyzed and emulated. Indeed, he admits in the poem "Eve" to deliberately cultivating this uncouth aspect of her personality in order to elicit these kinds of comments:

I'll give you brandy
or wine
whenever I think you need it
(need it)
because it whips up
your mind and your senses
and brings color to your face
—to enkindle that life
too coarse for the usual,
that sly obscenity
that fertile darkness
in which passion mates—
reflecting the lightnings of creation—

(*CEP*, 377–78)

The poet's apparent solicitude in the opening lines of this passage ("I'll give you brandy / or wine") is undermined by the subsequent qualifier, "whenever I think you need it." By means of this subtle assertion, Williams becomes the dominant, controlling figure in the scenario; he is the one to determine when, and if, Elena "needs" a drink. Several questions arise regarding this arrangement. For whose benefit is the alcohol being administered— mother's or son's? And exactly what "need" is being met? According to the remainder of the passage, alcohol is a vivifying tonic that restores color to Elena's wizened face and "whips up" her mind and senses. In short, the beverage rejuvenates her, crumbling her carefully constructed wall of puritanical inhibitions and enkindling the hidden core of passion and "sly obscenity" that drives her being.

The association Williams makes at the end of the passage between coarseness and the "lightnings" of artistic creation is crucial to understanding the reasons for his seemingly manipulative treatment of his mother. He believed that in order to be an artist it was necessary to not only acknowledge and accept one's unconscious, libidinal impulses, but to actively harness them. By exposing and fostering the earthy underside of Elena's character, the poet discovered the wellspring of her creative energy, as well as the source and prototype of his own. Through her example, he learned that the beautiful and sublime were not antithetical to the sordid and ugly, but complementary components of a single whole, like the virgin and whore in book 5 of *Paterson*. The pragmatic counsel she offers him in the memoir, "When you have no heart for anything, make it from your bowels" (*YMW*, 90), was well heeled throughout his life and work, as the following poem, "Fragment," reveals:

My God, Bill, what have you done?

What do you think I've done? I've
opened up the world.

Where did you get them? Marvellous
beautiful!

Where does all snot come from? Under
the nose.

Yea-uh?

—the gutter, where everything comes
from, the manure heap.

(CEP, 453)

Elena's critical significance for Williams thus lay in "open[ing] up the world" to him, not by means of religious and ethical instruction, but rather by the unconscious example of her language, raucous humor, and habits of mind. The legacy he uncovers in her "heart's dark" involves the reconciliation and synthesis of moral polarities, the knowledge that sublimity and snot are products of the same "gutter, where everything comes / from, the manure heap." In this way, Elena incarnates the essence of his own aesthetic philosophy.

Yes, Mrs. Williams represents both the evidence and outcome of this realization, for in divulging the dualistic core of his mother's character, the poet himself simultaneously stands revealed. By obscuring the boundaries of their individual identities and encoding himself within the figure of Elena, Williams demonstrates the centrality of her role in his emotional and artistic life, as well as the degree to which she served as his anima. The memoir is therefore a truly pivotal work—a tribute, at once personal and interpersonal, to the muse, a testament of spiritual oneness, and an oblique exploration, as Williams himself put it, of "how I got that way: honestly out of my mother."[26]

5

The Possession of America

What is the place of my birth? The place of my birth is the place
where the word begins.

A Voyage to Pagany

When Williams published his first novel, *A Voyage to Pagany,* in 1928, he af-
fectionately dedicated it "To the first of us all my old friend Ezra Pound."
Given the novel's European setting and examination of the deep psychic tensions which exist between the old and new worlds, one may assume that the
"first" alluded to in the dedication is Pound's expatriation from the United
States in 1908. On a less literal level, however, Williams was also acknowledging Pound's preeminence as an instigator and indefatigable advocate of the new
in American poetry. Although Williams did not choose to follow the same path
his friend had blazed, he recognized that he had undeniably benefited from
Pound's influence and example, and used the occasion of the novel's appearance to pay public tribute to him.

Pound returned the compliment in similarly public fashion, penning a review of *Pagany* for *The Dial* called "Doctor Williams' Position." This essay,
perhaps the shrewdest, most incisive critique of Williams ever produced by one
of his contemporaries, outlines a nexus of three issues—origin, identity, and
culture—which comprise the central preoccupations of both his life and art.
Through a close reading of this text, it is possible to identify the diverse factors
involved in Williams' obsessive but uneasy relationship to his physical and intellectual milieu—America in all its myriad and mythic implications. Interestingly, one of the most influential "factors" that emerges from the review proves
to be none other than the figure of Pound himself.

As its title suggests, the review contextualizes and subsumes *A Voyage to*
Pagany in a general discussion of the direction that Williams' literary career
had taken over the preceding two decades; in this way, Pound was able to
minimize the work's structural flaws, and simultaneously establish its questions
and thematic concerns as integral elements of a distinctive poetic stance. The

piece is also implicitly comparative in tone: Pound measures Williams' background and character in terms of its divergence from the standard of his own. Moreover, the critical judgements contained in "Doctor Williams' Position" are ultimately grounded in the authority of long-term, intimate association; the essay begins with the recounting of a story from Williams' childhood that Pound had heard many years earlier:

> There is an anecdote told me by his mother, who wished me to understand his character, as follows: The young William Carlos, aged let us say about seven, arose in the morning, dressed and put on his shoes. Both shoes buttoned on the left side. He regarded this untoward phenomenon for a few moments and then carefully removed the shoes, placed shoe a that had been on his left foot, on his right foot, and shoe b, that had been on the right foot, on his left foot; both sets of buttons again appeared on the left side of the shoes.
> This stumped him. With the shoes so buttoned he went to school, but . . . and here is the significant part of the story, he spent the day in careful consideration of the matter.[1]

The genealogy of this anecdote—from Elena to Pound to the reader—is noteworthy in that a subtle shift has occurred in the narrative's meaning and emphasis as a result of the process of transmission. The impulse underlying Elena's original telling of the tale is personal—to assist the youthful Pound in understanding her son's character by sharing with him what she perceived to be a key facet of it. In Pound's rendition, however, the anecdote assumes primarily aesthetic connotations, becoming a paradigm of Williams' poetic sensibility. The development of man and poet are thus conflated: the child's thoughtful contemplation, analysis, and resolution of a small, mundane mystery represent both the origin and analogue of the mature artist's relationship to the phenomenal world.

Pound's praise of his friend's reflective habit of mind is twofold: he first acknowledges its intrinsic value as the foundation of "any literary process,"[2] then more specifically stresses its uniqueness among American writers of his own generation. In Pound's estimation, Williams' attempt to understand things in their "natural colors and shapes"[3] favorably distinguished his work from that of his compatriots by preventing him from "grabbing ready-made conclusions, and from taking too much for granted."[4] This flattering assessment proves, however, to have ambiguous and subversive undertones. The singularity of Williams' perspective not only elevates him above the literary mainstream, but distances and isolates him from it, thus implying that his writing, while significant, is also aberrant, atypical, and un-American in character. In this manner, Pound's evaluation simultaneously confers distinction and exclusion upon the poet; the privilege of Williams' position is effectively abnegated by its anomaly.

The ambivalence of Pound's remarks becomes increasingly evident when he attempts to particularize the distinction between Williams and other American writers by introducing himself and a variety of political concerns into the discussion:

I cannot . . . observe the nation befouled by Volsteads and Bryans, without anger; I cannot see liberties that have lasted for a century thrown away for nothing, for worse than nothing, for slop; frontiers tied up by an imbecile bureaucracy exceeding "anything known in
Russia under the Czars" without indignation.

And just by this susceptibility on my part Williams, as author, has no small advantage.
If he wants to "do" anything about what he sees, this desire for action does not rise until he
has meditated in full and at leisure. Where I see scoundrels and vandals, he sees a spectacle
or ineluctable process of nature. Where I want to kill at once, he ruminates.[5]

The moral indignation which Pound expresses at the corruption of traditional American liberties in this passage is proprietary in tone; by virtue of his
birthright and heritage, he imaginatively allies himself with the vision and
values of the Founding Fathers and rails against their debasement by contemporary politicians. Through the patriotic bombast of his rhetoric, Pound characterizes himself as a staunch American of long and socially prominent standing,
dedicated to the preservation and protection of the nation's first principles. His
"susceptibility" to anger serves as further proof of this conservative prerogative:
his vested interest in democratic values is so strong that he cannot sit back and
idly watch their decline. Instead, the legacy of the poet's ancestry both demands and entitles him to the public voicing of his displeasure.

Viewed in this context, Williams' calm, meditative stance is hardly the
"advantage" Pound deems it to be. The philosophical detachment which allows
him to perceive an "ineluctable process of nature" where Pound sees "scoundrels and vandals" derives primarily from a difference in background rather
than individual temperament. The objectivity and emotional distance of Williams' ruminations are symptomatic of a more profound personal and historical
detachment, namely, his position as an outsider in American society. Yet
Pound is not using the term "advantage" ironically; from his vantage point,
Williams' chief value as a writer lies in the paradoxical condition of being an
un-American American:

Carlos Williams has been determined to stand or sit as an American. Freud would probably
say "because his father was English" (in fact, half English, half Danish). His mother, as
ethnologists have before noted, was a mixture of French and Spanish; of late years (the last
four or five) Dr. Williams has laid claim to a somewhat remote Hebrew connexion, possibly
a rabbi in Saragossa, at the time of the siege. He claims American birth, but I strongly suspect that he emerged on shipboard just off Bedloe's Island and that his dark and serious eyes
gazed up in their first sober contemplation at the Statue and its brazen and monstrous nightshirt.

At any rate he has not in his ancestral endocrines the arid curse of our nation. None of
his immediate forebears burnt witches in Salem, or attended assemblies for producing pro-
hibitions. His father was in the rum trade; the rich ichors of the Indes, Hollands, Jamaicas,
Goldwasser, Curaoças provided the infant William with material sustenance. Spanish was not
a strange tongue, and the trade profited by discimination, by dissociations performed with the
palate. . . .

From this secure ingle William Carlos was able to look out of his circumjacence and
see it as something interesting but *exterior,* and he could not by any possibility resemble any

member of the Concord School. He was able to observe national phenomena without necessity for constant vigilance over himself, there was no instinctive fear that if he forgot himself
he might be like some really unpleasant Ralph Waldo. . . .
  One might accuse him of being, blessedly, the observant foreigner, perceiving American
vegetation and landscape quite directly, as something put there for him to look at; and his
contemplative habit extends, also blessedly, to the fauna.[6]

As the extravagant diction of this excerpt suggests, Pound is engaged here
in a process more akin to mythmaking than straightforward description. By emphasizing the exotic elements of Williams' ancestry and upbringing, he creates
a vivid—if not entirely accurate—image of the poet as "Carlos," raised on the
rich, intoxicating liqueurs of the West Indies and the musical cadences of the
Spanish tongue. Pound's embellishments, while obvious today to anyone familiar with the basic details of Williams' biography, were in all likelihood not so
apparent to readers of *The Dial* in 1928. It is thus possible that his highly
romanticized comments were taken literally and may have influenced the
character of the poet's early reputation. Nonetheless, in terms of specific historical facts, Pound's misstatements are numerous: Williams' father, for example, was not half-Danish, nor was he technically "in the rum trade." William
George had indeed worked briefly as a rum taster in Saint Thomas during his
youth (*YMW,* 9); however, after migrating to the United States in 1882, he held
a far less glamorous post as advertising manager of Lanman and Kemp, a New
York-based firm which produced a perfume called "Florida Water."[7] The selec-
tive slant of Pound's reporting capitalizes on the allure of the family's Caribbean ties; his priority lies in presenting an interesting story rather than a truthful
or complete one.
  Pound's adroit manipulation of mundane fact into mythos is, moreover,
not without its negative implications. In conjecturing that Williams was born
"on shipboard just off Bedloe's Island," he figuratively places his friend
offshore, within close sight of the harbor and the statue's "brazen and monstrous nightshirt," but not yet in possession of it. He thus insidiously denies the
legal basis of Williams' claim to American identity (United States citizenship),
and effectively renders him homeless, a native of no land. This sense of exclusion is reinforced by Pound's assertion that Williams "has not in his ancestral
endocrines the arid curse of our nation." The operative word here is the possessive adjective "our," which transforms the poet's alleged good fortune (freedom from a dread, but ill-defined, curse) into a grave liability—incontrovertible proof that he does not, and cannot, belong.
  Having thus invalidated Williams' personal and familial claim to American identity, Pound then proceeds to debar him from a larger, more metaphorical kinship—inclusion in the American literary tradition. The unqualified assurance with which he states that Williams "*could not by any possibility* resemble *any* member of the Concord School" (emphasis mine) reveals how vast and
insurmountable a gulf Pound wants to establish between Williams and the his-

torical canon of great American writers. The judgement is implicitly smug and elitist, articulated from securely within the boundaries of that venerable tradition. Although Williams, by virtue of his status as an outsider, is spared the dreaded prospect of being like "some really unpleasant Ralph Waldo," Pound himself must continually guard against this danger. His irreverent tone and assumption of casual, first-name intimacy in referring to the acknowledged colossus of nineteenth-century American letters as if he were a cranky old relative reflect the privileged proximity of his position. Moreover, as Pound employs it, the very notion of "resemblance" is freighted with a variety of symbolic meanings. On the one hand, it signifies direct lineal descent, the indelible mark of connection to, and continuity with, the past; on the other, it also represents a threat to individuation, the possibility of grotesque parody and recapitulation of the past rather than pure artistic invention. For Pound, the figure of Emerson looms as a powerful progenitor whose influence must be cast off in order to develop his own poetic voice. Williams, in contrast, is completely detached from the legacy of literary "resemblance," and thus has neither fixed exemplars nor ghostly antagonists to contend with. Unfortunately, however, this condition also implies that the poet lacks context, occupies no particular or definable place. Williams exists rather on a remote, insubstantial periphery, the "observant foreigner" whose clear, inquisitive gaze is directed at an "interesting" but inevitably "exterior" American landscape.

Pound does not go so far, however, as to deny Williams an audience. In fact, he claims that the detachment of Williams' viewpoint has won him a small but select number of admirers abroad because "here at last was an America treated with a seriousness and by a process comprehensible to a European."[8] He continues: "One might say that Williams has but one fixed idea, as an author; i.e., he starts where a European would start if a European were about to write of America: sic: America is a subject of interest, one must inspect it, analyze it, and treat it as subject."[9] Once again, we have evidence of the sophistical nature of Pound's argument, the way in which he twists the apparent meaning of a statement through rhetorical sleight of hand. His assertion that Williams has "but one fixed idea" as a writer can be interpreted either as praise of his sustained, purposeful focus or disparagement of his limited, monocular vision. Through the dissonance of these possible interpretations this "compliment," like so many of the others Pound bestows on Williams in the essay, proves to be perfidious and implicitly critical.

But what is most puzzling and treacherous about Pound's evaluation is that, after taking such pains to deny Williams' American identity and exclude him from the nation's literary tradition, he can nonetheless describe his colleague's position as a "secure ingle." Pound's use of the archaic term "ingle" here is suggestive in that it links Williams with the unfortunate figure of Odysseus's crew member, Elpenor, whom the Greek leader encountered in his descent to the underworld in Pound's Canto 1 (published 1917). Like Williams,

Elpenor occupied an ingle, but suffered disastrous consequences as a result. In response to Odysseus's question—"How art thou come to this dark coast?"— Elepenor states:

> Ill fate and abundant wine. I slept in Circe's ingle.
> Going down the long ladder unguarded,
> I fell against the buttress,
> Shattered the nape-nerve, the soul sought Avernus.[10]

In the context of this tale, the ingle is a lofty, exposed place, which appears comfortable, inviting, and secure, but ultimately proves precarious and fatal. Moreover, the adversity of Elpenor's fate persists beyond death since Odysseus and his men, in their haste to depart from Circe's isle, neglected to bury his body. He is thus an outcast in Hades, condemned to restless, eternal wandering, and begs Odysseus to return and fulfill his obligation:

> But thou, O King, I bid remember me, unwept, unburied,
> Heap up mine arms, be tomb by sea-bord, and inscribed:
> A man of no fortune, and with a name to come,
> And set my oar up, that I swung mid fellows.[11]

These instructions offer further insight into Elepenor's character. The epitaph he chooses, for example, reveals a belief that although he was considered more unlucky than illustrious in life, posterity will accord him a favorable reputation. In addition, through the visual emblem of the oar set up over his grave, Elpenor indicates that, despite the isolation of his death, he wants to be remembered as an integral part ("mid fellows") of a team pursuing a common goal.

The parallels between Elpenor's plight and that of Williams are numerous and tantalizing; however, within the scope of the present discussion, the crucial point of convergence is location. Williams' modern ingle was no more "secure" than Elpenor's ancient one, and Ezra Pound undoubtedly knew it. By the time "Doctor Williams' Position" was published in 1928, the two poets had been acquainted for more than a quarter of a century; thus, the range and depth of their association extended beyond familiarity with one another's personal traits to their respective families. During their college years at Penn, Pound has been a frequent guest at the Williams home in Rutherford, and when he returned briefly to the States in 1910 to be treated for a case of jaundice, he visited 131 Passaic Avenue on several occasions. Given his interest and proficiency in foreign languages, Pound must have enjoyed the unique polyglot character of the Williams household, and perhaps even conversed with his friend's parents in Spanish and French. Moreover, as the anecdote which begins "Doctor Williams' Position" and the remarks about William George's work in the rum trade reveal, Pound was privy to the family's intimate stories of the past, and had first hand knowledge of the chaotic, ethnic jumble that constituted Williams' background. He was also aware that the exotic legacy of the Indies was a problematic one for Williams in that the lack of well-established roots induced feelings of uneasiness and inadequacy. In fact, this very issue lies at the heart of *A Voyage to Pagany,* the novel Pound ostensibly set out to review in "Doctor Williams' Position." Towards the end of that text, the main character, Dev Evans, who is a thinly disguised version of Williams himself, rejects the monuments and culture of the Old World in favor of returning to New Jersey, stating: "I can never be at home here. There is a deep loss in me that comes of my inheritance. Years ago I was lost—I am not of this club [of expatriates]. That is what I am, a great zero" (*VP,* 240). Pound's refusal to acknowledge this "loss" and its adverse effects on Williams' psyche suggest that he did not see his friend as he actually was, but rather through the distorted imaginative lens of what he wanted him to be.[12] He reinvents Williams according to a subjective conception which flatters and selfishly advances his own stature. In comparison to Williams' "Mediterranean equipment,"[13] Pound's ancestry seems remarkably stable, coherent, and homogeneous—more inherently American and, by implication, superior.

In many respects, the complex emotional configuration of Pound and Williams' relationship is a modern version of the fictional boyhood friendship between Tom Sawyer and Huck Finn—affectionate but rivalrous, predicated upon and sustained by a distinct sense of inequality. Pound, like Tom, came from a respectable family; he was "well-brung up and had folks at home that had characters."[14] He was also—again like Tom—a voracious reader, and spent decades berating and bullying Williams about his insufficient learning. The interminable reading lists that characterize Pound's half of their extensive correspondence ("If you'll read Yeats and Browning and Francis Thompson and Swinburne and Rossetti you'll learn something about the progress of English poetry in the last century. . . . You are out of touch. That's all"[15]) strongly echo Tom's typical criticism of Huck: "Why, hain't you ever read any books at all?—Baron Trenck, nor Casanova, nor Benvenuto Chelleny, nor Henry IV, nor none of them heroes?"[16] The condescending airs that both individuals assume in these statements illustrate the egotistical manner in which they elicit deference from their friends by making them feel ignorant and inferior. Stylish and blatantly precocious, securely ensconced within the social mainstream, Pound and Tom Sawyer, become powerful, yet not altogether positive role models for Williams and Huck, the outcasts whose connections to the past and their immediate environments are tenuous at best.[17]

Interestingly, the evolutions of the two friendships follow a similar pattern as well. In order to achieve full maturity and autonomy, both Williams and Huck had to recognize the shortcomings of their "models," and consciously choose to diverge from the examples which had been set for them. Williams' struggle to extricate himself from Pound's pervasive influence was accomplished gradually, over the course of nearly his entire adult life. Even as late as 1948, after publishing more than thirty books, discernible traces of an inferiority complex lingered, as the following passage from a letter to Babette Deutsch reveals: "I look at what I have done, with *Paterson* for instance, and though at times I am impressed, at other times I find little to praise in my attempts. Laid beside the vigors of some of Pound's cantos, not only the vigor but the sensitiveness to the life in a thousand phases, I feel like a boor, a lout, a synthetic artist" (*SL,* 264).

The self-deprecating nouns Williams uses in comparing himself with Pound here are quite telling; both "boor" and "lout" are pejorative social epithets which denote an individual with coarse manners who is utterly devoid of breeding and refinement. Within the context of the letter, however, the criteria for social esteem and literary value are conflated, so that Williams' lack of cultivation makes him a "synthetic" or fraudulent artist, whereas Pound, by virtue of his ancestry and deportment, is the real thing. What is especially insidious about this correlation is that the figure largely responsible for instigating Williams' feelings of deficiency is Pound himself. Thus, the letter's diction unconsciously reveals how crucial a role Pound played in shaping his friend's poetic self-image. He was the master and mentor—"il miglior fabbro"—in relation to whom Williams was destined to play the eternal disciple. It was a tiresome and severely restrictive role. In 1954, only nine years before his death, Williams would complain in a letter to Pound about the oppressiveness of this stance: "Ain't it enuf that you so deeply influenced my formative years without your wanting to influence also my later ones?" (*SL,* 324).

Pound's assessment of Williams' foreignness in his 1928 review represents only one facet of a lengthy, and occasionally ill-tempered, debate between the two men on the subject of American identity. And despite its persistently subversive undertones, "Doctor Williams' Position" reflects a rare, relatively cordial moment in that ongoing dialogue; there is, for example, nothing equivocal about Pound's praise of the "indispensable component of texture"[18] in Williams' writing, or his assertion that "no one else now writing would have given us the sharp clarity of the medical chapters"[19] in *Pagany*. This skillful blending of admiration and ambivalence complicates the essay, making its already subtle bias more elusive. Williams himself appears to have been pleased with Pound's evaluation; in a letter written in late 1928, he makes no mention of the jibes concerning his "Mediterranean equipment" and emergence "just off Bedloe's Island," but states:

> Dear Ezrie: Nothing will ever be said of better understanding regarding my work than your article in *The Dial.* I must thank you for your great interest and discriminating defense of my position. Without question you have hit most of the trends that I am following with the effect that you have clarified my designs on the future which in turn will act as encouragement and strength for me. (*SL,* 108)

Notwithstanding the ironic double entendre of the phrase, "*discriminating* defense," Williams chose in this instance to overlook his friend's presumption of hereditary prerogative and concentrate instead on charting his future literary course along the lines of Pound's specific encouragements. There were, however, numerous other occasions on which such restraint was impossible. In a letter dated only "Spring 1926," for example, Williams lashes out at Pound for grossly misinterpreting his character and work, for making him into something he is not:

> All I ever asked, even of you, is that you SEE me and not through glasses guaranteed and specially fabricated to miscolor and distort everything they come against. I do object to that. Look—if you have any eyes at all—and forget for a moment what happens to be itching you at the time. It may for a moment permit you to get a little pleasure without aching to make me something I ain't.
>
> You talk like a crow with a cleft palate when you repeat your old gag of heredity, where you come from or where I come from. Do you really agree that place matters? Or time either? (*SL,* 69)

Because the letter from Pound which provoked this outburst has not yet been published, the precise historical circumstances underlying Williams' response cannot be ascertained; nonetheless the tenor of his complaint makes the context reasonably clear. He condemns Pound's blinding egotism and penchant for invidious comparison of their backgrounds and ancestries, stating that heredity is merely an "old gag" that doesn't amount to anything. This allusion is intriguing because the term "gag" can refer to either a joke or an object thrust into the mouth (usually of a victim) to prevent speech. The beauty of Williams' statement is that it simultaneously allows both interpretations: Pound's continual "crowing" about his superior ancestry is an old and malicious joke intended to stifle Williams' speech (the medium of his art) which, however, backfires on its perpetrator by revealing a "congenital" defect in Pound's own speech.

The most vitriolic exchange in this debate, however, was inspired by a 1917 letter from Pound, portions of which Williams subsequently incorporated into the prologue of *Kora in Hell,* as proof that "E.P. is the best enemy United States verse has" (*I,* 26). Williams' editing of that letter emphasizes the arrogance of his friend's character, so that the rhetorical excesses of Pound's criticism become a tacit form of self-incrimination. Significantly, he omits an affectionate remark which occurs early in the letter and provides a mitigating context for the attack that follows it a few paragraphs later: "I had no ulterior or hidden meaning in calling you or the imaginary correspondent an 'American' author. Still what the hell else are you? I mean apart from being a citizen, a good fellow (in your better moments), a grouch, a slightly hypersensitized animal, etc.? Wot bloody kind of author are you save Amurkun (same as me)?"[20]

Whether Williams dismissed this momentary expression of solidarity as insincere or removed it on the grounds that it deflated the intensity of Pound's subsequent vituperation is unclear. Certainly, in the form in which the letter appears in *Kora,* there is nothing subtle or ambivalent about Pound's attitude:

> . . . God knows I have to work hard enough to escape, not *propagande,* but getting centered in *propagande.* And America? What the hell do you a blooming foreigner know about the place? Your père only penetrated the edge, and you've never been west of Upper Darby, or the Maunchunk switchback. Would Harriet, with the swirl of the prairie wind in her underwear, or the virile Sandburg recognize you, an effete Easterner, as a REAL American? INCONCEIVABLE!!!!
>
> My dear boy, you have never felt the whoop of the PEEraries. You have never seen the projecting and protuberant Mts. of the SIerra Nevada. WOT can you know of the country?
>
> You have the naive incredulity of a Co. Clare emigrant. But I (der grosse Ich) have the virus, the bacillus of the land in my blood for nearly three bleating centuries.
>
> (Bloody snob. 'eave a brick at 'im!!!). . . .
>
> I was very glad to see your wholly unAmerican poems in the L. [ittle] R. [eview]
>
> Of course Sandburg will tell you that you miss the "Big drifts," and Bodenheim will object to your not being sufficiently decadent.
>
> (You thank your bloomin gawd you've got enough Spanish blood to muddy up your mind, and prevent the current American ideation from going through it like a blighted colander.)
>
> The thing that saves your work is *opacity,* and don't you forget it. Opacity is NOT an American quality. Fizz, swish, gabble of verbiage, these are echt Amerikanisch. (*I,* 11)

Although the terms of Pound's argument differ slightly from those of *The Dial* essay, the conclusion is identical: Williams is not a genuine American. The criterion he employs in this case is not native birth, but a vaguely Whitmanic sense of experience and imaginative "possession" of the country's varied topography, from the "whoop of the PEEraries" to the "projecting and protuberant Mts. of the SIerra Nevada." As an "effete Easterner," Williams lacks this expansive understanding of the continent's mass, and thus his claim to American identity is tenuous and questionable. Pound situates Williams on a literal and cultural fringe, granting him a meagre foothold on the northeast seaboard: "Your père only penetrated the edge, and you've never been west of Upper Darby, or the Maunchunk switchback." In comparison to "der grosse Ich," whose possession of America is so complete that the very "bacillus of the land" has infiltrated his ancestral bloodline for nearly "three bleating centuries," Williams is the provincial newcomer, whose knowledge of the land of his birth is fragmentary and imperfect.

It is within this comparative framework that the significance of Williams' second deletion from Pound's letter emerges. After the parenthetical statement "Bloody snob. 'eave a brick at 'im!" there is an ellipsis, where the original text reads as follows:

> You (read your Freud) have a Vaterersatz, you have a paternal image at your fireside, and you call it John Bull.

Your statement about my wanting Paris to be like London is a figment of your own diseased imagination.

"I warn you that anything you say at this time may later be used against you." The Arts vs. Williams.

Or will you carry my head on a platter? Or would you like it brought over to be punched? A votre service, M'sieu. I am coming to inspect you.

I of course like your Old Man, and I have drunk his Goldwasser.[21]

In the first and last lines of this passage, Pound offers Williams a potential solution to his dilemma of cultural identity—a solution embodied in the figure of Williams' British father. Given Pound's strong Anglophilic tendencies, his attraction to, and appreciation of, William George is perfectly understandable; his assertion, "*I of course* like your Old Man, and *I* have drunk his Goldwasser" (emphasis mine), suggests that an affectionate rapport exists between the two men which the younger Williams unfortunately does not share. In Pound's estimation, Williams need look no further than his own "fireside" for a suitable image upon which to base his personal and poetic identity. In other words, he should ally himself, through the figure of his father, with the richness of the British tradition. Moreover, Pound interprets his friend's rejection of that option as a classic symptom of neurosis: "You (read your Freud) have a Vaterersatz, you have a paternal image at your fireside, and you call it John Bull." The term "Vaterersatz" refers to the landmark "Little Hans" case history (or as it is officially known, "Analysis of a Phobia in a Five-Year-Old Boy," published in 1909) in which Freud analyzes the Oedipus complex. In this text, Hans shifts the hostile, rivalrous impulses he feels towards his father onto an object (horses) which serves as a father substitute (*Vaterersatz*). The boy's phobia of horses, the outward symptom which brings the case to Freud's attention in the first place, has a positive function in that it allows Hans to hide his anger and yet express it at the same time.[22] Freud's task, as analyst, is to bring the repressed association between father and horse back to consciousness so that the real issue—rivalry over possession of the mother—can be resolved. Pound's allusion implies that Williams' personal antagonism towards his father is oedipal in nature, and that the *Vaterersatz* he has chosen to express this hostility is England. Assuming the role of analyst, Pound urges Williams to recognize the adverse effects of this substitution and to renounce his denial of the British tradition by separating William George from the cultural stereotype of "John Bull."

Williams' suppression of this passage suggests that Pound's assertions may have been painful or embarrassing to him, striking too uncomfortably close to a truth which he himself was unwilling to admit. When replaced in its original context, however, the passage—or more accurately, Pound's letter as a whole—greatly clarifies his perception of Williams. Convinced that his friend's background and work were "wholly unAmerican," Pound envisaged two alternate identities for him. The first, and clearly more preferable option in Pound's mind, was to become "William Williams," scion of a distinguished Englishman;[23] the other lay in the sensual, exotic persona of "Carlos," whose mind was "muddied up" by Spanish blood and produced poetry notable for its opacity and incoherence. Considering the diversity of Williams' heritage, Pound was probably mystified (as well as a bit disgusted) that the self-image his friend ultimately chose to promulgate was that of the patriotic, small-town physician. Because Pound regarded his own American identity as a limitation, something to be evaded, transcended, and eventually reclaimed from the safe distance of the European continent, he utterly failed to understand the magnitude of Williams' need to become American. He thus continually berated his friend's decision to remain in Rutherford, and issued repeated warnings about the dangers of provincialism, as in the French quotation at the end of his 1917 letter:

> L'amour excessif d'une patrie a pour immédiat corollaire l'horreur des patries étrangères. Non seulement on craint de quitter le jupe de sa maman, d'aller voir comment vivent les autres hommes, de se mêler à leurs luttes, de partager leurs travaux; non seulement on reste chez soi, mais on finit par fermer sa porte.[24]

Williams' struggle to establish a uniquely American identity is deeply and inextricably entangled with his relationship to Ezra Pound; their friendship forms the critical backdrop of that undertaking. Pound served as both inspiration and foil for Williams, advising, provoking, criticizing—forcing him with each installment of their correspondence to rigorously define and defend his position. The powerful endurance of this influence is illustrated by an episode in the *Autobiography* which describes how Pound's mere mention of "Old Doc Williams of Rutherford, NJ" during one of his World War II Radio Rome broadcasts was enough to land a suspicious FBI agent on Williams' doorstep:

> "Are you a loyal American citizen?" he said looking me steadily in the eye. I was embarrassed.
> "Of course I'm a loyal American citizen, I-I-I've spent my whole life, generally speaking, for my country, trying to serve it in every way I know how. I've even written a book about it."
> "What book?"
> "It's called *In the American Grain*—and many articles and critical essays . . . I'll get you the book if you want it." (*A*, 317)

The flustered, fiercely patriotic nature of Williams' response to the agent's insinuation of disloyalty reveals that, even at this late stage in his career, the poet remained somewhat insecure about his status as an American. Pound, whose blueblooded endeavor to preserve the values of the Founding Fathers would soon end in charges of treason, still retained the power to undermine his friend's cultural identity from afar.

One of Williams' earliest and most vociferous attempts to exorcise Pound's influence is the polemical prologue to *Kora in Hell*. In many respects, the angry, defiant tone of this piece comprises an indirect response to Pound's suppressed comment about William George and *Vaterersatz*. Williams prefaces his expurgated text of the letter with an anecdote which is intended to weaken the bond between his father and Pound:

> During this same visit in 1910 . . . my parent had been holding forth in downright sentences upon my own "idle nonsense" when he turned and became equally vehement concerning something Ezra had written: What in heaven's name Ezra meant by "jewels" in a verse that had come between them. These jewels—rubies, sapphires, amethysts, and whatnot, Pound went on to explain with a good deal of determination and care, were the backs of books as they stood on a man's shelf. "But why in heaven's name don't you say so then?" was my father's triumphant and crushing rejoinder. (*I*, 11)

Contrary to Williams' description, his father's comment is hardly a "triumphant and crushing rejoinder," but rather a candid tip on avoiding poetic obfuscation. Evidently Pound thought so too. Upon finding his personal correspondence unexpectedly in print, he dashed off a series of three letters to Williams in two days (11 and 12 September 1920) in which he stated: "Re the dialog with your old man . . . we did talk about 'Und Drang' but there the sapphires certainly are not anything but sapphires, perfect definite visual imagination. However, upshot (which you don't certainly, imply) is that your old man was certainly dead right."[25] Rather than disrupting the spiritual alliance between Pound and William George, Williams' anecdote serves to intensify it; Pound not only thoroughly defends the elder man's judgement, but laments his passing in terms suggesting the loss of a homeland: "Have I a country at all . . . now that Mouquin is no more, and that your father has no more goldwasser, and the goldwasser no obescent [*sic*] bonhomme to pour it for me?"[26] Ironically, it is Williams himself who becomes the adversary due to his biased reporting of the incident.[27]

In this same series of letters, Pound also chastized Williams for a more damaging and egregious misrepresentation:

> And you might in fairness have elaborated my quotation on *virus*. There is a blood poison in America; you can idealize the place (easier now that Europe is so damd shaky) all you like, but you haven't a drop of the cursed blood in you, and you don't need to fight the disease day and night; you never had to. Eliot has it worse than I have—poor devil.
>
> You have the advantage of arriving in the milieu with a fresh flood of Europe in your veins, Spanish, French, English, Danish. You had not the thin milk of New York and New England from the pap; and you can therefore keep the environment outside you, and decently objective.[28]

This letter contains all the major tropes of Pound's critique of Williams which would appear eight years later in *The Dial:* the "blood poison" and "curse" of America, Williams' "advantage" of recent arrival in the land, and the "objectivity" and "exteriority" of his relation to that environment. In this regard, "Doctor Williams' Position" can be viewed as an outgrowth of the prologue to *Kora,* an explication and attempted justification of the offensively elitist attitudes expressed in Pound's 1917 letter. The intricate network of cross-references linking the two texts accurately reflects the complexity of the friendship itself.

But in terms of Williams' assertion of cultural identity, the primary significance of the prologue lies in his articulation of the aesthetic battlelines which would remain operative throughout his lifetime. In announcing his decision to remain in the United States, Williams positions himself in direct opposition to expatriate writers like Pound and Eliot, as well as the entire British literary tradition, embodied in the figure of critic Edgar Jepson: "I wish that I might here set down my 'Vortex' after the fashion of London, 1913, stating how little it means to me whether I live here, there, or elsewhere so long as I can keep my mind free from the trammels of literature, beating down every attack of its retiarii with my mirmillones" (*I,* 16).

Williams' stance throughout the prologue is that of the defiant individualist (very much in the tradition of members of the "Concord School" whom Pound had said his friend could not "possibly" resemble), marching to the beat of a different drummer and openly deriding the conformity of the pack: "I praise those who have the wit and courage, and the conventionality, to go direct toward their vision of perfection in an objective world where the signposts are clearly marked, viz., to London. But confine them in hell for their paretic assumption that there is no alternative but their own groove" (*I,* 27).

The constellation of opponents Williams posits for himself in the prologue implicitly includes the figure of his father, the Englishman who spent the majority of his adult life in the United States but refused to become a citizen, maintaining that in his line of work it was easier to carry British rather than American papers.[29] Williams not only rejects Pound's advice to distinguish his personal difficulties with William George from the mythos of "John Bull," but expands the negative associations of that *Vaterersatz* to include a generally conservative habit of mind, style of speech, and poetic model which he intuitively distrusted. "Britons make the best policemen the world has ever witnessed" (*I,* 21), he declares, evoking an image of uniformed guardians of public order as the emblem of a cultural tradition based on formal authority and restraint. One such "policeman" singled out for an especially venemous attack is Edgar Jepson, the critic who had pronounced T. S. Eliot's work the best of modern American verse. What especially rankled Williams about Jepson's critique was his identification of the figure of Prufrock with "the soul of that modern land, the United States" (*I,* 24). The aplomb with which Williams denies this designation is noteworthy in a work characterized largely by defensiveness and insecurity; moreover, the nature of the denial itself illuminates the philosophical ground upon which the poet staked his contrary position:

I cannot question Eliot's observation. Prufrock is a masterly portrait of the man just below the summit, but the type is universal; the model in his case might be Mr. J.

No. The New World is Montezuma or, since he was stoned to death in a parley, Guatemozin who had the city of Mexico leveled over him before he was taken. (*I*, 24)

In contrast to the expatriates' adoption of a foreign homeland and cultural tradition, Williams chose to reside in the land of his "more or less accidental birth" (*A*, 178), and to firmly ally himself with the New World. As the above passage intimates, this alliance would be formed through an imaginative connection to the American past—not, however, that of the British colonial enterprise, but a more remote, exotic past of Indians and the Spanish conquest—the violent struggle between old and new worlds typified in the doomed, heroic resistance of Montezuma and Guatemozin. Thus, in the prologue to *Kora*, Williams takes the first step towards supplanting the *Vaterersatz* in all its myriad manifestations with a more sympathetic, ethnically diverse New World tradition, whose image he also discovered at his own fireside—in the figure of his mother. Significantly, the prologue opens with an anecdote about Elena in which she is described as "an impoverished, ravished Eden but one as indestructible as the imagination itself" (*I*, 7), a rich, paradisal garden, now despoiled but not ruined—a symbol, in other words, of America itself.[30] Through his establishment of Elena as a poetic model, Williams made a conscious choice which determined the subsequent direction of his career. Rather than founding his cultural identity, as Pound advocated, on his British patrilineage, Williams turned instead to the multifaceted ethnic heritage—French, Spanish, Dutch, Jewish—of his mother. As he states in the introduction to *Yes, Mrs. Williams:*

In the West Indies, in Martinique, St. Thomas, Puerto Rico, Santo Domingo, in those days, the races of the world mingled and intermarried—imparting their traits one to another and forgetting the orthodoxy of their ancient and medieval views. It was a good thing. It is in the best spirit of the New World. . . .

The great variety of the world—the tropic fruit—Fruitful—the flowers, Renoir; variety important because it allows mutation, the aspects of a life—from enough viewpoints to ascertain more accurately, the truth and the character of the good. (*YMW*, 30, 130–31)

Williams' empathic identification with Elena combines aesthetic and ethnic dimensions; she is not only a muse in the general sense of poetic inspiration, but specifically a New World muse, through whom he could gain possession of America. The organic imagery he employs in the above passage, "tropic fruit—Fruitful—the flowers," expresses the nature of Elena's role in this undertaking. Through her diverse racial heritage, she becomes a metaphorical seed, representing the potential for establishing American roots. Yet, as far as Ezra Pound was concerned, Williams was making the wrong choice, and apparently he did not hesitate to let his friend know it. In *I Wanted to Write a Poem,* Williams resentfully recalls that Pound's obvious preference for William George led him to slight Elena: "Pound met my mother and father. He liked my father very much. My mother? I suppose he was conscious of her. He allowed her to exist" (*IW,* 8). For his part, Williams made periodic attempts to persuade Pound of Elena's intrinsic value, as the following excerpt from a letter written at the beginning of Pound's confinement at St. Elizabeth's Hospital illustrates:

> Mother, who will be 90 the day before Christmas, always asks after you with the most intense interest. She feels you belong to her clan, the artists. She has forgiven you completely for all the faults the others have imputed to you; she does not believe them. . . . She has in her possession everything in the papers relating to you. Poor old thing, she's deaf as well as half blind. I'm amazed at her spirit.[31]

Despite this poignant expression of Elena's loyalty and support for him as a fellow artist, Pound ultimately remained unconvinced of her primacy in Williams' life and imagination. In the *Autobiography,* Williams states: "Ezra's insistence has always been that I never laid proper stress in my life upon the part played in it by my father rather than my mother. Oh, the woman of it is important, he would acknowledge, but the form of it, if not the drive, came unacknowledged by me from the old man, the Englishman" (*A,* 91).

The poet's affiliation with his mother represents, in effect, a "counterstress," born not only of the "sexual shock" alluded to in "To Daphne and Virginia," but a deep antipathy for the patriarchal cultural tradition he identified with his father, T. S. Eliot and, above all, Ezra Pound.[32] In "Letter to an Australian Editor," he describes Pound's achievement as "a strik[ing] back toward the triumphant forms of the past, father to father. No mother necessary," and warns that the price of cutting oneself off from the "supplying female" is literary sterility.[33] For Williams, the mother, as individual and metaphor, was absolutely necessary; what she "supplied" was a viable path to American identity. Just how important the "woman of it" was for the poet can be seen in nearly all his work, which is to say, as he did, "There is, of course, more" (*PB,* 78).

In February 1917, some nine months before Pound blasted, "And America? What the hell do you a blooming foreigner know about the place?" from London, Williams wrote to Marianne Moore seeking her advice about the title of his soon-to-be-published third book. The poet's description of himself in this letter illustrates yet another facet of his ambition to project a distinctly American identity:

> I'm going to have a book, as I told you. . . . But the title bothers me.
> You see I am a mixture of two bloods, neither of them particularly pure. Yet there is always in me a harking back to some sort of aristocracy—probably of the gallows or worse—that will have a hand in all my democratic impulses. Then again there is a certain broad-

fingered strain in me that will always be handling an axe for budding King Charles Firsts.
So I torture myself through life. But there are acute moments that seem distillations of agony
and this is one of them.
    I want to call my book:
        A Book of Poems:
        AL QUE QUIERE!
                —which means: To him who wants it—but I like the Spanish just as I
like a Chinese image cut out of stone: it is decorative and has a certain charm. But such a
title is not democratic—does not truly represent the contents of the book, so I have added:
        A Book of Poems:
        AL QUE QUIERE!
        or
        The PLEASURES OF DEMOCRACY.
    Now I like this conglomerate title! It is nearly a perfect image of my own grinning mug
(seen from the inside), but my publisher objects—and I shake and wobble. Help me, O lead-
ing light of the Sex of the Future. (*SL*, 40)

The antagonistic split in consciousness that Williams melodramatically
outlines in this letter, which manifests itself in an emotional tug of war between
aristocratic and democratic impulses, reflects a fundamental uncertainty about
who he is and how he wants to be perceived by others. Rather than aligning
himself unequivocally with one ideology or the other, he wavers and, as a result, experiences acute moments of "torture," "agony," and despair. He symbolically attributes this painful vacillation to hereditary causes: "You see I am
a mixture of two bloods, neither of them particularly pure," and seeks to establish a synthesis whereby these antithetical drives will coalesce and har-
monize. The "conglomerate title" the poet selects for his text, *Al Que Quiere*
or *The Pleasures of Democracy,* achieves such a synthesis by fusing the old
(Spanish/aristocratic) and new (American/democratic) worlds, and thus mirrors
his "own grinning mug (seen from the inside)." Unfortunately, however, his
choice is rejected by the publisher, most likely on the grounds that it is too
lengthy and cumbersome. Williams takes this rejection personally; the incident
becomes a metaphor for his cultural dilemma, signifying a lack of public acceptance of his mixed heritage.

This image of emotional polarities inducing tension within the self is one
which Williams frequently used to characterize his situation. In the introduction
to *Yes, Mrs. Williams,* for example, he states: "Our family is among those who
came to America from Europe through the West Indies—so that in the United
States—since they still owned slaves in Puerto Rico—I feel more southern
than the southerners, and by virtue of my father, who was born in England, as
northern as if I had come from Maine" (*YMW,* 29). The pattern of oppositions
proposed in this passage—north/south, Maine/Puerto Rico, coldness/warmth—
clarifies the antagonism between aristocratic and democratic impulses mentioned in the letter to Marianne Moore by identifying the divergent connotations
Williams associated with each of his parents. His father represented cool detachment, his mother warmth, passion, and sensuality. And while these associ-

ations convey an implicit preference for the latter, both this passage and the letter itself indicate that the primary legacy of the poet's mixed blood was divisiveness and confusion—an internalized "civil war," north versus south, by which he himself was enslaved. Williams' determination to establish an American identity was strongly motivated by a desire to reconcile these antagonistic aspects of his ancestry; however, as time passed, he realized that the synthesis he had hoped to achieve between them was all but impossible. A choice between the two strains was inevitable, and he ultimately allied himself with the "south" represented by Elena. In *A Voyage to Pagany*, Williams imaginatively isolates and explores the disparate alternatives which his cultural inheritance afforded by splitting himself into two characters, Dev Evans and his expatriate sister Bess: "Evans was like his mother. 'Bess is like the old man—purged,' her brother sometimes said" (*VP*, 15). And a bit later in the novel, this exchange occurs:

> Can it be that we are children of the same parents? Dev said to her.
> From America expect anything! Bess replied. . . .
> She was her father's daughter while Dev was of the southern side of his family which was so mixed that no one ever had been quite certain what they were, except that there was a strong Basque strain there associated with the somewhat mythical name of Hurrard. (*VP*, 27)

Despite their radically different temperaments and attitudes toward America, Dev and Bess have a strong and, as the end of the novel reveals, frankly erotic affection for one another. "Live here with me. . . . You need me—and you are mine, blessed man" (*VP*, 241), Bess entreats her brother in chapter 37, but her proposal must be rejected, just as his counteroffer that they buy a farm together in rural New Jersey must be. The impossibility of reconciling the two divergent strains of the family background—of achieving symbolic union—is emphasized by several allusions to incest and the tale of Sigmund and Siglinde. And so, brother and sister separate, she remaining in the old world, he sailing back to the new. The novel's concluding lines reaffirm Williams' commitment to America and also implicitly acknowledge the ascendancy of maternal influence on his character: "In the morning they were in the waters off Maine, *going south, south*. . . . So this is the beginning" (*VP*, 256; emphasis mine).

The exact "beginning" of the poet's privileging of the figure of his mother over that of his father is difficult to pinpoint. Certainly, it was already firmly in place by the publication of *Pagany* in 1928, and can be detected at least a decade earlier in the prologue to *Kora in Hell*. The formation of this spiritual allegiance thus dates back to the earliest phases of Williams' literary career when, torn between the models of Keats and Whitman, he searched for an authentic poetic voice, and earlier still to the experiences and natural inclinations of his childhood. In the opening chapters of the *Autobiography*, for example, Williams makes repeated reference to his father's prolonged absences from home during his youth, suggesting, as Paul Mariani has noted, the existence of a "vacuum that was naturally—and overwhelmingly—filled by the presence of his grandmother and mother."[34] The following passage typifies the nature of the poet's reminiscences about his father:

> Those were lyrical years [at the Bagellon house]. Pop was away most of that time but there is one memory with which he is still intimately associated: the kite—and the stories of kites and his own childhood in the West Indies. It was a kite . . . taller than I . . . as only Pop could make things. He flew it from the yard one day after readjusting the rag tail a few times and lashed it to the rail of the back porch. In the morning . . . it was still magnificently flying, the cord as tense as a fiddle string. I remember holding it with my hand and feeling the tug and vibration. (*A*, 8)

The ambiguous semantic connection between the first two sentences of this excerpt tacitly relegates the father to the utmost periphery of his son's emotional life. Were those early years "lyrical" in spite of William George's absence or perhaps because of it? The sense of ambivalence is further amplified by the poet's paucity of recollection—"there is *one* memory with which he is *still* intimately associated"—that of a kite proudly aloft in the distance, anchored to home by a thin cord tense with vibration—a perfect analogue for William George's relation to the family as a whole. The other aspect of Williams' memory, however, brings the father closer to earth:

> His accounts of his travels muleback over Costa Rica, the eating of the patés of black ants when caught short for a meal far out in the mountains held me rapt. His story of Bluebeard's castle, from his own childhood in St. Thomas, he made thoroughly familiar to me, as well as the story of the great earthquake and tidal wave that followed it in the early seventies. (*YMW*, 6)

These tales of exotic adventure, guaranteed to fire the imagination of any child, represent isolated moments of social contact between father and son. William George was, by nature, a taciturn, reserved, "curiously mild" (*YMW*, 7) man; the role of raconteur was one he assumed only on occasion. His stories, at least in the poet's memory, were exceptions which punctuated unbearably long stretches of silence.

Given the circumstances, it is not surprising that Williams begins the introduction to *Yes, Mrs. Williams* in this way:

> Determined women have governed my fate. Brought up on stories of my family, to whom I was devoted though I did not always approve of them, I made my way looking under every stone if need be to get on in the way I wanted to go.
> My mother was half French, out of Martinique, the other half was a mixed breed, the Hohebs, Monsantos, I have already written too much about them. Her mother, Meline Hurrard or Hurrand, was of Basque stock. My father was English, typically English, as I learned to know him during my growing years. Obstinate but gentle in his nature, always a true gentleman, he never became a citizen of the United States though he made no objection to my remaining one after I had been born in the country. (*YMW*, 3)

Figure 7. Williams Family, ca. 1899
Left to right: William George, William Carlos, Elena, and Edgar

The poet's elliptical description of himself in this passage illustrates several crucial aspects of his relationship to his family. It suggests, first of all, an ambivalent bond of devotion and disapproval, of simultaneous attachment and emotional distance. Secondly, it implies a sense of individual direction and purpose, a specific "way" that Williams "wanted to go" in order to achieve a desired goal which, though unnamed, appears to be American identity. Lastly, the image of "looking under every stone if need be," which immediately follows the reference to family stories, reveals a curiosity about the past and determination to examine what lay hidden beneath the surface.

Williams' quest for roots began, quite logically, with his immediate progenitors, two immigrants who had come to the United States from the West Indies just one year prior to his own birth. Due to the extensive peregrinations of their ancestors, however, neither of the poet's parents knew much about family history. As he points out in *Yes, Mrs. Williams:*

> Nothing is known of our family beyond the last three generations and not all of that—other than vague rumors, enticing, irritating, scandalous—racially doubtful in certain cases. But there was vigor and sensibility, even intelligence—on both sides.
>
> We are of those who came to the United States through the West Indies. On one side, the maternal, no one knows how long ago the originals had gone there, but on the other no earlier than in the 1850s. The later move by William George Williams and his wife, nee Raquel Elaine Rose Hoheb, came years later. We are the first to have been born here. (*YMW*, 132)

Cut off from their geographical points of origin and concomitant networks of relatives and friends, the elder Williamses viewed the past as an obscure welter of meaningless events. Though seemingly indifferent to their fate, both individuals were unquestionably victimized by it, becoming lifelong emotional transients who lived in, but never truly inhabited, the various environments in which they found themselves. Neither William George nor Elena nurtured any affection for the islands where they spent the greater portions of their youths,[35] nor did they feel a particular affinity for the homeland they had adopted as adults. In all the years the elder Williamses lived in America, they never integrated themselves into the mainstream of society, but remained perennial outsiders—distant, isolated, aloof.

As a young man, Williams was deeply troubled by his parents' foreignness, their estrangement from the environment he regarded as home. Upon reaching adulthood, he resolved to alter the aimless, itinerant course of the family's history by asserting that he was, in fact, truly American. In an often-quoted 1939 letter to critic Horace Gregory, he states:

> Of mixed ancestry I felt from earliest childhood that America was the only home I could possibly call my own. I felt it was expressly founded for me, personally, and that it must be my first business in life to possess it; that only by making it my own from the beginning to my own day, in detail, should I have a basis for knowing where I stood. (*SL*, 185)

Although this statement refers specifically to the composition of *In the American Grain,* for the second edition of which Gregory was then writing a preface, it has broad, multifaceted applications to the poet's life. The sentiments he expresses in the letter, read in conjunction with his foreword to the 1925 text, imply that his "possession" of America was to be accomplished principally through language. Thus, in order to learn about the country's various founders and heroes, he turned directly to primary sources—their "letters, journals, and reports of happenings":

> Where I have found noteworthy stuff, bits of writing have been copied into the book for the taste of it. Everywhere I have tried to separate out from the original records some flavor of an actual peculiarity the character denoting shape [*sic*] which the unique force has given. . . . It has been my wish to draw from every source one thing, the strange phosphorus of the life, nameless under an old misappellation. (*IAG,* v)

In more personal terms, Williams' strategy for possessing America was twofold: he would create a spiritual and geographical locus of familial activity by permanently settling in the town where he had been born and, from this niche, would attempt to learn as much about his own ancestry as possible. He could, in this way, incorporate the vagaries of his family's past into the larger continuum of the nation's history and erect a stable foundation upon which his descendants could build. Yet, unlike Williams' research for *In the American Grain,* this task did not entail the use of libraries or dusty archives; it was instead an oral project, with information gleaned from familiar, living sources—his parents. According to an unpublished version of *Yes, Mrs. Williams,* the poet perceived his father and mother as "Adam and Eve . . . they seem to have come more or less . . . out of the earth. There were cousins, West Indian ladies—Benny—this one or that—but there was no other background. It didn't lead anywhere. This was the origin."[36] Williams' investigation of this origin involved piecing together the "vague rumors" his parents had heard about their ancestors, along with their own fragmentary impressions of the past, and weaving them into a cohesive whole. He would try, in the words of *Paterson,* to interrelate this chaotic "mass of detail . . . on a new ground, difficultly / . . . pulling the disparate together to clarify / and compress" (*P,* 20).

Given the dearth of available resources, the poet's undertaking was especially arduous and frustrating. In attempting to reconstruct the paternal side of his family's history, for example, he met with an absolute dead end. His grandmother, Emily Dickenson Wellcome, was an orphan, and thus had no knowledge of her progenitors or ethnic roots. This massive lacuna was further widened by the mystery surrounding her alleged first husband and the name Williams itself. Emily adamantly refused to discuss William George's father, who was reputed to have been either a minister's son or an ironworker (*A,* 167), curtly dismissing all questions about the subject with the statement, "The past is for those who lived in the past. Cessa!" (*P*, 239). At one point, she apparently revealed her first husband's identity to William George, but made him swear on the grave of his half-sister Rosita not to divulge the secret, and he never did. Williams was endlessly tantalized by this enigma; over the years it became an imaginal free space in which he could indulge his wildest romantic fantasies. In part 1 of the introduction to *Yes, Mrs. Williams*, for example, he speculates that since the surname of Emily's adoptive parents was Godwin, she may have had some contact with Percy Bysshe Shelley and other "supporters of the principle of free love. God knows the intimacies of my grandmother and the set that surrounded her in those years; we have only evidence of it in her devotion to the name of Godwin which she gave her [youngest] child" (*YMW*, 6).[37]

The potent appeal of this speculation lies in a possible link to a famous ancestor, none other than the romantic poet Percy Bysshe Shelley. The train of Williams' fantasy serves to create an alternate ancestry for himself, one which would significantly make him a direct descendant of the British literary tradition rather than its antagonist. In this regard, the fantasy closely corresponds to Freud's description of the way in which children fabricate "family romances" by replacing one or both parents—usually the father—with more exalted individuals.[38] Notwithstanding the absurdity of identifying his grandmother with Shelley (who died in 1822, most likely before Emily herself was born),[39] the fantasy reveals how desperately Williams desired to connect himself to the past and establish some sort of fixed heritage. Also, one cannot help but discern the shadowy presence of Ezra Pound as an impetus for the development of this theory. After all, what better way to put the Anglophilic grandnephew of Henry Wadsworth Longfellow in his place than to present oneself as a lineal descendant of the author of "Prometheus Unbound"? The sheer insubstantiality of the "Godwin connection" prevented Williams from ever staking his personal poetic identity upon that claim; however, he seems to never have entirely abandoned the theory. The mystery of his father's paternity haunted him until the end.

On a more pragmatic note, Williams also attempted—and dismally failed—to gather genealogical information from his father. Because William George had left England at the age of five, he remembered nothing about his birthplace or relatives. In the introduction to *Yes, Mrs. Williams*, the poet summarizes the frustration of his endeavor:

> All my life, I had been interested in my father's head, its size. He wore a 7½ hat. I frequently tried it on, its shape and general attitude facing the world. Who was he? He was too young when he quit England to remember anything and his own mother was adamant in her refusal to disclose what I most wanted to know. There is one daguerreotype showing a brilliant and self-confident smile on that small face, a picture showing a London photographer's label. That is all. He was an intelligent and handsome child. (*YMW*, 6)

Like the excerpt from the *Autobiography* quoted earlier, this passage divulges yet another facet of the paucity of information Williams associated with his father. A single daguerreotype of his happy, youthful face comprises the sole tangible artifact of an otherwise inaccessible past. The poet's description of his fascination with William George's hat poignantly illustrates his inability to penetrate beyond the stiff facade of his father's character and learn the secret of his identity.

Moreover, the poet found it difficult to communicate with the elder man due to his retiring habits. "My father was too English for me to be able to talk with him animal to animal" (*SL,* 127), he complained to Ezra Pound in 1932, some fourteen years after William George's death. But if the remark expresses regret over a lost opportunity for productive dialogue, it also places the burden of responsibility for that failure entirely on the figure of the father. The remoteness and strict formality Williams observed in his progenitor's character was typified by the clipped, precise, exasperatingly articulate style of his "pure St. Thomas English" (*YMW,* 14). The poet's negative reaction to his father's discourse, which forms the basis of his later hostility towards the British tradition itself, originated in his perception of it as a barrier to intimacy.

The only poem Williams addressed to his father before the elder man's death on Christmas Day, 1918, is suggestively entitled "Invitation." Originally published in *Al Que Quiere* (1917), the lyric was omitted for unknown reasons when that text was reprinted in both the *Complete Collected Poems* (1938) and the *Collected Earlier Poems* (1951). Although not a particularly memorable work, "Invitation" is nonetheless historically significant in that it marks the moment of Williams' conscious acknowledgment of Elena's primacy in his life and psyche. The piece attempts to summarize, through a process of careful enumeration, William George's contributions to the development of his son's character. As the opening lines indicate, the father's chief value for the poet appears to have been his discerning choice of a spouse:

> You who had the sense
> to choose me such a mother,
> you who had the indifference
> to create me,
> you who went to some pains
> to leave hands off me
> in the formative stages—
> (I thank you most for that, perhaps)
>
> but you who
> with an iron head, first
> fiercest and with strongest love
> brutalized me into strength,
> old dewlap,—

I have reached the stage
where I am teaching myself
to laugh.

Come on,

take a walk with me.[40]

The conciliatory gesture Williams makes in the concluding lines of the poem is tempered by the deeply ambivalent tone of the remarks that precede it. The qualities for which he thanks William George are largely negative—indifference, detachment, and a fierce, if well-intentioned, emotional brutalization. Lines 5–8 are freighted with an especially bitter irony: the poet compliments his father for a lack of contact, for leaving "hands off me / in the formative years," alluding possibly to his protracted travels in Central and South America, or to a more subtle, metaphorical distancing, then he adds the parenthetical comment: "I thank you most for that, perhaps." The positioning of the adverb "perhaps" here sharply undercuts the meaning of the preceding clause, and tersely conveys the submerged resentment the poet harbored against his father. Overall, the lyric implies that William George signified absence for the poet rather than a strong, supportive presence or role model. Even the hope of reconciliation held out by the title—an "invitation" to take a walk together—is compromised by a description Williams gives of the "walking tours" which he, his father, and his brother made on various summer vacations around the turn of the century in the memoir's introduction: "I remember how we used to take the road, fifty or sixty feet apart, not talking together for a half an hour, perhaps longer" (*YMW,* 34).

Thus, through a combination of natural affinity, historical circumstance, and paternal default, Elena became the vehicle for Williams' achievement of American identity. Yet, as *Yes, Mrs. Williams* amply demonstrates, the poet's task was still beset with substantial difficulties. Although Elena had access to a greater range of historical information than either William George or Emily, her knowledge of the past was also scattered and imperfect. But even so, she possessed one distinct advantage over her husband and mother-in-law: she loved to talk about the past, and divulged its details freely (except when it came to the sensitive question of her own age) to her son. Williams never succeeded in constructing a unified narrative out of the isolated bits of information his mother provided; however, through patient and persistent inquiry over the years, he managed to uncover a skeletal genealogy that formed the basis of a general historical understanding. In one of the memoir's italicized interpolations, Williams attempts to plot out his maternal lineage, but does not get very far before the family tree dissolves into uncertainty:

Figure 8. Elena, 131 West Passaic Avenue, Rutherford, ca. 1917

"Sorrow is my own yard"
("The Widow's Lament in Springtime")

> This "Contemporary" is my mother—
> Raquel Ellen Rose Hoheb
> whose mother was
> Meline Hurrard
> of Martinique and
> whose father was
> Solomon (I think) Hoheb,
> half brother of the Enriquez of ??
>
> (*YMW*, 60)

Interestingly, this information is presented in the form of a poetic fragment— incomplete, mysterious, evocative, but nonetheless a beginning. Elena serves as a bridge, the sole link spanning the generations, a "contemporary" to her son as well as a living remnant of the past. "I am the Surropa," she proudly exclaims in the memoir, "You know, what is left in the bottom of the bottle. I am the sediment. I am the last of the Mohicans" (*YMW*, 51).

As the equivocation concerning Elena's father in this "poem" indicates, her knowledge of his ancestral background was extremely hazy, most likely because she was only eight at the time of his death. Williams' account of her patrilineage in the memoir reflects this uncertainty; he qualifies his assertions with "apparently" and "most likely" to acknowledge their status as educated guesswork rather than fact:

> The Monsantos, Enriquezes, and Hohebs are all mixed up in the telling about them. Apparently the Hohebs came from Holland—Amsterdam most likely. Carlos tried for years to locate some connection, or even to trace the name, but without success of any sort. She [Elena] remembers oil portraits in Dutch costume. But Cousin Sissy hated old things and all were lost or destroyed finally. Hoheb, the father, was of a first marriage and the half brothers Enriquez were often in his hair. How many generations there had been of them in Puerto Rico and how they had mixed with the Spanish there is completely lost. (*YMW*, 53)

What is most striking about this passage is its pervasive sense of loss and rupture from the past—Williams' namesake Uncle Carlos seeking in vain for the origins of the name Hoheb, the paintings of Dutch ancestors "all . . . lost or destroyed," the family's history in Puerto Rico "completely lost." Furthermore, in investigating the maternal branch of Elena's ancestry, the poet discovered a similar rift separating past and present—a rift epitomized by a natural catastrophe:

> When Mt. Pelée [in Martinique] exploded in 1902, the last of the Hurrards in America are supposed to have been blown to eternity. So that the only ones continuing the blood are ourselves. They had a liqueur business in St. Pierre, so I have heard the rumor. Very good stuff, though I had never heard of it before—nor heard of it since: Hurrard & Cie. (*YMW*, 52–53)

This image of a violent eruption blotting out the past by extinguishing all of Elena's maternal relations became a powerful metaphor for Williams of the inaccessibility of history. As in the case of his father, he was once again confronted with a dead end, an impenetrable lava wall behind which the past and its attendant secrets were irretrievably entombed. The poet was thus thrust back upon the resources immediately at hand—in other words, upon Elena herself, stalwart survivor of the cataclysm of the past, sole transmitter of the "somewhat mythical" Hurrard bloodline to the United States. Though past generations of the family were "completely lost," she nonetheless was "still here" (*YMW*, 53). By recording her memories, Williams could prevent this misfortune from being repeated yet again. The fragility of Elena's solitary tie to an exotic island past enhanced her symbolic significance in the poet's eyes, as he states in the memoir's introduction:

> No way to speak of her other than by first setting up a sign, as in a dream, to the overwhelming beauty of the world and its overwhelming, such as the destruction of St. Pierre by the explosion of Mt. Pelée in 1902. Not that St. Pierre was so particularly beautiful—though such towns have their voluptuous plenty in spite of a certain heterogeneity of moral background. (*YMW*, 32)

The literal fact of Pelée's explosion is here transformed into a symbolic analogue of Elena's character. Moreover, as the first two lines of the passage indicate, the establishment of this "sign," which Williams indirectly ascribes to an unconscious process of condensation, comprises an essential prerequisite for speaking about her. He thus "dreams" an image of his mother, identifying her with the "overwhelming beauty of the world and its overwhelming." The poet's repetition of the word "overwhelming" in two antithetical contexts within this short phrase suggests that the existence and destruction of beauty are related aspects of a single phenomenon. By shifting the term's usage from adjective to noun, modifier to substantive, he reveals that the potential for violent eruption is inherently contained in the "overwhelming beauty" of the tropical setting itself. In its conflation of mother and landscape, the passage is reminiscent of Williams' description of Elena in the prologue to *Kora in Hell* as an "impoverished, ravished Eden." St. Pierre is a modern avatar of the paradisal garden, and its violent "overwhelming" reenacts the primal myth of the loss of Eden.

Elena incarnates America for the poet in two disparate ways: the heterogeneity and "voluptuous plenty" of her ethnic background typify the "melting pot" concept of the nation, and the fateful circumstances of her life—from her youth in Puerto Rico, to "three miraculous years" (*YMW*, 5) as an art student in Paris, to the profound disappointment of her return and emigration to suburban New Jersey—parallel the despoiling of the continent's natural beauty. Interestingly, Elena did not like the United States, and never considered herself an American; it was only through her son's imaginative reinterpretation of her life and character that she assumed this quasi-mythical status. In the memoir, she vehemently expresses disaffection with the place:

I never wanted to come to America. When my father was dead and my mother died, my brother asked me, Where do you want to go? To America? Noooo! To France? Yesss! I never wanted to come here, Never, never. And yet when I came back from France, I came here. And here I am. I was married here. I have lived here and probably I will die here. And rot here. brrr. I hate that. I hate it. But don't put me any monument [*sic*]. Put it to your father if you want, but not to me. Let me rot. Brr. No I can't think of it. (*YMW*, 96)

In this statement, Elena's strong-willed resentment is counterpointed by a feeling of helplessness at the hands of fate itself. As Williams learned in his conversations with her over the years, this was one of her most characteristic modes of self-description: the unfortunate individual thwarted by circumstances beyond her control. Although sympathetic to his mother's plight, the poet also understood that her assessment was not entirely accurate. In the italicized interpolation which "responds" to the above passage, he intimates that the difficulty of Elena's situation was exacerbated by her tendency to dwell on the past to the point of excluding the present: "Memories—old and sweet, the crushing turn, ghosts—associated though with the solid part of her life, children, home, possessions—never realized because of the mirage of the past—Little left of Martinique, but the stories of the Hibaros—the common people—proverbs" (*YMW*, 96). As much as he appreciated these stories and proverbs, Williams recognized the inherent danger of a loss of perspective and detachment from reality whereby the "solid part of her life" (significantly, the part with which he was associated) was supplanted by the "mirage of the past." The memoir's purpose is therefore twofold: to not only link the poet with previous generations of his family, but to reestablish Elena's connection to the present moment.

Another, even more cryptic interpolation, which occurs a few pages later in the text, also concerns Elena's spiritual detachment from her immediate surroundings. The sequence, though dreamlike in tone, is in fact a childhood reminiscence; the scene is the Bagellon house, a rambling estate on the outskirts of Rutherford where the Williamses lived when the poet and his brother were small. Elena, generically described as "the mother" (no possessive pronouns attached), gazes down from a balcony at the children playing in the yard. The pose is heavily symbolic: her physical separation from the boys denotes a profound alienation from their world. Though they are completely at home in this environment, she is culturally displaced and socially isolated:

Ten miles deep inside its sleeping form a little boy whom later she would fit into her hollowness, her son—preordained by chance—free to run, now that it was April, ran. His legs seemed to bounce by themselves under him, he scarcely knew they could go so fast—or that they were legs—He desired and, riding his pleasure, he arrived and took.

It was all in a great yard with a painted wooden fence of boards, cut out into a scroll design and painted green and red—that stood above his head—but he could peek through and see the people passing.

Behind him his smaller brother, six years old or less, came following while the mother leaned upon the balustrade of the balcony that encircled the house and watched them play.

> There above them, as they played, leaned nothing of America, but Puerto Rico, a foreign
> island in a tropical sea of earlier years—and Paris of the later Seventies. (*YMW,* 116)

The syntax of the final paragraph is especially curious. Williams omits the subject of the sentence, thereby equating his mother with two distant—and foreign—places that she dearly loved: Puerto Rico and Paris. The impersonality of this statement is thematically connected with the obscure reference which begins the passage: "Ten miles deep inside its sleeping form a little boy whom later she would fit into her hollowness, her son."[41] The womblike hollowness alluded to here, into which Williams is later "fit," signifies both the vicarious fulfillment of Elena's artistic ambitions through her son and his creation of an American identity through her. Though she herself, at least from the vantage point of the poet's childhood memory, possessed "nothing of America," she offered a starting point from which this identity could evolve.

The pathos of Elena's situation—her physical presence in a land she despised and was emotionally estranged from, as well as her reliance on the poet to change or at least mitigate those circumstances—is powerfully evoked in one of the memoir's most lyrical interpolations:

> Neither one thing or the other, grotesques were drawn on the walls of grottos, half human,
> half leaves—whatever the fancy made obligatory to fate. So in her life, neither one or the
> other, she stands bridging two cultures, three regions of the world almost without speech—
> her life spent in that place completely out of her choice almost, to her, as the Brobdingna-
> gans to Gulliver. So gross, so foreign, so dreadful, to her obstinate spirit, that has neither
> submitted nor mastered, leaving her in a néant of sounds and sense—Only her son, the
> bridge between herself and a vacancy as of the sky at night, the terrifying emptiness of non-
> entity. (*YMW,* 94)

The vital reciprocity of the mother-son relationship is illustrated by Williams' usage of the term "bridge" to describe both their roles. Elena bridges "two cultures and three regions of the world," and thus links the poet to a crucial, if ill-defined, past, whereas he "bridges" the gap between her and the contemporary world of Rutherford, thereby protecting her from "the terrifying emptiness of non-entity" caused by social isolation. As the hyperbolic tone of this phrase implies, Williams appears to have momentarily succumbed to his mother's penchant for romanticizing her plight; her sentimental self-image of passive victimization her converges with his own imaginative reading of her character. What is most puzzling about the passage, however, is not the melodramatic description of Elena's "obstinate spirit that has neither submitted nor mastered," but the assertion that she stands "almost without speech," when the memoir itself is filled with evidence to the contrary. Moreover, it was in his mother's hybrid dialect—that curious melange of colloquial expressions, foreign words, and nonstandard syntax—that the poet found his key to the possession of America. In contrast to the heavily Anglicized diction of her hus-

band, Elena's speech represented the linguistic analogue of the New World's
ethnic diversity. Quite possibly, the phrase refers to her condition shortly after
arriving in the United States in 1882. As she recalls in the memoir:

> When I first came here, I knew some words, but no more than that. . . . When you are learning a language many funny things happen. I can remember how it impressed me when Julie Monsanto said, "What a cheek!" I thought that was awful funny. I can still see her. What a cheek! And they would say "boids." At first I didn't know what they were saying. Then I found out it was "birds." I thought that was the way to say it because in St. Thomas they would say "bierrds." (*YMW*, 8, 121)

Elena's delight in the nuances of colloquial English constituted an important impetus in her acquisition of the language and incorporation of it into her unique style of discourse. For Williams, his mother's speech signified a triumphant fusion of Old and New World elements into a distinctly American entity, a synthesis which she was unfortunately unable to achieve in other aspects of her life: "An exotic little figure. I can see her treading carefully across the frozen snow she never learned as a child to walk on balancedly. Pathetic, but resistant—resilient even, unwilling to look on, walking forth anyway, walking" (*YMW*, 95). This anecdote of Elena's determined attempt to walk on a slippery, unfamiliar surface has a symbolic resonance, illustrating that she did in fact make an active, if unsuccessful, attempt at cultural adaptation.

Williams' admiration for her resilience and tenacity manifests itself most clearly in his fascination with her language. In one of the "Writing Plans" for the memoir, his description of Elena's speech sounds remarkably similar to his definition of the American idiom: "[It is] not English, but a new start from a new base."[42] This implicit connection between Elena and Williams' poetic language expands her already considerable sphere of aesthetic influence. Not only is she her son's muse, but the literal wellspring of the American idiom. In an unpublished draft of the memoir, Williams copies out one of his mother's sayings (recorded on pages 41 and 89 of *Yes, Mrs. Williams*) in stanzaic form, as if it were a poem:

> Caracoles! I have danced, danced—
> like a hurricane—and they were
> always foreigners

This passage is followed by several notations:

> Speech (actual)
> actual three line poem
> 3 versions
> _____
> Remembered:
> Corrected:

Actual note refound:

Where I got my line?[43]

These notations, particularly the stunning last sentence, provide direct evidence that Williams' interest in Elena's speech was closely allied with the development and formal evolution of his own poetry. The cadences of her eccentric, multilingual dialect ("Can you see with that light?" he asks her at one point in the memoir, and she responds, "Much, yes! with a bow" [*YMW*, 120]) comprise both an inspiration and immediate source of his poetic measure. Additional confirmation of this intriguing connection is offered by another draft of the memoir wherein a letter Elena wrote to Williams from her summer cottage on the Connecticut shoreline has been typed into a poem, with a marginal comment—this time not in Williams' hand—stating, "Bill's technique":

> As I don't want to write a letter
> for just asking a question, I say
> please inquire from Sonny where he
> left or put the ax—he used sometimes.
> Nobody else but he had it. If he
> had only given it to me to keep.[44]

The rhythm and tone of this "poem" bear an uncanny resemblance to Williams' own lyric, "This is just to Say." Yet what is most revealing about the passage is the anonymous marginalia of one of the poet's many typists, which indicates that the similarities between Elena's language and the poet's were tangible and obvious enough to be discerned by others. Williams' own awareness of this connection deepened and perpetuated the intense emotional bond which he had felt for his mother since birth, and compelled him to return again and again to the composition of her "biography," despite the persistent problems he experienced with it. For Williams, Elena represented the essential generative source of life, of love, of language—of poetry itself. His famous response to the question "But this language of yours, where does it come from?" asked by an "obvious Britisher" at a City College of New York lecture in the early 1950s is thus somewhat of a misstatement. "From the mouths of Polish mothers," he retorted; however, the Polish mothers, encountered during his long obstetrical practice, came later. The first mouth out of which Williams' American language came was that of his own French, Spanish, Dutch, and Puerto Rican mother, Elena.

6

His Mother's Son: *Paterson*

> *one unlike the other, twin*
> *of the other, conversant with eccentricities*
> *side by side*
>
> Paterson, Book 1

In 1939, Williams wrote enthusiastically to Louis Untermeyer concerning his plans for the book he had been preparing about his mother over at least the previous decade: "I hope to make her biography . . . one of my major works—if not *the* major one."[1] This conception of Elena's biography as a potential magnum opus is both puzzling and paradoxical, since the end result of the poet's labor, published twenty years later in the form of *Yes, Mrs. Williams,* occupies a distinctly minor place in his canon. The complete incongruity of the ambition articulated in the letter and the slender, fragmentary volume Williams ultimately produced, which, by his own admission, was "not . . . a good book,"[2] raises several questions: What happened? Why was the poet unable to bring the project to its intended fruition? And, most significantly, what relationship does the memoir have to his true magnum opus, *Paterson?*

According to Mike Weaver, in the two decades that elapsed between Williams' letter to Untermeyer and the appearance of *Yes, Mrs. Williams,* "most of its preoccupations with family history had found their way into *Paterson,* freshly prompted by his visit to Puerto Rico in the spring of 1941."[3] Indeed, a dramatic displacement of creative energy and source material seems to have occurred between Elena's biography and the epic in the early forties. This shift can be partly attributed to the poet's mounting frustration with his inability to find a suitable form for representing his mother's life; however, since both texts stem from a common impulse—namely, Williams' quest for origins—the reasons underlying his reorientation of priorities are deeper and more intimately connected to an evolving sense of selfhood. In giving *Paterson* precedence over the memoir, Williams was taking the final step in his possession of America, attempting to achieve, through the imaginative fusion of man and city, the fulfillment of a New World identity which had its essential source in the figure of Elena. Because the diversity of his ethnic background mirrored that of the Passaic region itself, this conflation of poet and place was especially appropriate: "By the middle of the century—the mills had drawn a heterogeneous population. There were in 1870, native born 20,711, *which would of course include children of foreign parents;* foreign 12,868 of whom 237 were French, 1,420 German, 3,343 English . . . 5,124 Irish, 879 Scotch, 1,360 Hollanders and 170 Swiss" (*P,* 10; emphasis mine).

Despite its patriarchal title, *Paterson* neither excludes nor denies the power of the female; in fact, the invisible binding presence which makes possible the intergenerational succession from father to son is the mother: "Oh most powerful connective, a bead / to lie between continents through / which a string passes" (*P,* 179). Yet, in terms of the Oedipus myth, by producing a male heir the mother also becomes a divisive influence, an object of desire interposed between spouse and child. No such antagonism exists within the poem, however, because the roles of son and father merge in the figure of Williams himself. As in Wordsworth's statement, "The child is the father to the man,"[4] in *Paterson* it is only through the poet's filial acknowledgment of the spiritual and cultural "connective" supplied by Elena that he can attain the authoritative position of American patriarch. In large measure, then, Paterson is his mother's son, and *Yes, Mrs. Williams* is the maternal subtext and complement of the long poem. Like the elements of air and water described in book 1, each work is "unlike the other," yet simultaneously "twin of the other," and when examined "side by side" their respective eccentricities become a source of mutual elucidation.

Evoked by brief phrases, allusions, and place names, Elena's presence floats unobtrusively throughout all five books of *Paterson.* At various points in the text, such as book 3, section 3, it is possible to identify her voice directly: "Let me see, Puerto Plata is / the port of Santo Domingo" (*P,* 136). In general, however, Williams' technique is far more subtle and opaque: he invokes Elena by encoding distinctive features of her character into descriptions of himself. The poet thus obliquely acknowledges his indebtedness to her through a process of symbolic incorporation, a melding of individual traits akin to that which occurs in *Yes, Mrs. Williams.* Although she is an avatar of the poem's female principle, Elena's status differs from that of the "Innumerable women, each like a flower" mentioned in book 1, women who by their very multiplicity stand in external, albeit loving, relation to the "one man—like a city" (*P,* 7). This particular flower, Raquel Helene *Rose,* exists, in contrast, within the figure of Paterson, forming a crucial, animating component of the man/city himself.

The first allusion to Elena in *Paterson* appears midway through book 1, prompted by Williams' recollection of the rough landing his seaplane made off the coast of Haiti in 1941. This memory engenders thoughts of the family's history and his own violent rupture from the past:

(Thence Carlos had fled in the 70's
leaving the portraits of my grandparents,
the furniture, the silver, even the meal
hot upon the table before the Revolutionists
coming in at the far end of the street.)

                                              (*P*, 26)

Williams then makes a quick associative leap from past to present, shifting his thoughts from his namesake uncle, the surgeon Carlos Hoheb, to Elena herself by inserting a letter from "T." (Alva Turner) which begins: "I was over to see my mother today" (*P*, 26). While some of the letter's details do not correspond exactly to the poet's situation, its depiction of the mother-son relationship is quite apt. The mother is characterized as an aged and sickly individual who, despite her debility, persists in "always trying to do something for her children," especially "T.," whom "she thinks more of . . . than any child she has" (*P*, 26–27). This favoritism causes him to be protective of her, as when he discovers her mending his trousers and gently admonishes: "Mother, you can't do that for me, with your crippled head" (*P*, 26).

Like "T.'s" mother, Elena was also crippled, both in body and, towards the end of her life, in mind. There is, however, a still deeper symbolic connection at work here. Several pages before Turner's letter, Williams presents a description of yet another "crippled head," that of Peter the dwarf:

> His face from the upper part of his forehead to the end of his chin, measures *twenty-seven inches* . . . his eyes and nose are remarkably large and prominent, chin long and pointed. . . . His body is twenty-seven inches in length. . . . He has never been able to sit up, as he cannot support the enormous weight of his head; but he is constantly in a large cradle, with his head supported in pillows. (*P*, 10)

Throughout *Paterson*, the deformed dwarf represents an analogue of the poet, so that the resemblance between the mother's "crippled head" and that of Peter implicitly includes the figure of Williams. This subliminal association is strengthened in book 2 when the dwarf undergoes a metamorphosis, becoming a grotesque:

> As there appears a dwarf, hideously deformed—
> he sees squirming roots trampled
> under the foliage of his mind by the holiday
> crowds as by the feet of the straining
> minister. From his eyes sparrows start and
> sing. His ears are toadstools, his fingers have
> begun to sprout leaves (his voice is drowned
> under the falls)

                                              (*P*, 83)

In the *Yes, Mrs. Williams* manuscripts at Yale, the poet uses the title "A Grotesque" for at least six different drafts of his mother's anecdotes, suggesting that he closely allied her with this concept;[5] yet only one such reference survives in the published version of the text: "Neither one thing or the other, grotesques were drawn on the walls of grottos, half human, half leaves—whatever the fancy made obligatory to fate. So in her life, neither one or the other, she stands bridging two cultures, three regions of the world, almost without speech" (*YMW,* 94). This description of Elena's ambivalent cultural status— that she is "neither one thing or another"—parallels the dwarf's transformation from the human to vegetative in which his original features remain discernible, but are nonetheless changed ("From his eyes sparrows start and / sing. . . . his fingers have / begun to sprout leaves"). The grotesqueness of both figures lies in their bridging of two distinct realms, with the alienating effect of belonging to neither. But the most significant similarity between the two passages is that, as a result of their circumstances, both individuals are denied language: Elena stands "almost without speech" and the dwarf's voice is "drowned under the falls." The true horror of the grotesque then, for Williams, is silence; as the lines immediately following the dwarf's metamorphosis warn:

> Poet, poet! sing your song quickly! or
> not insects but pulpy weeds will blot out
> your kind.

(P, 83)

The elaborate network of correspondences linking Turner's letter, Elena, Peter the dwarf, and Williams typifies the subjective, highly associative logic which governs the overall structure of *Paterson.* The inclusion of diverse details, as well as their exact placement within the text's collage, is determined by the progression of the poet's own thoughts. The unity of its discrete pieces ("Make it of *this,* this / this, this, this, this" [*P,* 141]), while not always apparent to the reader, derives from the stream of the man/city's consciousness.

Another, more clearly identifiable example of Williams' incorporation of Elena's character traits into depictions of himself occurs in book 1, section 3, the lyric beginning, "How strange you are, you idiot!" As the deprecating direct address of the opening line indicates, the poet's strategy is dialogic; the conversation, however, is internalized, conducted between divergent aspects of the self. Williams playfully derides his artistic pretensions of "mastery" and immortality, juxtaposing his ephemeral existence with the cyclical processes of natural regeneration, embodied in the blooming of the "livid rose." Not only will the rose outlast the poet, it will literally "overtop" him in death when, buried beneath the earth, he shall "no more speak, or / taste or even be" (*P,* 30). The response to this morbid observation, signalled by the narrative shift from second to first person, acknowledges the fallacy of the speaker's previous presumption of "mastery," but simultaneously implies a refusal to abandon the pursuit of that goal: "My whole life has hung too long upon a partial victory" (*P,* 30). By referring to his endeavor as a "partial victory" rather than a partial defeat, the poet emphasizes its positive aspects; yet the impetus to achieve complete "victory" over nature is quickly deflated by the complacent attitude he expresses in the succeeding stanza:

> But, creature of the weather, I
> don't want to go any faster than
> I have to go to win
>
> (*P*, 30)

The poet's emotions are, like the weather, variable and inconstant; moreover, having articulated these contrary sentiments, he feels no need to clarify or reconcile them, but instead thrusts that responsibility back onto "you," his other half (and also, by implication, onto the reader), issuing the cryptic imperative: "Music it for yourself." This awkward, ungrammatical statement, in which the noun "music" has been transformed into a verb meaning something on the order of "to sound it out," is in fact a variation of one of Elena's favorite adages, "Figure to yourself." Williams employs this saying in "From My Notes about My Mother" as part of his rationale for the choppy, nonnarrative style of the memoir, which mimics his family's characteristically indirect manner of discourse:

> Perhaps my way of telling you this isn't exactly what you might prefer or expect, but in this family you are expected to understand what is said and interpret, as essential to the telling, the way in which it is told—for some reason which you will know is of the matter itself. That is to picture it. "Figure to yourself," as my mother would often say—obviously translated directly from the French.[6]

In effect, Williams "translates" his mother's original translation from the French, creating an aphorism uniquely suited to the purposes and contexts of his American poem. By substituting the term "music" for "figure," he shifts the emphasis of his injunction from the visual to the aural, and suggests that the relationship between his conflicting emotions is contrapuntal—that together they comprise complementary strands of a single, euphonic whole.

At this point in the lyric the dialogue abruptly ceases, and a third-person narration begins. The change in point of view does not, however, signify a corresponding change in subject; rather, the "you" and "I" of the initial conversation have converged in the figure of "he." The poet is at home, an environment of mundane particulars (a stray hairpin, linoleum, lavender lotion) that is at once reassuring and tedious. After musing upon a time when he will no longer "speak or taste or even be," he experiences a renewed appreciation for the information provided by the senses, and focuses his entire attention on them. Because he is alone, and presumably unobserved, the poet can indulge in idle activities, such as intently and unselfconsciously watching his thumb roll "about the tip of his left index finger" (*P*, 30); the irony of Williams' presentation lies in exposing this private moment to public view, so that the poet's utter absorption in these trivial actions becomes additional confirmation of just how strange and idiotic he really is.

In these stanzas, Williams systematically explores one sense after the other, moving from touch ("He picked up a hairpin from the floor / and stuck it in his ear . . .") to sight ("The melting snow / dripped from the cornice by his window / 90 strokes a minute—") to smell ("his hands / strong of a lotion he had used / not long since"), and finally to hearing ("the faint filing sound" made by the motion of his thumb). But in the center of this progression he describes a phenomenon which, though tangentially connected to sight, has more to do with the "mind's eye," or imagination:

> He descried
> in the linoleum at his feet a woman's
> face
>
> (*P*, 30)

This momentary "vision" of a face in the linoleum is a familiar trick played by the senses, a metamorphosis of the inanimate to animate, sparked by the unconscious association of a pattern or shape in the object itself with an image in the mind of the perceiver. Williams' reference to the phenomenon may have been intended to illustrate how the senses serve as stimuli for the imagination; in addition, it establishes a substantive link between mother and son. After breaking her hip in the early thirties, Elena was unable ever to walk again and, as a result, spent most of the last two decades of her life confined to bed. She amused herself in a variety of ways: reading, observing the seasonal changes and continual parade of human activity outside her window, and reminiscing about the past; however, as her cataracts worsened, she was eventually deprived of most of these diversions as well. Elena thus grew increasingly dependent upon an innate visionary capacity, which manifested itself in a preoccupation with dreams and the fanciful transformation of her all-too-familiar surroundings:

> She saw faces in the fringes of rugs and curtains as she sat with unfocused eyes in contemplation which, when you went to look directly at them, disappeared. Everywhere, faces, beautiful and grotesque made by a stray thread in a woven fabric, in a pattern of wallpaper— faces, staring, in contemplation—children, madonnas. Lions and also dogs.[7]

The poet's vision of a face at his feet, combined with the apparent purposelessness of his other actions, suggests that, like Elena, he too is confined in a severely restrictive environment and resorts to similarly imaginative means to alleviate his boredom and help pass the time. His ultimate escape, however, comes not from immersion in the minutiae of sense experience, but from complete detachment from objective reality. This transition is indicated by a sudden loss of hearing; the acute sensitivity which allowed the poet to perceive the faint noise made by his thumb and forefinger only a line earlier vanishes without warning ("of / earth his ears are full, there is no sound"). The imagery of this line links Paterson the man with the mythical giant embedded in the local landscape, but also evokes the inevitability of death and man's final resting place in the earth.[8] Confronted once again with the troubling prospect of his own mortality, Paterson creates a hyperbolic fantasy of bardic power:

> :And his thoughts soared
> to the magnificence of imagined delights
> where he would probe
>
> as into the pupil of an eye
> as through a hoople of fire, and emerge
> sheathed in a robe
>
> streaming with light

(P, 31)

As James E. B. Breslin has observed, this passage is comic in tone; conceding "no tension between dream and reality, Paterson becomes the bacchic seer . . . [and thus] slips into the romantic mode, another false start."[9] The "romantic mode" was one Williams perennially associated with his mother— her nostalgic aesthetic, tales of Paris in the 1870s, thwarted ambitions of greatness and, above all, her rarified and sublime concept of the artist. "A poet to me is transfigured to the ideal, soar[ing] to the lofty strain of the heart and soul," she wrote once in a letter to her son; his task is "to bring us the beautiful emotions our sensitive inner soul craves."[10] In his youth, Williams was deeply influenced by these ethereal values, and their lingering appeal is evident in his lyrical description of "the magnificence of imagined delights," though counterbalanced by a mature recognition of their unreality. His repetition of the verb "probe," for example, allies this exalted image of the poet garbed "in a robe / streaming with light" with the unflattering depiction that appears earlier in the passage; both are differeng phases of the same idiotic sensibility. The "shocking" and "disgusting"[11] act of probing around the inside of one's ear with a hairpin is rendered innocuous through a transformation of the literal into the figurative—Paterson probes "*as* into the pupil of an eye / *as* through a hoople of fire" (*P,* 31). These similes distance the actions described, safely removing them from the realm of physical reality.

The poet's metaphorical identification of his thoughts with trees "from whose leaves streaming with rain / his mind drinks of desire" in the subsequent lines signals the beginning of yet another movement within the lyric. The Blakean vision gradually fades, and Paterson is reconnected to his immediate environs, instilled with a new, more positive sense of selfhood that allows him to confidently assess his present status and accomplishments. The point of view shifts once again, reverting to the conversational style of the lyric's beginning, with the crucial difference that it is now a monologue rather than a dialogue. The antagonistic voice which earlier addressed the poet as "you" has been silenced, suggesting a successful reconciliation of dissonant elements within the ego. Although "I" poses a series of insistent questions throughout the passage, they are rhetorical in nature, and receive no response:

> Who is younger than I?
>   The contemptible twig?
> That I was? stale in mind
>   whom the dirt
>
> recently gave up? Weak
>   to the wind.
> Gracile?
>
> (*P*, 31)

This comparison between the tree and "contemptible twig" juxtaposes the poet's present circumstances with those of his youth; rather than dwelling on the imminence of death, he enumerates the hard-won advantages of maturity. In contrast to the "mere stick that has / twenty leaves" (*P*, 32), he has mass, strength, solidity, and well-developed roots, and thus can haughtily exclaim: "I stand and surpass / youth's leanness." Another aspect of the poet's "convolutions" is his exploration and mapping of the "green and / dovegrey countries" of his own mind, an inner world which the twig, in its narrowness, does not even know exists. Williams describes the relationship between past and present in terms of organic growth—the tree's development of annular rings around the original twig:

> I enclose it and
>   persist, go on.
>
> Let it rot, at my center.
>   Whose center? . . .
>
> My surface is myself
> Under which
>
> to witness, youth is
>   buried. Roots?
>
> Everybody has roots.
>
> (*P*, 32)

The imagery of incorporation, read in conjunction with the three previous allusions to Elena, suggests that the passage is a tacit acknowledgement of her influential role in Williams' development. In particular, the equivocations, "my center / whose center?" and "My surface is myself / under which / to witness, youth is / buried," imply the poet's recognition of the "otherness" of his origins, a disparity between the tree's superficial, mature appearance and the animating core from which it sprang. "Everybody" indeed "has roots," but the pervasiveness of Elena's presence in the lyric—the remembered adage, the face descried in the linoleum, the image of the poet "transfigured to the ideal"—intimates that in Williams' case, these roots are strongly maternal.

As the lyric's repeated references to mortality demonstrate, the subject was very much on Williams' mind during the composition of *Paterson*. Book 1 was published in 1946, when the poet was sixty-three; book 5 appeared twelve years later, when he was seventy-five. But it was not only the prospect of his own demise that troubled Williams. The forties were the last years of his mother's life, and throughout the decade—until 7 October 1949, to be precise—he watched, with a mixture of awe and profound apprehension, her struggle against the inevitable. The atmosphere in which he wrote books 1–3 of the epic were pervaded by anxiety and the threat of imminent loss, stemming from the dissolution of his sole remaining tied to the past—his mother. Moreover, Elena's decline was a slow and uneven one; she would periodically sink into unconcsciousness and seem on the verge of death, and then, almost miraculously, recover. It was a time of morbid uncertainty and prolonged stress for the poet, of helpless waiting punctuated by flashes of hope and despair. On Good Friday, 1949, some six months before Elena died, he wrote to Ezra Pound:

> For the past week I've been watching Mother getting ready to die—in her 93rd year. She's not dead yet, not that one, but she's only conscious by moments. That's all she needs, moments, in which to assert herself in her own particular way—by sitting bolt upright in bed (a thing she hasn't done in ten years) and telling off the really wonderful British couple who, "hearts of oak," are caring for her—by God's word. It's a sight all right, no question about that. . . . But what a fight![12]

According to an unpublished version of the *Autobiography,* the poet's deathwatch actually began some seven years earlier, when Elena was hospitalized at the end of 1941. After visiting her on New Year's Day, 1942, with Ann and Irving Taylor, the British couple mentioned in the above letter to Pound, Williams returned home and made the following notes:

> The beauty and exhilaration expressed on her face before impending death astonished and reassured me. I drank at it eagerly. It seemed the face of a believer. She had been unhappy so long, so miserably distressed, in such pain—and no mind left to stabilize her, nothing left but what spirit she could muster to complain or drive at me with a momentary fire of anger. I was disheartened—not to say disgusted and embittered. Hatred before the spectacle she presented, a horrible body and a mind quite as horrible, obstinate, vindictive, suspicious of those to whom she was most beholden—but the summative finality of death is impressive, that it could bring out something of loveliness from that wreckage still leaves me inspired. . . .

I could see . . . death, the lover to whom she was giving herself completely and with satisfaction—a satisfaction I have never seen in her face during my entire lifetime. . . . Intensely selfish in her ecstatic moment, all release, as if she had never loosed herself to love—for I know it in my own heart what she was, she had cut the bonds and was leaving us.[13]

This narrative depicts Elena in a moment which the poet mistakenly believed was her last: the "finality of death" presses upon her, and in preparation for that moment, she has already "cut the bonds" of earthly attachment, leaving her loved ones behind. Williams' response to the scene combines fascination and repugnance; Elena has become for him a universal symbol of the horrible but lovely "wreckage" of a human life. On the one hand, he regards her as a guide; her behavior and outlook, as she stands poised on the threshold of the unknown, "inspires" him. Her mood of exhilaration assuages his own fears of death, and thus he drinks at it "eagerly." Yet, on the other hand, he is also disgusted by the degenerative changes of his mother's body and mind, and considers her a lamentable "spectacle." Although he never openly admits it, resentment and a sense of abandonment are crucial elements in the poet's emotional response to Elena's impending demise. In characterizing death as a lover to whom she gives herself completely, Williams implicitly places himself in the role of a rival suitor, whose quest is unsuccessful. His embitterment derives largely from jealousy that the love she "had never loosed herself to" in life is now released, selfishly directed towards something in which he has no part. The vehement statement, "for I know it in my own heart what she was," conveys how genuinely wounded and surprised he is by this development—at finding himself jilted, supplanted in his mother's affections by death itself.

Interestingly, the narrative has a postscript written several days later, after it became evident that this was not to be the occasion of Elena's death:

Following that New Year's farewell—there was the recovery. The drowsiness and slow deterioration with occasional flashes of memory:

"Once I was on the ferryboat and there was a man there with a little girl with sore eyes that he was taking to the doctor in New York. Her eyes were all inflamed and covered with matter. He took out his handkerchief. It was black, black as if he had used it to wipe the floor. He wet it with his saliva and cleaned her eyes with it. I suppose it didn't do her any harm! I was struck by it."

And love—before her eyes! Before her injured eyes, to the last breath, dogging her steps to the very end.[14]

These cyclical bouts of "dying" and recovery, which recurred several times during the forties, deepened Williams' awareness of the tenacity with which Elena clung to life. The vividness of her momentary returns to consciousness and epiphanic recollection of distant, mundane memories—such as that of the man and sick child aboard the ferry—constituted a powerful lesson for him. Through his mother, the poet realized that memory was a vivifying resource, a potent charm against death. Her example provided the inspiration for one of his most famous lyrics, the "descent" passage in book 2:

> The descent beckons
> as the ascent beckoned
> Memory is a kind
> of accomplishment
> a sort of renewal
> even
> an initiation, since the spaces it opens are new
> places
> inhabited by hordes
> heretofore unrealized
>
> (*P*, 77)

The context in which this lyric appears offers yet another illustration of the way in which Williams encodes aspects of his mother's character within himself. Having ascended to the summit of Garrett Mountain, Paterson is about to begin his descent homeward; the literal downward journey, however, assumes symbolic connotations of the "descent" from middle to old age. Day's end corresponds to life's end, and the poet begins musing upon the "nul" that "defeats it all"—death. The lyric is immediately preceded by a proverb which, like the beginning of the "How strange you are, you idiot" passage in book 1, contrasts the seasonal regeneration of nature with man's mortality:

> But Spring shall come and flowers will bloom
> and man must chatter of his doom . . .
>
> (*P*, 77)

The poem challenges this clichéd formulation of doom by proposing a constructive alternative to such futile "chatter"—the act of remembering one's past. The inherently optimistic view that memory is in itself an "accomplishment" and "renewal" can be directly traced to Elena. Throughout *Yes, Mrs. Williams,* the poet presents numerous examples of his mother's habit of giving herself "mental exercises—anything to pass the time."[15] She would recall, for instance, with great specificity and painstaking attention to detail, the layout and furnishings of her childhood home in Mayagüez, or attempt to enumerate the names of all her acquaintances there:

> Today just to pass the time, I was trying to remember all the people that were in Mayagüez, when the Dodds were living in Ponce. They were all foreigners. Merle de Lauris, very fine people. Mr. Merle was a tall man. I remember as a child I used to admire him. Miss Merle married some Italian count. I can't remember his name. I was trying to squeeze my mind. (*YMW*, 43–44)

The act of "squeezing" one's mind, plundering its rich storehouse of memories, impressed Williams as a creative response to the plight of old age—

a means of sustaining interest in, and connection to, life itself. In a 1948 letter to Charles Abbott, he commented on this phenomenon:

> Cheer up! . . . and be sure no matter what phase is ending and what beginning, the next one, with proper respect to ourselves, will always contain as much of interest as the last. I have this from my mother at ninety-two [actually one hundred and one]. I am amazed at her ability to find *some*thing of interest, even if it has to be hallucinations, in every moment of her life.[16]

This reference to the productive use Elena made of her hallucinations indirectly clarifies Williams' paradoxical characterization of memory in the lyric as a process of simultaneous "renewal" and "initiation." His assertion that memory serves not only as a means of recapturing the past but also of making discoveries in the present—opening up "new places / inhabited by hordes / heretofore unrealized"—stems from a recognition of the integral role which imagination plays in the endeavor. Through the faculty of memory, experience is transformed and reshaped according to an individual's subjective perception of it; in this respect, the act of remembering resembles the creation of fantasies. Both are processes of conscious fictionalizing, which differ not so much in substance as in their degree of detachment from objective reality. The poet's use of the term "hordes" to describe the inhabitants of these mysterious "new places" reinforces the link between memory and fantasy and also points to his mother as the informing presence behind the lyric as a whole. In a broad sense, the words "hordes" connotes an image of the mind teeming with thoughts which are animate but not individuated, a swarming human mass moving across an indefinite interior landscape. Although the image itself is vague and impersonal, its origin lies in one of Elena's most bizarre visions, which Williams recorded in the poem "Another Old Woman":

> Throngs visit her:
> We are at war
> with Mexico—to
> please her fancy—
>
> A cavalry column
> is deploying
> over a lifeless terrain
> to impress!

(CLP, 205)

The "throngs" of cavalry soldiers that Elena saw in her mind's eye were, in the poet's estimation, no more or less fantastic than the shadowy figures recalled from her youth in Mayagüez; in fact, the exercise of reminiscing about the past facilitated these inner visions by honing her powers of creative visualization and opening up previously unexplored channels of the mind. In this way, "a world lost" yields naturally to "a world unsuspected," as the imagination beckons and beguiles the individual to enter the mind's increasingly remote reaches. Significantly, Williams never regarded his mother's hallucinations as evidence of senility, but rather an expedient, albeit extreme, "compensation" for her failing eyesight (*YMW,* 19). The notion of compensation, of the mind's ability to transform apparent loss into gain, underlies the entire "descent" passage. Furthermore, the philosophy that "no defeat is made up entirely of defeat," while universal in application, was arrived at inductively through the poet's observation of one particularly compelling example—Elena. Her resilience in coping with the numerous misfortunes which befell her over the course of a long lifetime offered incontrovertible proof for him that:

> The descent
>   made up of despairs
>   and without accomplishment
> realizes a new awakening   :
>   which is a reversal
> of despair.

(*P,* 78)

The story of Elena's defeat—the financial constraints which cut short her Parisian education and prevented the fulfillment of her grand artistic ambitions—was one Williams knew well; indeed, it formed the core of her personal mythos, and had been inculcated in him since childhood. As she characterized her fate in a 1921 letter to her eldest son, "In [all] the vital things in my life, when near getting the goals I desired—like unto Tantalus, it would be so, that I could not reach them. Like being suddenly awakened from a nice dream without seeing the end."[17] The poet assessed and reinterpreted this myth of defeat many times throughout his life, questioning the veracity of his mother's romantic self-representation, and ultimately distilled its essence into a single, late poem entitled "The Painting":

> Starting from black or
> finishing
> with it
>
> her defeat stands
> a delicate
> lock
>
> of blonde hair dictated
> by the
> Sorbonne
>
> this was her last
> clear
> act

a portrait of a
child
to which

she was indifferent
beautifully
drawn

then she married and
moved to
another country

(PB, 27)

The abstract nature of Elena's defeat is concretized, made palpable, in the poem through the evocation of a single object—one of her last portraits, painted after her unhappy return to Puerto Rico from Paris in 1880. Williams does not systematically describe the work, commenting only that the image is "beautifully drawn" and that the child's delicate lock of blonde hair conforms to the contemporary aesthetic conventions "dictated by the Sorbonne." Rather, the painting's significance is symbolic; it functions in the Poundian sense of a "luminous detail," a brilliant moment of clarity which emerges out of, and subsequently fades into, indeterminate darkness, "starting from black or / finishing with it." The portrait, as a historical artifact, represents Elena's "last clear act," the final moment of purposefulness and independent direction in her life which preceded the capitulation of her artistic aspirations. The poem's last lines, "then she married and moved to / another country," poignantly evoke the abandonment of these goals; she marries a man instead of the dream of artistic greatness, and emigrates to a foreign country, leaving her idealized vision behind. Yet the poem's conclusion is not completely pessimistic since the end of Elena's youthful dream also heralds a new beginning, a fresh start in a new place—in other words, entry into another phase of life.

The romanticism of "The Painting" reveals the extent to which Williams was influenced by his mother's mythos of defeat; its power continued to resonate in his psyche long after her death. The impact it produced on him as a young man is illustrated by a letter written in 1915, at least forty years prior to the poem, in which he attempts to mitigate her sense of personal failure by explaining that a disparity always exists between aspiration and achievement:

Dearest Old Silly Mommy,

Of course you're a failure—what good would you be if you didn't think yourself a failure? It's the fineness of your appreciations alone that makes you discontented with yourself. You *are*—you exist, you feel, you aspire, you love and you hate—the deep inexplicable burning in your innermost heart is real—it isn't a sham—it isn't false—therefore how can you really dare to tell me you are a failure? Of course you wish you had painted great pictures—you wish you had followed your voice—you wish you had married differently—yes you do, at

Figure 9. Portrait of a Niece in Mayagüez by Raquel Helene Rose Hoheb Williams, ca. 1880

"This was her last/clear/act"
("The Painting")

times—you wish for self-confidence, happiness, pleasure—and when you have these last things you can't enjoy them.

In spite of everything you cannot free yourself—you fail to soar up into the sort of being you wish to be—therefore you call yourself a failure.

Mother dear—I also wish to do great works of art—to write great good poems—to help the poor and the unhappy—but young as I am who shall say that I will not be a failure?

Mother that does not bother me in the slightest degree—it never has. I want to succeed of course but—so long as I can live a passionate life—full of striving, full of eager attempts to the whole extent of the power that is in me I shall say that I have really lived—that I have been really worthy of you—yes of you for you are to me perfect. (*YMW*, xi–xii)

The letter's mawkish salutation, "Dearest Old Silly Mommy," is indicative of its overall tone and rhetorical strategy. Williams, aged thirty-two, affects an ingratiating, childlike pose, and lovingly chides his mother for the "silly" self-image she persists in cultivating. He tries to dispel her melancholic air of defeatism by flattering her extravagantly, stating that to his mind she is "perfect." Although he does acknowledge the failure of Elena's two career ambitions—painting great pictures and following her voice—he minimizes the gravity of that fact by attributing it to the "fineness" of her appreciations. In this way, he implicitly transforms the cause of her defeat into a veiled compliment: the goals she establishes for herself are so rigorous and idealized that no one could possibly attain them. The poet, who in 1915 was poised at the beginning of his own artistic career, admits in the letter to sharing these lofty aspirations, but stresses that his relation to them is more pragmatic than his mother's. For him, the act of striving, of making "eager attempts" to realize the power within, takes precedence over actual achievement—a belief he would maintain throughout his life, writing in *Paterson,* book 4: "*La Verture / est toute dans l'effort* . . . a quieting thought: / Virtue is wholly / in the effort to be virtuous" (*P,* 189).

Because he had not yet experienced an artistic defeat of the same devastating magnitude as Elena's, Williams tended, at this early stage in his career, to make light of her failure, and even to deny it as a means of shoring up her fragile ego. As he grew older, however, the poet's perception of her defeat changed in that he came to increasingly identify with it, and saw in her adaptation to adverse circumstances a model which he could emulate. The 1915 letter presages his recognition of the fundamental disparity between what Elena was and what she aspired to be in the statement "You *are*—you exist, you feel, you aspire, you love and you hate—the deep inexplicable burning in your innermost heart is real—it isn't a sham—it isn't false—therefore how can you really dare to tell me you are a failure?"

This same configuration of defeat and indomitable spirit recurs several decades later in the poet's assessment of his mother's character in the introduction to *Yes, Mrs. Williams:*

So grown old—in vain, a woman creates a son and dies in her own mind. That is the end. She is dead, she says. But that vigor for living, clinging desperately to the small threads of a reality which she thought to have left in Paris—the battle is against her. How continue to love in the fact of defeat? *Why am I alive? No one can realize what I have desired. I succeeded in nothing, I have kept nothing, I am nothing.*

That is the defeated romantic. It is not by any means a true picture. Despondency, discouragement, despair were violent periodic factors in her life. Under it lies the true life, undefeated if embittered, hard as nails, little loving, easily mistaken for animal selfishness. . . .

Witness her courage—difficulties quiet her, she is not led astray by false feeling. She remains unbroken. . . .

Don't think I don't know what old age does. You are nothing you wanted to be, true enough, what *you* wanted to be. But something is alive that maybe you did not want to be. Something is there for all that. . . . (*YMW*, 33–34)

After many years of sustained, daily interaction with Elena, observing the "deep, inexplicable burning in [her] innermost heart," Williams came to the conclusion that despite her perpetual aura of disappointment and despondency, she was not "dead," but relentlessly alive, "unbroken," and "undefeated if embittered." What is most interesting about this passage, however, is the manner in which Williams subtly entwines his fate with that of his mother. The statement, "So grown old—in vain, a woman creates a son and dies in her own mind," for example, suggests a process of not only physical but spiritual transmission—that as the inheritor of Elena's values and romantic ideals, he incarnates the possibility of realizing her thwarted ambitions. Yet several lines later, he asserts, "Don't think I don't know what old age does," indicating that he too has met with disappointment and failure, and "so grown old—in vain" like his mother.

At another point in the memoir's introduction, Williams explicitly attributes the cause of their individual defeats to Elena's idealism:

The truth and its pursuit was [*sic*] always at the front of my mother's mind. It was a long time before I came to realize how her romantic ideas had deceived her and me in the modern world which we in our turn had to push behind us to come up fighting or smiling, if we could make it, or just to find some sunny spot where we could stretch our bones, even if we had a broken hip like Mother, and not complain. (*YMW*, 20)

The struggle depicted in this passage pits the shared values of mother and son against those of an antagonistic "modern world" which must be pushed aside in order to create a viable niche for them. They labor in unison to "come up fighting or smiling," although here, as in the 1915 letter, Williams' emphasis is not on the outcome of the struggle, whether success or failure, but rather on the endeavor itself. The image of him and Elena seeking an idyllic haven "where we could stretch our bones, even if we had a broken hip like Mother" reflects the degree to which the poet imaginatively allied his fate with hers. He envisions the two of them as renegades, intimately bound together by the anomaly of their views; yet, on an unconscious level, the skewed syntax of his description proposes an even more radical unity. By joining a plural subject ("we") to a singular object ("a broken hip"), Williams tacitly assumes one of his mother's physical characteristics which, not at all coincidentally, happens to be a crippling disability—much in the same way as her "romantic ideas." Thus, in a metaphorical sense, he becomes her, and the causes of her "defeat" defeat him as well.

Williams also addresses the theme of his and Elena's mutual defeat in the poem "An Eternity," which was published in 1949 but composed in 1946–47,[18] at approximately the same time as the "descent" passage. In fact, "An Eternity" forms an illuminating corollary to this section of *Paterson* in that it documents the emotional crisis which the prospect of Elena's death precipitated for the poet, and outlines the same triumvirate of associations—memory, defeat, and love—in relation to her. The poem, apparently written in the aftermath of one of Elena's many skirmishes with death, begins with an entreaty; faced with the threat of permanent separation from her, Williams urges his mother to linger with him in the realm of the living:

> Come back, Mother, come back from
> the dead—not to "Syria," not there
> but hither—to this place.
>
> You are old, Mother, old
> and almost cold, come back from
> the dead—where I cannot yet join you.
> Wait awhile, wait a little while.
>
> (*CLP*, 182)

The insistent verbal repetition in these lines—"come back from the dead," "old . . . old and almost cold," and "wait awhile, wait a little while"—creates an incantatory effect,[19] as if Williams were weaving a spell to prevent Elena from slipping off into death. This impression is deepened by the poet's invocation of the obscurity of darkness as a prerequisite for communication between them:

> This
> winter moonlight is a bitter thing,
> I like it no better than you do.
> Let us wait
> for some darker moment of the moon.
>
> (*CLP*, 182)

Through the invisibility afforded by the absence of light, Williams fuses his past and present experience with that of his mother:

> —the night, the night we face
> is black but of no more weight than
> the day—the day we faced and were
> defeated and yet lived
> to face the night in which
> the fair moon shine—

> (*CLP,* 182)

In the poet's mind, the circumstances which he and Elena have encountered in life, represented by the generic images of "day" and "night," are identical, as are their respective responses to them. Her ability to survive defeat constitutes a model which he consciously imitates, aligning his destiny with the intricate pattern her life continuously unfolds before him.

Williams also uses this "darker moment of the moon" as an opportunity to make the rather startling confession to his mother, "Frankly, I do not love you." In light of his earlier plea that she not abandon him by dying, this declaration seems peculiar indeed; however, it proves to be only an attention-getting ploy, a prelude to announcing the existence of a mysterious, even more intimate bond between them which supercedes the power and duration of interpersonal love:

> The soul, my dear, is paramount,
> the soul of things
> that makes the dead moon shine. . . .
>
> It is the loveless soul, the soul
> of things that has surpassed
> our loves. In this—you live,
> Mother, live in me .
>   always.

> (*CLP,* 183)

By transmuting his love for Elena into an amorphous animating essence, "the soul of things," Williams is able to psychologically accept the inevitable fact of her death. Though their earthly relationship will eventually draw to a close, her presence will continue within him as an enduring spiritual legacy, typified in the memory of her obstinate resistance: "I remember how at eighty-five / you battled through the crisis and / survived!" (*CLP,* 183). The poet perceives himself as the inheritor of the life principle she incarnates: "In this—you live, / Mother, live in me / always."

As in "An Eternity," Williams invokes a symbolic darkness in the "descent" passage to signal the emergence of love:

> With evening, love wakens
>   though its shadows
>   which are alive by reason

> of the sun shining—
>> grow sleepy now and drop away
>>> from desire
>
> Love without shadows stirs now
>> beginning to waken
>>> as night
> advances.
>
>>>> (*P*, 78)

This allusion provides the first solid indication of a submerged personal perspective at work in the lyric; until this point, the poet had completely concealed himself behind the generality of his diction. Yet even here, the primary emphasis is not on the specific source from which this love springs or the objective toward which it is directed, but rather on the qualities of the emotion itself. Unencumbered by the "shadows" of self-consciousness and reason which typify its diurnal manifestations, the love that stirs at twilight is, like "the soul of things," an animating principle capable of transforming despair and loss into a "new awakening." As such, it comprises a crucial component of the descent.

In the lyric's concluding lines, the point of view suddenly shifts from the third to first person, revealing that Williams' depiction of the resource of memory derives in part from his own experiences; however, the narrative voice he employs is not singular, but plural:

> For what we cannot accomplish, what
> is denied to love,
>> what we have lost in the anticipation—
>>> a descent follows,
> endless and indestructible .
>
>>>> (*P*, 79)

His use of the pronoun "we" in this context is somewhat equivocal: it can be explained as a rhetorical convention denoting the universality of human experience, or refer to a much smaller, more literal unit—that of mother and son—whose bond of shared defeat is amply illustrated in both "An Eternity" and *Yes, Mrs. Williams*. The latter interpretation is reinforced by Williams' characterization of the "descent" as "endless and indestructible," which makes it, in effect, a metaphor for immortality. In this respect, the "descent" rhymes with "the loveless soul" mentioned at the end of "An Eternity" through which Elena lives in the poet "always," and also echoes his early depiction of her in the prologue to *Kora in Hell* as "an impoverished, ravished Eden but *one as indestructible as the imagination itself*" (*I*, 7; emphasis mine). Through his mother's example, Williams learned that life's defeats—the lack of substantive accomplishment, denial of love, and thwarting of anticipation—could be conquered by means of reliance on the mind's richest, most resilient resource—the imagination. Towards the end of his own life, he turned increasingly to the methods Elena had taught him for coping with old age, specifically, "squeezing the mind" to recover the diverse memories it contains. The poem "The High Bridge above the Tagus River at Toledo," first published in 1956,[20] is just such a "mental exercise," a detailed recounting of being pressed against an ancient stone bridge in Spain by a flock of sheep during his 1910 trip to Europe.[21] The poem's final lines pay tribute to its half-century of germination, the slow filtering of the incident through time into memory and dream, and its ultimate metamorphosis into art, where the scene is permanently preserved for posterity:

> The whole flock, the shepherd and the dogs, were covered
>   with dust as if they had been all day long on the road. The
>   pace of the sheep, slow in the mass,
> governed the man and the dogs. They were approaching the
> city at nightfall, the long journey completed.
>
> In old age they walk in the old man's dreams and still walk
>   in his dreams, peacefully continuing in his verse
>   forever
>
> (PB, 53)

Paterson, book 3, published in September 1949, is the section of the epic composed closest to the actual event of Elena's death; not surprisingly, it also contains the largest concentration of references to her in the text as a whole. As its title, "The Library," suggests, book 3 "considers the poet's relationship to the past, and to the literary tradition in particular."[22] Elena's presence here thus serves a dual function, dovetailing family history into a broader sense of the region's and nation's past, and also illustrating the pervasiveness of her influence on Williams' writing. At the beginning of section 2, for example, he meditates on the predicament of the contemporary writer, stating that in order "to write, nine tenths of the problem is to live" (*P*, 113), a generalization that leads to thoughts of how he personally resolved this financial dilemma through doctoring. Williams then imagines a chorus of clichéd comments from the populace of Paterson about his ability to combine medicine and poetry:

> We're so proud of you!
> A wonderful gift! How *do*
> you find the time for it in
>
> your busy life? It must be a great
> thing to have such a pastime.
>
> But you were always a strange
> boy. How's your mother?
>
> (P, 113–14)

To the collective mind of the community, writing is a hobby, a harmless, pleasurable activity designed to fill one's leisure hours, much in the same way as gardening or stamp collecting. They regard the poet with a mixture of pride, incredulity, and skepticism; like Peter the dwarf, he is one of the natural curiosities of the Passaic region. Although the superficiality of the public's response isolates Williams and trivializes his urgent search for a "redeeming language," it also posits a casual but vital link between Elena and his creativity. The associative logic of the statement "You were always a strange / boy. How's your mother?" implies that the townspeople connect his "strangeness," manifested in the writing of incomprehensible poetry, with the figure of his mother, as if she were its source. This perception limits the poet, relegating him to the eternally subservient status of a child, but also attests to his predominant spiritual inheritance—that regardless of his age, Williams remains his mother's son.

Moreover, the polite, perfunctory character of the question "How's your mother?" not only affirms the fact of Elena's continued existence, but illustrates the poet's filial role as her liaison to the community at large. Through him, her acquaintances send their greetings and expressions of concern—the small messages that connect her to a world of social intercourse in which she could not otherwise participate. Thus, in the words of *Yes, Mrs. Williams,* he becomes "the bridge between herself and a vacancy as of the sky at night, the terrifying emptiness of non-entity" (*YMW,* 94).

In contrast to the brief, anonymous query made about her in section 2, Elena speaks directly in the concluding section of "The Library." Her statement, which blurs the distinction between memory and inner vision in the same manner as the "descent" passage, occurs as part of the leaden flood of information that threatens to overwhelm the poet:

> Let me see, Puerto Plata is
> the port of Santo Domingo.
>
> There was a time when
> they didn't want any whites
> to own anything—to
> hold anything—to say, This
> is mine   .
>
> I see things,   .   .

(*P,* 136)

Once again, Elena has returned in imagination to the islands of her youth, gathering up the shards of memory as a solace in old age. Her fragmentary reminiscence begins and ends with "seeing," yet neither context in which the verb appears is literal. The first instance, "Let me see," is a figurative colloquial expression, signifying a process of concentration, the focusing of one's mental energies on a particular issue or problem (here, remembering Santo Domingo). The strategy is an effective one, engendering an "isolate fleck" (*CEP,* 272) of memory which, rather than idealizing the past, evokes a resonant tension within it. The narrative ends abruptly, however, and Elena's voice drifts off into a more remote, insubstantial world, the details of which she cannot describe. Only ghostly generalities remain: "I see things."

The question of ownership and possession raised in this reminiscence has, in addition, broad metaphorical implications for Williams' encoding of the figure of Elena within himself throughout *Paterson* as well as the rest of his work. In the introduction to *Yes, Mrs. Williams,* he uses proprietary terms to describe his attempt to capture and preserve her exotic fragrance:

> She is about to pass out of the world; I want to hold her back a moment for her to be seen because—in many ways I think she is so lovely, for herself, that it would be a pity if she were lost without something of her—something impressed with her mind and her spirit— herself—remaining to perpetuate her—for our profit. (*YMW,* 24)

The poet's desire to "hold back" his mother, to extract, appropriate, and perpetuate her essence through the creation of "something impressed with her mind and . . . spirit" which he could own and "profit" from became more frenzied and intense as her death drew closer. In the mid to late forties, he felt that all his previous efforts to represent her—in "Eve," "A Memory of Tropical Fruit," "Raquel Helene Rose," as well as the unfinished biography—had failed dismally, and thus allied the mimetic problem she posed with his ongoing struggle to write *Paterson.* In both cases, the dilemma was the same:

> How to begin to find a shape—to begin to begin again,
> turning the inside out: to find one phrase that will
> lie married beside one another for delight   .   ?
> —seems beyond attainment   .
>
> (*P,* 140)

Because Williams believed that "we know nothing, pure / and simple, beyond / our own complexities" (*P,* 3), the "shape" he ultimately settled on as a means of representing Elena was himself. Given her pivotal role in his personal and artistic development, he recognized that the best way to perpetuate her salient character traits was through an exhaustive depiction of his own, a "turning [of] the inside out" onto the page: "In this—you live, / Mother, live in me / always" (*CLP,* 183).

By acknowledging that Elena formed an integral facet of his identity, Williams was able to rationalize and effectively diminish the threat which her impending demise presented for him. He was losing only the companionship and reassurance of her physical presence, not "the soul of things" itself. Just prior to his climactic rejection of the past in favor of "the roar of the present" (*P,* 144) at the end of book 3, the poet makes two statements which illustrate

another, related aspect of this rationalization process—an attempt to emotionally distance himself from her in preparation for that final moment. The flip-
pant tone of the first remark reveals an uncharacteristically brusque and unsympathetic response to the debility of old age:

> Let's give the canary to that
> old deaf woman; when he opens his
> bill to hiss at her, she'll think he
> is singing
>
> (*P,* 143)

Although no specific bond is postulated between the unidentified speaker and
the "old deaf woman," their relationship is compromised by the ironic nature
of the proposed gift—a hissing canary. What the old woman will, because of
her hearing loss, perceive as a thoughtful gesture, a source of diversion and entertainment, in fact makes her the brunt of a practical joke. The motivation underlying this proposed prank is cathartic, a release of pent-up hostility and frustration; such malicious tendencies, as Williams notes in the memoir's introduction, are innately human:

> It is very difficult for a younger person to deal with the aged—unless he be a saint. Some-
> times she would drive me almost crazy with her fumbling, and she would notice it and beg
> my pardon so that the cruelty in my voice from the exasperation of it would have to be cut
> short. . . . There is an incentive arising from the weak and the defenseless that drives us
> devilishly to want to insult and even to kill them. It is bestial in a man to want to slaughter
> his old mother—so that he had better find an alternative. (*YMW,* 37, 35–36)

In contrast to the first statement, the second, which occurs only half a
page later in the poem, is more tender and intimate in tone; yet it can also be
interpreted as a veiled farewell:

> Did I do more than share your guilt, sweet woman. The
> cherimoya is the most delicately flavored of all
> tropic fruit   . Either I abandon you
> or give up writing
>
> (*P,* 144)

This passage, like the one about the canary, contains no indisputable proof that
the "sweet woman" being addressed is indeed Elena; however, the allusion to
tropical fruit, which Williams habitually associated with his mother,[23] strongly
suggests that she may be its subject. Moreover, the provocative series of disjointed assertions which the poet makes in relation to this alluring woman correspond to his complex and occasionally paradoxical symbolization of Elena as
mother, impossible beloved, and muse. In particular, the statement "Either I
abandon you / or give up writing" acknowledges a deep psychic tension between the poet's attraction to the feminine and his continued ability to write.

This antagonism, in specific terms of Elena, may refer to Williams' simultaneous fascination with her and frustrating failure to depict her in words. Although he recognizes that, in order to avoid the risk of creative paralysis, it is necessary to choose between the two conflicting desires, he reaches no decision in the passage. Because of their shared bond of secret, inexplicable guilt, the "sweet woman" cannot be easily dismissed or abandoned.

Additional evidence pointing to Elena as the subject of these two passages can be found in Williams' long poem, "Two Pendants: for the Ears," his most detailed account of her periodic spells of "dying" and recovery. The poem describes a particular episode, in all likelihood the last before her actual death, that took place over Easter weekend in April 1949, a serendipitous coincidence which the poet exploited in the text by thematically intertwining the pagan celebration of spring with the biblical account of Christ's crucifixion and resurrection and his mother's personal confrontation with death. A number of specific elements—references to tropical fruit, a pet canary, the difficulty of achieving accurate mimesis, and an irreverent attitude toward old age—link the poem back to *Paterson, book 3.*

But what is most striking about "Two Pendants" is the sense of helplessness Williams experiences in the face of Elena's imminent demise. The first section of the poem relates a nightmare in which the poet/physician arrives at a dark public plaza in the aftermath of a "terrific fight" (*CLP*, 214) between a tiger and its trainer. Both are gravely wounded and, although Williams wants to assist, the murky confusion of the situation as well as his own insecurity and fear prevent his intercession:

> I could
> make out nothing clearly and then
> did the logical thing: unarmed
> I saw that I was helpless and so
> turned and walked back to the others.
>
> (*CLP*, 216)

This dream forms the basis of Williams' response to another, more horrific nightmare from which he cannot "turn and walk back"—that of his mother's death. Part 2 of the poem, entitled "Elena," begins with a gesture of farewell:

> You lean the head forward
> and wave the hand,
> with a smile,
> twinkling the fingers
> I say to myself
> Now it is spring
> Elena is dying
>
> What snows, what snow
> enchained her—

               she of the tropics
               is melted
                       now she is dying

               The mango, the guava
               long forgot for
               apple and cherry
               wave goodbye

               now it is spring
               Elena is dying
                       Goodbye

                                              (*CLP*, 220–21)

These lines, like the poem "The Painting," offer a concise summary of the course of Elena's life—her poignant foresaking of an exotic tropical past, embodied in the mango and guava, for the pedestrian fruit of a more northerly climate, and her imprisonment by both the literal snow of that region and the emotional frigidity arising from her puritanical values. Despite the evident fondness of this description, it is also strangely dismissive; "She of the tropics / is melted," Williams declares, as though her death were a fait accompli. His prognosis, however, proves to be false or, at best, premature.

When told by the couple at the nursing home (who, though nameless, are undoubtedly Ann and Irving Taylor, the British "hearts of oak" Williams mentioned in the 1946 letter to Ezra Pound quoted earlier) that Elena is "not going to die—not now" (*CLP*, 221), Williams reacts in a peculiar manner. He denies and deflects the stressfulness of the situation by evading the subject altogether, introducing trivial, irrelevant information, such as the "fashionable grocery list" about which Mike Wallace questions him in *Paterson*, book 5:

               Listen, I said, I met a man
               last night told me what he'd brought
               home from the market:
               2 partridges
               2 Mallard ducks
               a Dungeness crab
               24 hours out
               of the Pacific
               and two live-frozen
               trout
               from Denmark
                                              (*CLP*, 221–22)

This pattern persists throughout the poem; Williams deliberately suppresses his feelings of anxiety and grief by shifting his thoughts away from Elena to other, peripheral concerns. For example, he interrupts an intense moment of painful inner questioning

> How can you weep for her? I
> cannot, I her son—though
> I could weep for her without
> compromising the covenant

> She will go alone.

with this:

> And Magazine #1 sues Magazine
> #2, no less guilty—for libel
> or infringement or dereliction
> or confinement

(CLP, 222)

The diversionary thought of litigation offers no substantive relief from the poet's problem because he too is guilty—derelict in the performance of his filial devotions—and thus his mind circles back to the ugly, inevitable fact: "Elena is dying (but perhaps not yet)" (*CLP*, 223). As son and physician, Williams can do nothing other than passively watch Elena's struggle and feebly apologize for his helplessness: "I'm afraid I'm not much use to you, Mother" (*CLP*, 226). As a writer, however, he can at least attempt to make "the language" accurately record the subtle complexities of her existence:

> the rumblings of a
> catastrophic past, a delicate
> defeat—vivid simulations of
> the mystery

(CLP, 228)

But the most horrifying moment of the poet's three-day nightmare is the discovery not of his own helplessness, but rather of Elena's inability to recognize him:

> Elena is dying.
> In her delirium she said
> a terrible thing:

> Who are you? NOW!
> I, I, I, I stammered. I
> am your son.

(CLP, 224)

The sense of emotional estrangement and dissolution of familial ties implied by Elena's question shocks Williams, momentarily reducing him to the status of a nonentity until he can stammer back a reply. Interestingly, he does not identify himself by name, but instead in terms of his filial relation to her. This assertion reestablishes the formal bond between them, and when she tells the poet, "Don't go. I am unhappy" (*CLP*, 224) in the subsequent line, he gladly stays, secure once again within the mutual dependency of their relationship.

Yet, on the third day, after the imminent danger of her death has passed, Elena begs Williams:

> Can't you give me
> something to make me disappear
> completely, said she sobbing—but
> completely!

to which he responds in an apparently loving, but obliquely hostile way:

> No I can't do that
> Sweetheart (You God damned belittling
> fool, said I to myself)

(CLP, 225)

The incongruity between his pleasant articulated reply and angry, parenthetical one derives from a combination of relief and frustration; both mother and son have been granted a temporary reprieve—she from death itself, he from mourning and disconsolate loneliness. But because he realizes that the final crisis has only been briefly deferred, the poet retains a remnant of the protective emotional armor which will help shield him against the pain of her ultimate loss.

The depiction of Elena as a fierce antagonist of death, mustering all her strength to fight against it, pervades the second part of "Two Pendants: for the Ears." "She fights so," Mrs. Taylor says; "You can't quieten her. . . . She's one of the wonders of the world I think" (*CLP*, 221, 228). This image is reaffirmed by the question of an anonymous ethnic voice that drifts into the poem:

> Is this a private foight
> or kin I get into it?
>
> This is a private fight.

(CLP, 224)

Williams is curiously silent about the end of this "private fight"; there are no poems which commemorate the fact of Elena's passing, and the event merits only a few lines in *Yes, Mrs. Williams:* "She died with a tranquil smile on her face, just went to sleep with pneumonia. What dream she was following at the moment of course we will never know" (*YMW*, 20). The poet's correspondence from October and November 1949 makes repeated mention of the serene circumstances of her death, but in a very formal, restrained way: "My stern, frivolous mother died Sunday evening" (*SL*, 268) and "My little mother died ten days ago or more. She just slept away . . ." (*SL*, 275). But perhaps his most revealing statement was to Louis Zukofsky: "She curious little thing that she was simply went to sleep. Whether or not I could have 'saved' her by giving penicillin the week before is something I have debated in my mind ever since her death. So that, in effect, I 'killed' her. In her coffin her features were astounding, an Egyptian princess."[23] Williams' speculation about the possibility of valiantly rescuing Elena from death and characterization of his failure to do so as metaphorical murder illustrate how difficult and traumatic her loss was for him to accept. Moreover, although the letter does not explicitly state this, part of the poet's fascination with his mother's "astounding features" as she lay in her coffin doubtlessly stemmed from a perception of the strong physical resemblance which existed between them. In the face of that aged "Egyptian princess," Williams saw his own face, and knew that his death would be next.[24]

Paterson, book 4, published in 1951, contains a mysterious, elegiac lyric about the funeral of an unidentified elderly woman who Williams says "had a private ticket" into heaven. The proximity of the poem's composition to Elena's death, along with several thematic elements within the piece itself, infer that she is its subject:

> She used to call me her
> > country bumpkin
> Now she is gone I think
> > of her as in Heaven
> She made me believe in
> > it   .   a little
> Where else could she go?
>
> > There was
> Something grandiose
> > about her   .
> Man and woman are not
> > much emphasized as
> such at that age: both
> > want the same
> thing . to be amused.
> > Imagine *me*
> at her funeral. I sat
> > way back. Stupid,
> perhaps but no more so
> > than any funeral.
> You might think she had
> > a private ticket.
> I think she did; some
> > people, not many,
> make you feel that way.
>
> > It's in them.

> Virtue, she would say .
> > (her version of it)
> is a stout old bird,
> > unpredictable. And
> so I remember her,
> > adding,
> as she did, clumsily,
> > not being used to
> such talk, that—
> > Nothing does, does
> as it used to do
> > do do! I loved her.

(P, 189–90)

    This lyric, in many respects, represents the culmination and synthesis of a lifetime of interpretive effort—a recitation of the poet's richly varied responses to his mother. As a requiem, its tone is purely celebratory, unmarred by the harshness and ambivalence that characterize "Two Pendants: for the Ears"; as a reminiscence, it demonstrates the creative use of memory which she taught him. Williams pays tribute in the poem to the rare, "grandiose" nature of Elena's ideals and aspirations, acknowledges her love of American colloquial expressions (as well as her consistently awkward use of them) and her desire in old age to "be amused"—a factor which played a central role in their collaborative translation of novels by Soupault and Quevedo in the twenties and thirties.

    Even more importantly, Williams hints at the interrelation of their identities in the passage: "Imagine *me* at her funeral. I sat way back," as if his continued existence beyond the fact of her death were somehow unthinkable or absurd. He attempts to put as much physical distance as possible between himself and her coffin in order both to assuage his grief and avoid confronting the spectre of his own mortality. At the time of Elena's death, the poet was sixty-six, retired from active hospital duty, and beginning to experience the health problems that attend old age[26]; a year and a half later, shortly before book 4 appeared, he suffered his first stroke. The descent was beckoning. In addition, his assertion, "Man and woman are not / much emphasized as / such at that age" minimizes the importance of gender distinctions among the elderly and thus implicitly blurs the boundaries between his identity and that of the deceased woman by establishing a fundamental bond of common humanity: "both / want the same / thing . . . to be amused" (P, 190).

    Lastly, the rhetorical question Williams poses about this woman's eternal life in heaven, "Where else could she go?" (P, 189), raises the issue of another sort of immortality—in literature. Within a few years of Elena's death, the poet realized that *Yes, Mrs. Williams* had to be brought to fruition; as he explained in a letter to Charles Abbott: "I had to get Mother down on paper as long as I had to keep thinking about her."[27] In *Paterson,* book 5, the only epic which contains no discernible personal reference to his mother, Williams, now an old man, employs—as she herself had so strikingly done—the resource of memory, and recalls their joint translation of a French novel:

> What has happened
>   since Soupault gave him the novel
>   the Dadaist novel
> to translate—
>   *The Last Nights of Paris.*
>   "What has happened to Paris
> since that time?
>   and to myself?"
>
>
>   A WORLD OF ART
>   THAT THROUGH THE YEARS HAS
>
>   SURVIVED!
>
> <div align="right">(<i>P</i>, 209)</div>

The omission of his maternal collaborator from the series of questions Williams asks here ("What has happened to Paris . . . and to myself?") has two possible causes. The first is that since the final revision of *Yes, Mrs. Williams* coincided exactly with the composition of book 5, the poet's preoccupation with Elena may have been channeled and redirected back into that work. Secondly, Williams' silence implies that perhaps, in her case, he already had the assurance of a positive answer: transformed into art through the agency of his imagination and pen, she would survive forever.

A short lyric in the *Pictures from Brueghel* sequence serves as an allegorical paradigm of Williams' relationship to his mother, as he ultimately interpreted it at the end of his life:

> The rose fades
> and is renewed again
> by its seed, naturally
> but where
>
> save in the poem
> shall it go
> to suffer no diminution
> of its splendor
>
> <div align="right">(<i>PB</i>, 39)</div>

The rose, traditional symbol of beauty, love, and evanescence, is an appropriate metaphor for Raquel Helene Rose, muse and maternal flower, who transmitted the secret of vitality, sustenance, and creativity to the "seed" of her son. In and through him, she was "renewed," and although he too would inevitably fade, the rich, multifaceted splendor of their relationship is permanently preserved in the fictive world of his writing. Mother and son, blossom and seed—

two interrelated aspects of a single entity. The fragrance of this "rose" pervades the entire canon of Williams' work, standing as testimony of how much she meant to him. Through his mother, the poet learned not only how to live and die, but that the power of the imagination withstands all.

Notes

Introduction

1. Quoted in Paul Mariani, *William Carlos Williams: A New World Naked* (New York: McGraw-Hill, 1981), p. 458.

2. Williams' narration of this incident in *I Wanted to Write a Poem* is even more vividly emphatic:

   > My grandmother had *seized* me from my mother as her special possession, *adopted me,* and *her purpose in life was to make me her own.* But my mother ended all that with a terrific slap in the puss. (*IW,* 26; emphasis mine)

3. Robert Lowell, "William Carlos Williams," *History* (London: Faber and Faber, 1973), p. 142. As Paul Mariani has noted, many of the poem's factual details are incorrect. In 1947, the first and only time Lowell visited 9 Ridge Road, Williams was sixty-four, not sixty-seven, and he had not yet suffered any of the "three autumn strokes" that Lowell mentions in the lyric. Despite these errors, Mariani asserts, Lowell "captured Williams in essence . . . the dress, the tough loving speech, the crack about sex, the warmth of the man. The rest was unimportant" (Mariani, *William Carlos Williams: A New World Naked,* p. 553).

4. Sigmund Freud, "The Theme of the Three Caskets," trans. C. J. M. Hubback in *On Creativity and the Unconscious* (New York: Harper Torchbooks, 1958), p. 75.

5. Paul Mariani, *William Carlos Williams: A New World Naked,* p. 84.

Chapter 1

1. Unpublished letter from William Carlos Williams to Charles Abbott, 9 November 1949, Poetry/Rare Books Collection, Lockwood Library, Buffalo, F 945.

2. Because Williams had signed a number of political statements and contributed work to left-wing magazines like *New Masses* in the thirties, he was suspected of being a communist sympathizer by McCarthyite witch-hunters in Washington. As a result, his consultantship at the Library of Congress, scheduled to begin in the autumn of 1952, was revoked pending a loyalty investigation. The full details of this bleak episode are recounted in Paul Mariani's *William Carlos Williams: A New World Naked* (New York: McGraw-Hill, 1981), pp. 651–62.

3. William Carlos Williams, *Selected Letters* (New York: McDowell-Obolensky Press, 1957), p. 298.

4. William Carlos Williams quoted in Mike Weaver, *William Carlos Williams: The American Background* (New York: Cambridge University Press, 1971), p. 259.

5. Mike Weaver's "Introduction to a Modern Portrait," written to accompany the posthumous publication of Williams' essay in the British little magazine *Form* (1 September 1966), reveals that Romano kept a diary while painting the poet's portrait in the autumn of 1951. On 27 September he made the following entry: "The only thing disturbing me was the reflection of the light in his eye-glasses. Something maddening—the light was, so strong I could not see Williams' face" (21). Weaver's commentary articulates the artist's problem a bit more fully. Although Williams' glasses reflected light, they also gave his face a certain youthful quality; "once removed, the poet [suddenly] became his age—the boyish enthusiasm gone, the bedside manner finally dropped. Instead the silky independence of Williams' mother was revealed" (21).

Because Weaver does not quote Romano's diary in its entirety in his article, it is difficult to surmise whether this perception of Elena's "silky independence" is the artist's or Weaver's own. The portrait itself, as Paul Mariani notes in his biography of Williams, bears a strong resemblance to photographs taken of Elena in old age: "[It] showed Williams indoors and seated, wearing a sports jacket, his right arm across his lap, his head resting on his left hand. The face was angular, almost fractured in a style recalling Cézanne, and it was striking how much Williams had come in these later years to resemble his mother" (641). This physical likeness makes Williams' metaphorical inscription of himself in the figure of Elena all the more powerful and uncanny; not only were their attitudes and responses to aging parallel, they even looked like one another as well.

6. Bram Dijkstra, ed., *A Recognizable Image: William Carlos Williams on Art and Artists* (New York: New Directions Books, 1978), pp. 198–99.

7. Bram Dijkstra, p. 199.

8. Bram Dijkstra, p. 200.

9. Ezra Pound, *Literary Essays* (New York: New Directions Books, 1935), p. 398.

10. William Carlos Williams quoted in Mike Weaver, *William Carlos Williams,* p. 164.

11. Bram Dijkstra, p. 199.

12. Unpublished manuscript, Beinecke Library, Yale University, Za Williams 275.

13. William Carlos Williams, "From My Notes about My Mother," ed. Edith Heal Berrien, *Literary Review,* vol. 1, no. 1, Autumn 1957, p. 9.

14. Unpublished letter, William Carlos Williams to Louis Untermeyer, 8 March 1939, Lilly Library, Indiana University.

15. Unpublished letter, William Carlos Williams to Winfield Townley Scott, W. T. Scott Papers, John Hay Library, Brown University.

16. Although Williams originally envisaged *Paterson* as a four-part structure—"a Trinity, with the inclusion of the dissonance of Pan" (Mariani, p. 699)—after completing book 4 he realized that a fifth book was necessary. The appendix to the poem, which contains notes for a projected sixth book, indicates that he regarded *Paterson* as an essentially open-ended work which would be concluded only by his own death.

Chapter 2

1. Williams articulates this belief in the last chapter of his *Autobiography,* entitled "The Poem Paterson": "The poet thinks with his poem, in that lies his thought, and that in itself is the

profundity" (*A*, 391). Cf. also "To Daphne and Virginia": "A new world is only a new mind /
And the mind and the poem / are all apiece" (*PB*, 76).

2. Quoted in Charles Olson, *Selected Writings* (New York: New Directions Books, 1966), p.
16.

3. For a more detailed discussion of this concept, see *Spring and All* in *Imaginations,* pp. 120–
23.

4. Oxford English Dictionary (New York: Oxford University Press, 1981), vol. 1, p. 24.

5. Hugh Kenner, *A Homemade World* (New York: William Morrow and Company, 1975), p.
60.

6. William Carlos Williams, "From My Notes about My Mother," ed. Edith Heal Berrien, *Literary Review,* vol. 1, no. 1, Autumn 1957, p. 12.

7. Unpublished letter, Poetry/Rare Books Collection, Lockwood Library, SUNY/Buffalo, F
1149.

8. William Carlos Williams, "The Little Red Notebook (1914)" in *William Carlos Williams Review,* vol. 9, nos. 1–2, Fall 1983, pp. 18, 20.

9. Ibid., p. 22.

10. Dickran Tashjian, *William Carlos Williams and the American Scene* (New York: Whitney
Museum of American Art, 1978), p. 105.

11. Rafael Arévalo Martínez, "The Man Who Resembled a Horse," in *New Directions 8,* 1944,
p. 319.

12. The unusual emphasis Williams placed on parental approbation of his work is best illustrated
by the traumatic results of his failure to secure that approval from his father. In the *Autobiography,* he records a powerful dream he had a few days after William George's death:

> I saw him coming down a peculiar flight of exposed steps, steps I have since identified
> as those before the dais of Pontius Pilate in some well-known painting. But this was
> in a New York office building, Pop's office. He was bare-headed and had some business letters in his hand on which he was concentrating as he descended. I noticed him
> and with joy cried out, "Pop! So, you're not dead!" But he only looked up at me over
> his right shoulder and commented severely, "You know all that poetry you're writing.
> Well, it's no good." I was left speechless and woke trembling. I have never dreamed
> of him since. (*A,* 14)

The last sentence of this passage is particularly revealing: the poet, utterly devastated by his
father's pronouncement, is momentarily robbed of language, the very medium of his art. In
order to protect himself from further injury, Williams psychically abnegates his elder by
banishing him from the realm of the imagination—the unconscious.

An unpublished note which Williams jotted to himself in 1938 while writing a piece on
Federico García Lorca for the *Kenyon Review* is equally trenchant:

> When I first told my mother than I had been asked to write a paper on Spanish literature, she forbade me to do it. What do *you* know about Spanish literature? More than
> you think. I'll prove it to you. Well I am at least supposed to be a practicing poet, in
> spite of what Pop used to think and anyway I'm going to do it. I'm going to get paid
> for it! No, she said. But I persuaded her. (Yale, Za Williams 267)

Given the highly defensive tone of this statement, one might be tempted to assume that it
was written by a rebellious adolescent engaged in a crisis of self-definition rather than by a

well-established fifty-five-year-old poet. The melodramatic quality of Williams' language intensifies this impression; although Elena was a complete invalid by the late thirties, he characterizes her as a stern, authoritative figure who forbids him to trespass on unfamiliar literary terrain. This bizarre imaginative aggrandizement of parental power is also evident in his disparaging allusion to William George. Some twenty years after his father's death, the poet had not yet recovered from the heavy blow which their ideological rift dealt to his ego, but instead remained bitter, resentful, and unsure. The passage thus exposes a vulnerable, childlike dimension of Williams' character that is usually concealed by the public mask of the genial writer/physician. "I'll prove it to you," he declares defiantly to his disapproving parents, and the measure of his success will be tangible and easily understood—money.

13. Rafael Arévalo Martínez, "The Man Who Resembled a Horse," p. 319.

14. Ibid., p. 309.

15. In this respect, it is extremely ironic that when Macaulay Books published the Soupault translation in 1929 Elena was not credited as a participant in the project; the work is attributed to Williams alone. This error is corrected in Ron Padgett's introduction to the 1982 reissue of the text by Full Court Press. Although it is, as Padgett notes, impossible to determine the extent of Elena's involvement in the translation, I believe her assistance went far beyond "help[ing] with difficult points and perhaps [making] a general review" as claimed in Philippe Soupault, *Last Nights of Paris* (New York: Full Court Press, 1982), p. 7.

16. Unpublished manuscript, Beinecke Library, Yale University, Za Williams 271.

17. The formal interrelation of Quevedo's text and Elena's biography is confirmed by a remark Williams made in a letter to James Laughlin on 7 June 1939: "I'm using the whole novella as a framework to hang my mother's biography on" (*SL*, 183).

18. William Carlos Williams, "Raquel Helene Rose," *Twice a Year*, nos. 5–6, Fall/Winter 1940–Spring/Summer 1941, p. 402.

19. Unpublished manuscript, Beinecke Library, Yale University, Za Williams 275.

20. Unpublished manuscript, Beinecke Library, Yale University, Za Williams 279.

21. Unpublished manuscript, Beinecke Library, Yale University, Za Williams 269.

22. The following two "writing plans" from the Beinecke Library at Yale illustrate alternative methods Williams considered for incorporating Quevedo's novella into the memoir:

Plan:

    1. Introduction (present day). The translation (mention the earlier one?) and preliminary remarks—her mood relative to stories: Quevedo—how during it remarks were picked up and jotted down. Laughter. A bit here and there quoted—representing the scope of the life. Order. Vitality. Anger.

(body)   2. Youth—entirely quoted. No remarks. No translation.

(mind)   3. France. Marriage. U.S. Spiritualism. Seances. Music. Painting. Unitarianism. (Quoted) but with remarks. Translation.

(soul)   4. Deafness and blindness. Age. The Translation carried through. Finis. Last quotations.

    5. Selected letters.

(Za Williams 269)

6 Chapters instead of 4

    1. Introductory—the conditions and place and time. Introduce the translation

    2. Youth—quote only

3. France and Marriage (perhaps just touch translation)
4. Today with some translation
5. Rest of translation almost by itself
6. Letters

(Za Williams 281)

23. Unpublished manuscript, Beinecke Library, Yale University, Za Williams 275.

24. Paul Mariani, *William Carlos Williams: A New World Naked* (New York: McGraw-Hill, 1981), pp. 467–68.

25. Unpublished manuscript, Beinecke Library, Yale University, Za Williams 278.

26. Ibid.

Chapter 3

1. In *I Wanted to Write a Poem,* Williams explains that the incorporation of "Raquel Helene Rose" into the translation's introduction was purely a matter of pragmatic expedience:

> Norman Holmes Pearson came to me in 1954, telling me about a group of men at Yale who had more or less sponsored a small offset printing firm. There was an opening for a book, "Did I have anything?" I fished out the Quevedo thing. It wasn't long enough. "Can't you add an introduction?" Pearson said. I looked through papers written twenty years ago and found an Introduction I'd started, stopped in the middle of a sentence. It needed more, so I wrote it. And the book, to be a book, still needed more. I had also found a piece about my mother, her childhood, so I made it into the true story of our work together on the translation. I was interested in this, didn't care anything about style. Perhaps this is the way to do certain things. Ezra Pound was tickled, thought it was the best piece of prose I'd ever written. *(IW, 91)*

2. The transition to "Raquel Helene Rose" in the introduction to *The Dog and the Fever* is similar, though not identical:

> So for the balance of this introduction, and counting on her natural sympathy for Quevedo to bridge the gap, I shall go on. . . . For what it is worth, tying it in where possible with the translation of this book, as I say, I shall speak from now on about my mother. I wrote this originally more than fifteen years ago to be part of her biography, to be incorporated with selections from her letters, but the occasion to publish has never arrived. I speak, then, as if my mother were still living. *(The Dog and the Fever,* pp. 14–15)

3. "Raquel Helene Rose," *Twice a Year,* nos. 5–6, Fall/Winter 1940–Spring/Summer 1941, p. 412; Introduction to *The Dog and the Fever,* p. 39.

4. Williams specifically mentions his sons and the subject of family history at another point in the introduction to *The Dog and the Fever;* however, this reference, like the one in the essay's conclusion, is also omitted in *Yes, Mrs. Williams.* The passage, which begins with a grandly rhetorical question ("What better preparation, my children, can I give you for facing the world, or what more difficult than this?" [p. 26]), concerns the possibility that Elena's father was a Jew. While it is impossible to determine whatever reasons—personal, political, or otherwise—the poet had for excluding this discussion, his action serves as further evidence of the deliberate breakdown of the memoir's historical perspective.

5. Phoebe Adams, "Lines for a Portrait," *Atlantic Monthly,* vol. 204, July 1959, p. 81.

6. Reed Whittemore, "What Is the Secret?," *Virginia Quarterly Review*, vol. 35, Autumn 1959, pp. 638–39.

7. Babette Deutsch, "Picture of a Poet's Mother," *New York Herald Tribune Book Review*, 21 June 1959, p. 4.

8. John Ciardi, "A Flame to Her Son," *Saturday Review*, 11 July 1959, p. 33.

9. Ibid., p. 33.

10. Unpublished manuscript, Beinecke Library, Yale University, Za Williams 271.

11. *In the American Grain*, which Thomas Whitaker describes as "a dialogical encounter with the New World" (*William Carlos Williams*, p. 78), uses the counterpoint of different voices as a means of expressing ideological dissension. In "The Founding of Quebec," for example, Williams conjoins two antithetical interpretations of Samuel de Champlain by setting them within the framework of a casual discussion between two friends, identified only as "I" and "you." These figures, whom Whitaker claims are actually "projected facets" of the poet himself (p. 84), typify the two divergent attitudes towards European settlement of the North American continent which underlie the entire text. This same dichotomy between nature and civilization assumes a mythological dimension in the dialogue of "De Soto and the New World." The mysterious "she" who addresses the Spanish explorer, seductively luring him on to inevitable destruction, symbolizes the savage beauty and power of the wilderness. Through the technique of personification, Williams ironically inverts the standard historical version of the colonizing effort by revealing that it was De Soto, the conqueror, who was ultimately conquered and claimed by the New World.

    Similarly, the female figure in book 2 of *Paterson* (pp. 82–85) is associated with nature (e.g., the rushing stream) as well as with language and poetic inspiration. The realtionship between this pervasive dialogic motif and Williams' theory of the androgynous artist is pursued in detail in chapter 4.

12. Notwithstanding the various clues in *January*, Williams' familiarity with Gris' aesthetic theories is positively established by his famous 1932 letter to Kay Boyle concerning the problem of contemporary poetic form, in which he states: "Why do we not *read* more of Juan Gris? He knew these things in painting and *wrote* well of them" (*SL*, 130; emphasis mine). See also Mike Weaver, *William Carlos Williams: The American Background*, pp. 41–42, and Rob Fure, "The Design of Experience: William Carlos Williams and Juan Gris," *William Carlos Williams Newsletter*, vol. 4, no. 2, 1978, pp. 10–19.

13. Daniel-Henry Kahnweiler, *Juan Gris: His Life and Work* (New York: Harry N. Abrams, 1969), p. 200.

14. Ibid., p. 200.

15. Unpublished manuscript, Beinecke Library, Yale University, Za Williams 275.

16. William Carlos Williams, "From My Notes about My Mother," ed. Edith Heal Berrien, *Literary Review*, vol. 1, no. 1, Autumn 1957, p. 8.

17. Williams apparently felt he had largely succeeded in achieving his goal, declaring in the *Autobiography* that, "Those last few years [of her life] I learned to know my mother pretty well" (*A*, 306). Yet despite the plethora of detailed information she revealed to him, Elena nonetheless carried three significant "secrets" to the grave with her: that she had been awarded three medals for her drawings in Paris, that she had been proposed to by a Frenchman several years before marrying William George, and most importantly, her true age. The poet discovered the first two secrets in the weeks immediately following his mother's death in October 1949, but did not receive official verification of her date of birth until a visit to Puerto Rico in 1956

(See Mariani, p. 596). His divergent responses to these bits of information are extremely interesting because they indicate how seriously he took the project of recovering Elena's past. Here, for example, is Williams' narration, written in a letter to a friend, of finding the three medals:

> My little mother died ten days ago or more. She just slept away, at almost 93. So there's that. When we, my brother and I, opened her big trunk in the attic, we found among other things three coin-shaped, bright-red cases large enough to hold say, a silver dollar. When we opened them we found in each a medal as bright as when it was first placed there, a prize in each case which she had won by her painting and drawing in Paris, at the School for Industrial Design, in 1877, 78, and 79. And in all these years she had kept those medals secret.
>
> What the devil are we alive for? To hide ourselves? When I think of how little my mother ever said to me of herself and her ambition I grind my teeth in fury. There is no sense to it. It is one of the cardinal sins that we do not break bounds one way or another and come out of our prehistoric caves. It's indecent and silly. . . . (*SL,* 275)

Rather than experiencing surprise, pleasure, and a sense of long-belated pride at this tangible evidence of his mother's accomplishments, Williams is furious. He feels hurt, cheated, and frustrated that she kept this facet of her life hidden from him. Elena's reticence thus becomes an example of one of humanity's "cardinal sins"—the inability to fully open ourselves to one another.

The second discovery is also described in a letter, this one to poet Selden Rodman:

> Somehow or other it is a sense of closeness, of opening the eyes above pettiness such as I got from an entirely different source today. My mother died a month ago at the age of 92. Among the objects that she left me was her Mass Book—for she had been a Catholic but renounced it years ago. In the book was a letter written in 1880 by a certain De Longueville. . . . It was a proposal of marriage from the young man, which apparently had been refused, for Mother married my father two years later. But she had not destroyed the letter—nor spoken of it to anyone, as far as I know, all her life. I wonder if she knew it was still in her Mass Book. If she did, she wanted me to see it, for the book was left especially to me, her oldest child.
>
> Well, that's the sort of continuation that the mind should have. . . . (*SL,* 277)

The measure of comfort Williams takes in Elena's bequest of the book to him illustrates how deep his need for intimacy with her was. He wants desperately to believe that after death, she is passing her romantic secret on to him—making him its guardian and steward— and thereby reestablishing the "sort of continuation the mind should have."

The profoundly traumatic effect Elena's death had on the poet is also reflected in the fact that he represses the exact date of its occurrence, recalling it to have been more recent than it actually was—one week rather than two in the first letter, four weeks rather than eight in the second. Curiously, it is only the third discovery, made seven years after the mother's demise, that appears in *Yes, Mrs. Williams.* With the passage of time, the pain of her loss had sufficiently abated so that Williams could deal with the information in a detached and objective manner:

> By the record in the Cathedral in Mayagüez, Puerto Rico, where she was born— Raquel Helene Rose Hoheb lived to be one hundred and two years old! Slightly more. I got it direct from the big book of the Recorder in the Mayor's office; he copied it out for me: December 24, 1847. . . .
>
> My mother had always told me she did not know when she was born but that it was close to Christmas. In fact it was on Christmas Eve, she was almost certain. Her uncertainty came from the fact that in Catholic countries, especially in such a country as

> Puerto Rico, they celebrate their Saint's Day preferably to the day of their birth. That, if she remembered correctly—and of course she did—occurred in August, Santa Rosa her patron saint. Birthdays for that reason meant little to her.
>   But 102 years! The record amazed me. (*YMW,* 51–52)

18. Unpublished manuscript, Poetry/Rare Books Collection, Lockwood Library, SUNY/Buffalo, B 11.

19. Unpublished letter from William Carlos Williams to Louis Zukofsky, 18 November 1948, Humanities Research Center, University of Texas, Austin.

20. Unpublished manuscript, Beinecke Library, Yale University, Za Williams 110.

21. Ibid.

Chapter 4

1. William Carlos Williams, "'Men . . . Have No Tenderness': Anaïs Nin's *Winter of Artifice*," *New Directions 7,* 1942, p. 432.

2. Ibid., pp. 432–33.

3. Ibid., p. 431.

4. Jerome Mazzaro, *William Carlos Williams: The Later Poems* (Ithaca: Cornell University Press, 1973), pp. 135–36.

5. William Carlos Williams, "From My Notes about My Mother," ed. Edith Heal Berrien, *Literary Review,* vol. 1, no. 1, Autumn 1957, p. 8.

6. Paul Mariani, *William Carlos Williams: A New World Naked* (New York: McGraw-Hill, 1981), pp. 462–63.

7. The essay, published in the inaugural issue of the Fairleigh Dickinson University *Literary Review,* is attributed solely to Williams and does not credit Edith Heal Berrien as the editor. I discovered her role in its production during a series of discussions with her at the William Carlos Williams Centenary Conference held at the University of Maine, Orono, in August 1983. According to Heal, Williams was pleased with the article, but "balked when I wanted to go further and try the vignette method for the entire manuscript." She has generously provided me with a photocopy of the letter Williams sent her regarding this matter on 4 November 1957:

> Dear Edith,
>   Whatever you do with the notes on my mother I hanced [*sic*] you last week keep the originals intact—including my title for them: Your Grandmother, My Son. Make copies of them, push 'em around as you please, we may adopt your version in the final draft, but I don't want to lose the first alignment of any part of it, including the cancelled versions which I included with the others. We'll get together when I get back but it is important to me to preserve the originals.
>   I didn't quite go along with you about a "small book," I decided at the time I should like to think that over. Not having the pages or what I had written on them very well in mind, I couldn't envision the problem.
>   We'll have to go slow, giving me time to study the matter—but it is up to me to make the final decisions.

The letter illustrates the poet's particularity about the memoir ("It is important to me to preserve the originals") as well as his strong determination, despite serious health problems, to maintain his autonomy in this project.

8. William Carlos Williams, "From My Notes about My Mother," p. 7.

9. Unpublished manuscript, Beinecke Library, Yale University, Za Williams 281.

10. Telephone interview with David McDowell, 18 February 1983.

11. I strongly suspect it was McDowell rather than Williams who went through the manuscript and determined which sections were to be italicized. The basis for this speculation is two passages in the text (pp. 79, 100) where statements made by Elena are erroneously attributed to the poet by virtue of their typeface. Moreover, since Williams himself was nearly blind by the time the memoir appeared, Flossie was largely responsible for the proofreading, which may in fact explain why the misattributions were never corrected. In any event, their presence in the text tacitly confirms its confusing nature and further complicates the reader's difficulty in distinguishing between mother's and son's voices.

    In addition, Williams' elliptical complaints about the book to Winfield Townley Scott suggest that he had serious reservations about the typographical innovation (perhaps because it clarified what he wanted left blurred and indistinct), but ultimately deferred to the wishes of his publisher:

    > I can't help but tell you that it will be far from a finished book when it is finally released—*too many people have had a hand in its composition and I am powerless to do anything about it.* At that Dave has done what he has had to do or there would have been no book at all. (Unpublished letter, Winfield Townley Scott papers, The John Hay Library, Brown University; emphasis mine)

12. Compare also *Imaginations,* pp. 264–65 and *Yes, Mrs. Williams,* pp. 101–4.

13. William Carlos Williams, "From My Notes about My Mother," p. 11.

14. Rod Townley, *The Early Poetry of William Carlos Williams* (Ithaca: Cornell University Press, 1975), p. 111.

15. John C. Thirlwall, "Portrait of a Poet as His Mother's Son," in *William Carlos Williams: The Critical Heritage,* ed. Charles Doyle (London: Routledge and Kegan Paul, 1980), pp. 324–25.

16. Longinus, *On Sublimity,* trans. D. A. Russell (Oxford: Clarendon University Press, 1965), p. 1.

17. James E. B. Breslin, *William Carlos Williams: An American Artist* (Chicago: University of Chicago Press, 1985), p. 6.

18. Unpublished letter from Elena Hoheb Williams to Mary Warner Moore, 8 January 1937, Rosenbach Library, Philadelphia, PA. Quoted in Mariani, *William Carlos Williams: A New World Naked,* p. 811.

19. Unpublished letter from Elena Hoheb Williams to William Carlos Williams, Beinecke Library, Yale University, Za Williams 274.

20. Unpublished letter from Elena Hoheb Williams to William Carlos Williams, undated, Beinecke Library, Yale University, Za Williams 274.

21. Linda Wagner, *The Prose of William Carlos Williams* (Middletown, CT: Wesleyan University Press, 1970), p. 192.

22. In his treatise *On Sublimity,* Longinus states: "Sublimity depends on elevation" (p. 17) and is the product of "a combination of wonder and astonishment" (p. 12).

23. Ibid., p. 8.

24. Ibid., pp. 36–37.

25. These anecdotes can be found throughout the memoir on pp. 62, 71, 84, 86, 90, 97, 109, 111, 114, 115, 120, 121, and 139.

26. William Carlos Williams quoted in Mike Weaver, *William Carlos Williams,* p. 259.

Chapter 5

1. Ezra Pound, "Doctor Williams' Position," *Literary Essays* (New York: New Directions Books, 1935), p. 389.

2. Ibid., p. 390.

3. Ibid., p. 390.

4. Ibid., p. 389.

5. Ibid., pp. 391–92.

6. Ibid., pp. 390–91.

7. Paul Mariani, *William Carlos Williams: A New World Naked* (New York: McGraw-Hill, 1985), p. 9.

8. Ezra Pound, "Doctor Williams' Position," p. 392.

9. Ibid., p. 392.

10. Ezra Pound, *The Cantos* (New York: New Directions Books, 1972), p. 4.

11. Ibid., p. 4.

12. Pound also arrogantly presumes that his interpretation of Williams exceeds the poet's own understanding of himself:

> There are plenty of people who think they 'ought' to write 'about' America. . . . There are also numerous people who think that the given subject has an inherent interest simply because it is American and that this gives it ipso facto a dignity or value above all other possible subjects; *Williams may even think he has, or may have once thought he had this angle of attack, but he hasn't.* ("Doctor Williams' Position," p. 392; emphasis mine)

13. Ezra Pound, "Doctor Williams' Position," p. 394.

14. Mark Twain, *The Adventures of Huckleberry Finn,* ed. Henry Nash Smith (Boston: Houghton Mifflin, Riverside Editions, 1958), p. 196.

15. Ezra Pound, *Selected Letters, 1907–1941,* ed. D. D. Paige (New York: New Directions Books, 1950), p. 8.

16. Mark Twain, *The Adventures of Huckleberry Finn,* p. 200.

17. It is interesting to note in this context that the 1928 letter in which Williams informed Pound that he had dedicated *Pagany* to him playfully mimics the ungrammatical, folksy diction of Huck Finn:

> And now, me old frien', lemme tell ya what I don las week. Havin' writ a novel what I always sez I would never in the world do (nothing does, does, does as it use to do, do, do!) why I sez to myself this is somethin'. Well, then who shall I hang it onto? Why, who else but my old friend and college chum Ezrie, sez I. So this is to let you

know that I writ it all out fine and high sountin and it'll be in print in the front of that there novel, as nice as you please. What do you think? Why it's dedicated to you. God help me. I hope you likes it. (*SL,* 100–101)

18. Ezra Pound, "Doctor Williams' Position," p. 395.

19. Ibid., p. 398.

20. Ezra Pound, *Selected Letters,* p. 123.

21. Ibid., p. 124.

22. Sigmund Freud, *The Sexual Enlightenment of Children,* ed. Phillip Rieff (New York: Collier Books, 1978), p. 8.

23. Interestingly, the signature Williams appended to *Poems* (1909), the volume his father heavily edited and corrected, was the British-sounding "William C. Williams." In both the *Autobiography* and *I Wanted to Write a Poem,* the poet explains that the choice of signature was a difficult one: "I had a great time making up my mind what my literary signature should be — something of profound importance, obviously. An advertising friend of my father's spoke up strongly for plain W. Williams. 'It's a common name,' he said, 'but think of the advantage of being *the* W. Williams.' To me the full name seemed most revealing and therefore better" (*A,* 108). In "Doctor Williams' Position," Pound refers to his friend at various points as both "William Williams" and "Carlos Williams."

24. "Excessive love of a country has as its immediate corollary a horror of foreign countries. Not only is one afraid to leave his mother's apron strings, to go see how other people live, to engage himself in their struggles, to share their work, not only does one stay at home, but he closes his door besides."

25. Ezra Pound, *Selected Letters,* p. 159.

26. Ibid., p. 159.

27. This conversation between Pound and his father clearly had symbolic resonance for Williams. He recounted it not only in the prologue to *Kora in Hell,* but in the *Autobiography* and *I Wanted to Write a Poem* as well. It is only in the first of these texts (i.e., the one chronologically closest to the event itself), however, that he describes his father's comment as "crushing" and "triumphant"; in the *Autobiography,* for example, he concludes the narrative with the neutral statement: "Ezra appears never to have forgotten the lesson" (*A,* 92). In light of Williams' sensitivity to his father's expressions of disapproval (articulated most clearly in the nightmare in which William George, speaking from beyond the grave, states: "You know all that poetry you're writing. Well, it's no good" [*A,* 14]), he seems to have derived some assurance from the fact that William George also regarded Pound's work as "idle nonsense."

28. Despite the persistent undercurrent of antagonism between them, Pound and Williams remained lifelong friends. The brunt of Williams' animosity towards the expatriate movement was instead directed at the "poor devil" whose American "blood poison" ran even deeper than Pound's — T. S. Eliot. The nearly comic proportions of Williams' vituperation against Eliot is extensively documented in Paul Mariani's biography. Eliot, for the most part, endured these affronts with a dignified, aristocratic mien yet, when an appropriate occasion arose, he did not hesitate to return fire. As the editor of Pound's *Literary Essays,* the collection in which "Doctor Williams' Position" appears, he amended the statement that "none of [Williams'] immediate forebears burnt witches in Salem" with the footnote, "We didn't burn them, we hanged them" (Ezra Pound, *Literary Essays,* p. 391).

29. William George's decision to remain a British citizen was a very sensitive issue for the poet, who referred to it many times throughout his work. In the preface to *Selected Essays,* for

example, he states: "I loved my father but never forgave him for remaining, in spite of every-thing we could say against it, a British subject. It had much to do with my violent partisan-ship toward America. Not that we discussed this openly—it would have been better for both of us if we had—but it was, I am sure, always at the back of our thoughts." Even in "Adam," his 1936 elegy for William George, he describes him as:

> God's handyman
> Going quietly into hell's mouth
> for a paper of reference—
> fetching water to posterity
> a British passport
> always in his pocket—
> muleback over Costa Rica
> eating patés of black ants
>
> *(CEP, 373)*

30. An extensive literature exists on the trope of American as an Edenic garden. Among the major critical texts are: Leo Marx, *The Machine in the Garden: Technology and the Pastoral Ideal in America* (New York: Oxford University Press, 1964); R. W. B. Lewis, *The Amer-ican Adam: Innocence, Tragedy, and Tradition in the Nineteenth Century* (1955. Reprint, Chicago: University of Chicago Press, Phoenix Books, 1966); Henry Nash Smith, *Virgin Land: The American West as Symbol and Myth* (1950. Reprint, New York: Random House, Vintage Books, 1961); and more recently, from a feminist perspective, Annette Kolodny, *The Lay of the Land* (Chapel Hill: University of North Carolina Press, 1975).

31. William Carlos Williams, "Letters to Ezra Pound, 1946–49." Notes by James Laughlin. *Grand Street,* vol. 3, no. 2, Winter 1984, pp. 110–11.

32. In Walter Sutton's 1960 interview with Williams, the poet specifically links these three fig-ures:

> I went along with Pound. Later on he switched to Eliot and his *Waste Land,* which I admired too, but I was intensely jealous of this man, who was much more cultured than I was, and I didn't know anything about English literature at all. But when I recognized what he was doing I didn't like it at all. He was giving up America. And maybe my attachment to my father, who was English and who had never become an American citizen influenced me because I was—You know, the Oedipus complex between father and son—I resented him being English and not being American. And that was when Eliot was living in England and had given up America. (Int, 47)

33. William Carlos Williams, "Letters to an Australian Editor," *Briarcliff Quarterly,* vol. 3, no. 2, October 1946, p. 208.

34. Paul Mariani, *William Carlos Williams: A New World Naked,* p. 10.

35. In the memoir Williams notes that although his parents maintained regular contact with numerous West Indian acquaintances and often housed visitors from the islands in Ruther-ford, they themselves never expressed a desire to return there:

> She never went back to her native land, neither one of them did for that matter. It was only a short ship's journey and dozens of others came to our house in the course of the thirty years and were returned—while Pop at least sailed all around the place, to Central America, everywhere. But she never did more than to go to Paris and Geneva with us boys. I don't think she ever thought of going. Then after the Spanish-American War she flatly refused, bitterly, in fact. (YMW, 131)

This deliberate physical dissociation from the past mystified the poet, who himself made two separate trips to the Caribbean, the first in 1941, the latter fifteen years later. These excursions, which combined business (conferences, public readings, etc.) and pleasure, were partially inspired by Williams' passionate interest in family history. During the 1956 trip, made while he was actively revising *Yes, Mrs. Williams* for publication, he stopped in both Mayagüez and St. Thomas to see and explore the places where his mother and father had grown up (see Mariani, p. 729).

36.   Unpublished manuscript, Beinecke Library, Yale University, Za Williams 277.

37.   See also the *Autobiography* (pp. 4, 23, 167–68) and *Selected Letters* (pp. 284–85).

38.   Sigmund Freud, "Family Romances," *The Sexual Enlightenment of Children*, trans. James Strachey (New York: Collier Books, 1978), pp. 41–45.

39.   Paul Mariani, *William Carlos Williams: A New World Naked*, pp. 4–5.

40.   Quoted in John Thirlwall, "The Lost Poems of Williams Carlos Williams, or The Past Recaptured," *New Directions 16*, 1957, pp. 18–19.

41.   A manuscript variant of this passage at the Beinecke Library substitutes the word "husband" for "son," providing additional confirmation of the strongly oedipal configuration of the mother-son relationship alluded to throughout this chapter (Za Williams 283).

42.   Unpublished manuscript, Beinecke Library, Yale University, Za Williams 269.

43.   Unpublished manuscript, Beinecke Library, Yale University, Za Williams 271.

44.   Unpublished manuscript, Beinecke Library, Yale University, Za Williams 274.

Chapter 6

1.   Unpublished letter, William Carlos Williams to Louis Untermeyer, 8 March 1939, Lilly Library, Indiana University.

2.   Unpublished letter, William Carlos Williams to Charles Abbott, 29 June 1959, Poetry/Rare Books Collection, Lockwood Library, SUNY/Buffalo, F 994.

3.   Mike Weaver, *William Carlos Williams: The American Background* (New York: Cambridge University Press, 1971), p. 159.

4.   William Wordsworth, *Poems*, volume 1, ed. John O. Hayden (New Haven: Yale University Press, 1977), p. 357.

5.   Unpublished manuscript, Beinecke Library, Yale University, Za Williams 271 and 280.

6.   William Carlos Williams, "From My Notes about My Mother," ed. Edith Heal Berrien, *Literary Review*, vol. 1, no. 1, Autumn 1957, p. 7.

7.   Ibid., p. 10.

8.   Critics have interpreted this line in a variety of ways; James E. B. Breslin, for example, makes the poet an active agent, and the filling of his ears with earth a symbolic choice: "Paterson characteristically gets impatient with this kind of absorptive activity, closes the senses . . . and lets his visionary imagination take over" (*William Carlos Williams: An American Artist*, p. 183). Benjamin Sankey, on the other hand, avoids the issue of volition: "The probing in Paterson's ear has symbolic force: a page later Williams comments, 'of / earth his ears are full. . . .' There is no sound (that is, for the moment, perhaps, he fails to hear the riddling challenge of the Falls)" (*A Companion to William Carlos Williams' Paterson*, p. 61).

9. James E. B. Breslin, *William Carlos Williams: An American Artist*, p. 184.

10. Unpublished letter, Elena Hoheb Williams to William Carlos Williams, undated, Beinecke Library, Yale University, Za Williams 271.

11. Walter Scott Peterson, *An Approach to Paterson* (New Haven: Yale University Press, 1967), p. 38.

12. Williams Carlos Williams, "Letters to Ezra Pound, 1946–49." Notes by James Laughlin. *Grand Street*, vol. 3, no. 2, Winter 1984, p. 119.

13. Unpublished manuscript, Beinecke Library, Yale University, Za Williams 18.

14. Ibid.

15. William Carlos Williams, "From My Notes about My Mother," p. 7.

16. Unpublished letter, 7 April 1948, Poetry/Rare Books Collection, Lockwood Library, SUNY/ Buffalo. Quoted in Emily Mitchell Wallace, "A Musing in the Highlands and Valleys: The Poetry of Gratwick Farm," *Williams Carlos Williams Review*, vol. 8, no. 1, Spring 1982, p. 36.

17. Unpublished letter, Elena Hoheb Williams to William Carlos Williams, Beinecke Library, Yale University, Za Williams 274.

18. My dating of the lyric's composition is based on internal evidence—Williams' description of the present moment in relation to his mother's age: "At ninety, the strangeness of death / is upon you" (*CLP*, 182). Because he mistakenly believed Elena had been born in "1855 or thereabouts" (*YMW*, 32), the date alluded to in "An Eternity" is, in all likelihood, 1946; it was not until 1956 that he discovered her actual date of birth was 24 December 1847 (*YMW*, 51).

19. James E. B. Breslin has commented on a similar effect created by Williams' verbal repetition in the "descent" passage (See *William Carlos Williams: An American Artist*, p. 188).

20. The poem, which appears in *Pictures from Brueghel*, was first printed in the inaugural issue of the Australian little magazine, *Edge* (See Emily Mitchell Wallace, *A Bibliography of William Carlos Williams*, p. 230).

21. See also the prose account in the *Autobiography*, p. 123.

22. Benjamin Sankey, *A Companion to William Carlos Williams' Paterson* (Berkeley: University of California Press, 1971), p. 116.

23. Quoted in Paul Mariani, *William Carlos Williams: A New World Naked*, p. 595.

24. Ibid., p. 597.

25. See *Imaginations*, pp. 322–24 and *Yes, Mrs. Williams*, pp. 65–67.

26. In 1946, Williams underwent two successive hernia operations (the second was required to correct the work of the first); in 1948, he experienced his first heart attack (See Mariani, pp. 533–34, 556).

27. Unpublished letter, William Carlos Williams to Charles Abbott, 29 June 1959, Poetry/Rare Books Collection, Lockwood Library, SUNY/Buffalo, F 994.

Bibliography

Works by William Carlos Williams

Autobiography. New York: New Directions Books, 1967.
The Build-Up. New York: New Directions Books, 1968.
Collected Earlier Poems. New York: New Directions Books, 1966.
Collected Later Poems. New York: New Directions Books, 1967.
Dear Ez: Letters from William Carlos Williams to Ezra Pound. Ed. Mary Ellen Solt. Bloomington, IN: Frederic Brewer Press, 1985.
"Emanuel Romano." Introduced and edited by Mike Weaver. *Form* (Cambridge, England), vol. 1, no. 2, September 1966.
The Embodiment of Knowledge. Ed. Ron Loewinsohn. New York: New Directions Books, 1961.
The Farmers' Daughters. New York: New Directions Books, 1961.
"From My Notes about My Mother." Ed. Edith Heal Berrien. *The Literary Review*, vol. 1, no. 1, Autumn 1957.
"The Great Sex Spiral, A Criticism of Miss Marsden's 'Lingual Psychology.'" *The Egoist*, vol. 4, nos. 3 and 7, 1917.
"The Ideal Quarrel." *The Little Review*, vol. 5, no. 3, December 1918.
Imaginations. New York: New Directions Books, 1970.
Interviews. Ed. Linda Wagner. New York: New Directions Books, 1976.
In the American Grain. New York: New Directions Books, 1956.
In the Money. New York: New Directions Books, 1940.
I Wanted to Write a Poem: The Autobiography of the Works of a Poet. Ed. Edith Heal. New York: New Directions Books, 1978.
"Letters to Ezra Pound, 1946–1949." Notes by James Laughlin. *Grand Street*, vol. 3, no. 2, Winter 1984.
"Letter to an Australian Editor." *Briarcliff Quarterly*, vol. 3, no. 2, October 1949.
Many Loves and Other Places. New York: New Directions Books, 1961.
"'Men . . . Have No Tenderness': Anaïs Nin's *Winter of Artifice*." *New Directions 7*, 1942.
"Notes toward an Autobiography." *Poetry*, vol. 74, no. 2, May 1949.
Paterson. New York: New Directions Books, 1963.
Pictures from Brueghel. New York: New Directions Books, 1962.
"Prose about Love." *The Little Review*, vol. 6, no. 2, June 1918.
"Raquel Helene Rose." *Twice a Year*, nos. 5–6, Fall/Winter 1940, Spring/Summer 1941.
A Recognizable Image: William Carlos Williams on Art and Artists. Ed. Bram Dijkstra. New York: New Directions Books, 1978.
Rome. *Iowa Review*, vol. 9, no. 3, Summer 1978.
Selected Essays. New York: New Directions Books, 1969.

Selected Letters. Ed. John C. Thirlwall. New York: McDowell, Obolensky, 1957.
Selected Poems. Ed. Charles Tomlinson. New York: New Directions Books, 1985.
"Some Notes toward an Autobiography." *Poetry,* vol. 72, nos. 3 and 5, June and August 1948.
Something to Say: William Carlos Williams on Younger Poets. Ed. James E. B. Breslin. New York: New Directions Books, 1985.
"Three Professional Studies." *The Little Review,* vol. 5, nos. 10–11, February–March 1919.
A Voyage to Pagany. New York: New Directions Books, 1970.
White Mule. New York: New Directions Books, 1937.
William Carlos Williams—John Sanford: A Correspondence. Foreword by Paul Mariani. Santa Barbara, CA: Oyster Press, 1984.
Yes, Mrs. Williams. New York: New Directions Books, 1982.

Secondary Sources

Adams, Phoebe. "Lines for a Portrait." *Atlantic Monthly,* 204, July 1959.
Altieri, Charles. "Presence and Reference in a Literary Text: The Example of Williams' 'This Is Just to Say.'" *Critical Inquiry,* vol. 5, Spring 1979.
Baldwin, Neil. *To All Gentleness: William Carlos Williams, The Doctor Poet*. New York: Atheneum Books, 1984.
Baldwin, Neil, and Steven Meyers: *The Manuscripts and Letters of William Carlos Williams at SUNY/Buffalo: A Descriptive Catalogue*. Boston: G. K. Hall and Co., 1978.
Barthes, Roland. *Camera Lucida: Reflections on Photography*. New York: Hill and Wang, 1981.
―――. *Critical Essays*. Trans. Richard Howard. Evanston: Northwestern University Press, 1972.
Bernstein, Michael. *The Tale of the Tribe: Ezra Pound and the Modern Verse Epic*. Princeton: Princeton University Press, 1980.
Borroff, Marie. "William Carlos Williams: The Diagnostic Eye." In *Medicine and Literature*. Ed. Enid Rhodes Peschel. New York: Neale Watson Academic Publications, 1980.
Breslin, James E. B. *From Modern to Contemporary: American Poetry, 1945–1965*. Chicago: University of Chicago Press, 1984.
―――. *William Carlos Williams: An American Artist*. Chicago: University of Chicago Press, 1985.
Bruns, Gerald. "De Improvisatione." *Iowa Review,* vol. 9, no. 3, Summer 1978.
Ciardi, John. "A Flame to Her Son." *Saturday Review,* 11 July 1959.
Coles, Robert. *William Carlos Williams: The Knack of Survival in America*. New Brunswick: Rutgers University Press, 1975.
Conarroe, Joel. *William Carlos Williams'* Paterson: *Language and Landscape*. Philadelphia: University of Pennsylvania Press, 1970.
Cushman, Stephen. *William Carlos Williams and the Meanings of Measure*. New Haven: Yale University Press, 1985.
Deutsch, Babette. "Picture of a Poet's Mother." *New York Herald Tribune Book Review,* 21 June 1959.
Dickie, Margaret. *On the Modernist Long Poem*. Iowa City: University of Iowa Press, 1986.
Dijkstra, Bram. *Cubism, Stieglitz, and the Early Poetry of William Carlos Williams: The Hieroglyphics of a New Speech*. Princeton: Princeton University Press, 1969.
Doyle, Charles. *William Carlos Williams and the American Poem*. New York: St. Martin's Press, 1982.
―――, ed. *William Carlos Williams: The Critical Heritage*. London: Routledge and Kegan Paul, 1980.
Duplessis, Rachel Blau. "Pater–Daughter." *Soup 4,* 1985.
Frank Waldo; Lewis Mumford; et al., eds. *America and Alfred Stieglitz: A Collective Portrait*. New York: Aperture Books, 1979.

Fredman, Stephen. *Poet's Prose: The Crisis in American Verse*. New York: Cambridge University Press, 1983.

Freud, Sigmund. *The Interpretation of Dreams*. Trans. James Strachey. New York: Avon Books, 1978.

―――. *The Sexual Enlightenment of Children*. Trans. James Strachey. New York: Collier Books, 1978.

―――. "The Theme of the Three Caskets." Trans. C. J. M. Hubback. In *On Creativity and the Unconscious*. New York: Harper and Row, 1958.

―――. "The Uncanny." Trans. Alix Strachey. In *On Creativity and the Unconscious*. New York: Harper and Row, 1958.

Friedman, Melvin J., and John B. Vickery, eds. *The Shaken Realist*. Baton Rouge: Louisiana State University Press, 1970.

Fure, Rob. "The Design of Experience: William Carlos Williams and Juan Gris." *William Carlos Williams Newsletter*, vol. 4, no. 2, Fall 1978.

Gelpi, Albert. "Stevens and Williams: The Epistemology of Modernism." *Wallace Stevens: The Poetics of Modernism*. Cambridge: Cambridge University Press, 1985.

Goodridge, Celeste. "Private Exchanges and Public Reviews: Marianne Moore's Criticism of William Carlos Williams." *Twentieth Century Literature*, vol. 30, nos. 2–3, 1984.

Graham, Theodora Rapp. *Woman as Character and Symbol in the Work of William Carlos Williams*, Ph.D. diss., University of Pennsylvania, 1974.

Guimond, James. *The Art of William Carlos Williams: A Discovery and Possession of America*. Urbana: University of Illinois Press, 1968.

Hoffman, Daniel, ed. *Ezra Pound and William Carlos Williams: The University of Pennsylvania Conference Papers*. Philadelphia: University of Pennsylvania Press, 1983.

Kahnweiler, Daniel-Henry. *Juan Gris: His Life and Work*. New York: Harry N. Abrams, 1969.

Kenner, Hugh. *A Homemade World*. New York: William Morrow, 1975.

―――. *The Pound Era*. Berkeley: University of California Press, 1971.

―――. "With the Bare Hands." *Poetry*, vol. 80, no. 5, August 1952.

Kronick, Joseph. *American Poetics of History: From Emerson to the Moderns*. Baton Rouge: Louisiana State University Press, 1984.

Laughlin, James. "A World of Books Gone Flat." *Grand Street*, vol. 3, no. 2, Winter 1984.

Levin, Gail. "Wassily Kandinsky and the American Literary Avantgarde." *Criticism*, vol. 21, Fall 1979.

Lloyd, Margaret Glynne. *William Carlos Williams's* Paterson: *A Critical Reappraisal*. Rutherford: Fairleigh Dickinson University Press, 1980.

Longinus, Robert. *On Sublimity*. Trans. D. A. Russell. Oxford: Clarendon Press, 1965.

Lowell, Robert. *Selected Poems*. New York: Farrar, Straus and Giroux, 1976.

Mariani, Paul. "The Hard Core of Beauty." *Sagetrieb*, vol. 3, no. 1, 1984.

―――. *William Carlos Williams: A New World Naked*. New York: McGraw-Hill, 1981.

―――. *William Carlos Williams: The Poet and His Critics*. Chicago: American Library Association, 1975.

Marling, William. *William Carlos Williams and the Painters: 1909–1923*. Athens: Ohio University Press, 1982.

Martínez, Rafael Arévalo. "The Man Who Resembled a Horse." Trans. William George Williams and William Carlos Williams, *New Directions 8*, 1944.

Martz, Louis. *The Poem of the Mind*. New York: Oxford University Press, 1966.

Matthews, Kathleen. "Competitive Giants: Satiric Bedrock in Book I of William Carlos Williams' *Paterson*." *Journal of Modern Literature*, vol. 12, 1985.

Mazzaro, Jerome. *William Carlos Williams: The Later Poems*. Ithaca: Cornell University Press, 1973.

Miller, J. Hillis. *The Linguistic Moment: From Wordsworth to Stevens*. Princeton: Princeton University Press, 1985.

————. *Poets of Reality: Six Twentieth Century Writers.* Cambridge: Harvard University Press, 1966.

————, ed. *William Carlos Williams: A Collection of Critical Essays.* Englewood Cliffs: Prentice-Hall, 1966.

Myers, Neil. "Williams' 'Two Pendants for the Ears.'" *Journal of Modern Literature,* vol. 1, no. 4, May 1974.

Nash, Charles. "Women and the Female Principle in the Works of William Carlos Williams." *Publications of the Missouri Philological Association,* vol. 3, 1978.

Nash, Ralph. "The Use of Prose in *Paterson.*" *Perspective,* vol. 6, Autumn 1953.

Neumann, Erich. *The Origins and History of Consciousness.* Princeton: Princeton University Press, 1973.

Olson, Charles. *The Maximum Poems.* Ed. George F. Butterick. Berkeley: University of California Press, 1983.

————. *Selected Writings.* New York: New Direction Books, 1966.

————. *The Special View of History.* Berkeley: Oyez Press, 1970.

Oren, Michael. "Williams and Gris: A Borrowed Aesthetic." *Contemporary Literature,* vol. 26, 1985.

Paul, Sherman. *The Music of Survival.* Urbana: University of Illinois Press, 1968.

Pearce, Roy Harvey. *The Continuity of American Poetry.* Princeton: Princeton University Press, 1961.

Pearson, Norman Holmes. "Williams, New Jersey." *Literary Review,* vol. 1, no. 1, Autumn 1957.

Perloff, Marjorie. "The Man Who Loved Women: The Medical Fictions of William Carlos Williams." *Georgia Review,* vol. 34, Winter 1980.

Peterson, Walter Scott. *An Approach to Paterson.* New Haven: Yale University Press, 1967.

Pound, Ezra. *ABC of Reading.* New York: New Direction Books, 1934.

————. *The Cantos.* New York: New Direction Books, 1972.

————. *Literary Essays.* New York: New Direction Books, 1935.

————. *Selected Letters, 1907–1941.* New York: New Direction Books, 1971.

Quevedo, Don Francisco. *The Dog and the Fever.* Trans. William Carlos Williams and Raquel Helene Williams. Hamden: Shoe String Press, 1954.

Quinn, Sister M. Bernetta. *The Metamorphic Tradition in Modern Poetry.* New Brunswick: Rutgers University Press, 1955.

————. "Paterson: Landscape and Dream." *Journal of Modern Literature,* vol. 1, no. 4, May 1971.

Rapp, Carl. *William Carlos Williams and Romantic Idealism.* Hanover, NH: University Press of New England, 1984.

Rexroth, Kenneth. *American Poetry in the Twentieth Century.* New York: Seabury Press, 1973.

Rheingold, Joseph C. *The Mother, Anxiety, and Death.* London: J. & A. Churchill, 1967.

Riddel, Joseph. *The Inverted Bell: Modernism and the Counterpoetics of William Carlos Williams.* Baton Rouge: Louisiana State University Press, 1974.

Rodgers, Audrey T. "The Female Presence: Women in the Poetry of William Carlos Williams, 1910–1950." *American Poetry,* vol. 3, no. 2, 1986.

Rosenthal, M. L., and Sally M. Gall. *The Modern Poetic Sequence: The Genius of Modern Poetry.* New York: Oxford University Press, 1983.

Rosenthal, Mark. *Juan Gris.* New York: Abbeville Press, 1983.

Sanford, John. "On Rereading *In the American Grain.*" *View from This Wilderness: American Literature as History.* Santa Barbara, CA: Capra Press, 1977.

Sankey, Benjamin. *A Companion to William Carlos Williams'* Paterson. Berkeley: University of California Press, 1971.

Sayre, Henry. *The Visual Text of William Carlos Williams.* Urbana: University of Illinois Press, 1983.

Schevill, James. "Notes on the Grotesque: Anderson, Brecht, and Williams." *Twentieth Century Literature,* vol. 23, 1977.

Schmidt, Peter. "Some Versions of Modern Pastoral: William Carlos Williams and the Precisionists." *Contemporary Literature,* vol. 21, no. 3, 1980.

Schwartz, Murray M. "'The Use of Force' and the Dilemma of Violence." *Psychoanalytic Review,* vol. 59, no. 4, 1972.

Simpson, Louis. *Three on the Tower: The Lives and Works of Ezra Pound, T. S. Eliot, and William Carlos Williams.* New York: William Morrow, 1975.

Soupault, Philippe. *Last Nights of Paris.* Trans. William Carlos Williams and Raquel Helene Williams. New York: Full Court Press, 1982.

Steiner, Wendy. *The Colors of Rhetoric: Problems in the Relation between Modern Literature and Painting.* Chicago: University of Chicago Press, 1982.

Tapscott, Stephen. *American Beauty: William Carlos Williams and the Modernist Whitman.* New York: Columbia University Press, 1984.

Tashjian, Dickran. *William Carlos Williams and the American Scene, 1920–1940.* Berkeley: University of California Press, 1979.

Terrell, Carroll F., ed. *William Carlos Williams: Man and Poet.* Orono: National Poetry Foundation, 1983.

Thirlwall, John C. "The Lost Poems of William Carlos Williams." *New Directions 16,* 1957.

———. "William Carlos Williams' *Paterson.*" *New Directions 17,* 1961.

Townley, Rod. *The Early Poetry of William Carlos Williams.* Ithaca: Cornell University Press, 1975.

Untermeyer, Louis, ed. *Modern American Poetry: A Critical Anthology.* New York: Harcourt, Brace, 1936.

Vazquez-Amaral, Jose. "Williams' Poem to Neruda." *Rutgers Review,* vol. 1, no. 2, Spring 1967.

Waggoner, Hyatt H. *American Poetry from the Puritans to the Present.* New York: Delta Books, 1968.

Wagner, Linda Welsheimer. *The Poems of William Carlos Williams.* Middletown: Wesleyan University Press, 1964.

———. *The Prose of William Carlos Williams.* Middletown: Wesleyan University Press, 1970.

———. *William Carlos Williams: A Reference Guide.* Boston: G. K. Hall, 1978.

Walker, David. *The Transparent Lyric: Reading and Meaning in the Poetry of Stevens and Williams.* Princeton: Princeton University Press, 1984.

Wallace, Emily Mitchell. *A Bibliography of William Carlos Williams.* Middletown: Wesleyan University Press, 1968.

Weaver, Mike. *William Carlos Williams: The American Background.* New York: Cambridge University Press, 1971.

Whitaker, Thomas R. *William Carlos Williams.* New York: Twayne Publishers, 1968.

Whittemore, Reed. "What Is the Secret?" *Virginia Quarterly Review,* vol. 35, Autumn 1959.

———. "William Carlos Williams: 'The Happy Genius of the Household.'" Washington, D.C.: Library of Congress, 1984.

———. *William Carlos Williams: Poet from Jersey.* Boston: Houghton Mifflin, 1975.

Williams, William George. "Translations from the Spanish." *Others,* vol. 3, no. 2, August 1916.

Index